Hollywood Heroines

Women in *Film Noir* and the Female Gothic Film

by
Helen Hanson

I.B. TAURIS
LONDON · NEW YORK

10063842

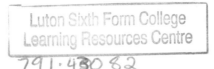
Published in 2007 by I.B.Tauris & Co Ltd
6 Salem Road, London W2 4BU
175 Fifth Avenue, New York NY 10010
www.ibtauris.com

In the United States of America and Canada distributed by
Palgrave Macmillan a division of St. Martin's Press, 175 Fifth Avenue,
New York NY 10010

ISBN: (PB) 978 1 84511 561 6
ISBN: (HB) 978 1 84511 562 3

A full CIP record for this book is available from the British Library
A full CIP record is available from the Library of Congress

Library of Congress Catalog Card Number: available

Designed and Typeset by 4word Ltd, Bristol, UK
Printed and bound by TJ International Ltd, Padstow, Cornwall, UK

This book is dedicated to my family,
Don and Margaret, Liz and John, Ed and Sue,
with love and thanks

Contents

List of Illustrations

Acknowledgements

I acknowledge the University of Exeter and the Arts and Humanities Research Council for funding the time for me to pursue this project. I am also grateful for a travel grant from the British Academy, which allowed me to present some of the material on working-girl investigators in *film noir* at the South Atlantic Modern Languages Association Conference in Atlanta in November 2005. Thanks to Mark Osteen for inviting me to join the panel, and to Julie Grossman for her enjoyable and valuable correspondence about women and *film noir*. I also thank Philippa Brewster at I.B.Tauris for her interest in the project and editorial help, and Annette Kuhn and Yvonne Tasker for their support for the book.

I am most grateful to colleagues past and present who have provided mentorship and encouragement, and who have taught me a great deal. Thanks are due to the Department of English at the University of Southampton, where I benefited enormously from the positive culture for postgraduate research: particular thanks to my PhD supervisor Linda Ruth Williams, and to Caroline Blinder, Mike Hammond, Tim Bergfelder and Pam Cook. I was also lucky to have spent time in the Department of Film and Television Studies at the University of Warwick: thanks are due to José Arroyo, Charlotte Brunsdon, Jon Burrows, Richard Dyer, Ed Gallafent, Rachel Moseley, Victor Perkins, Ginette Vincendeau and to Helen Wheatley, who shared thoughts on the gothic with me.

My colleagues in the Department of English at the University of Exeter are such a remarkable bunch of people that I hardly know where or how to start acknowledging them. I am sincerely grateful for the generosity of the working atmosphere there, which is marked by a real excitement about ideas and how to take them forward. Particular thanks are due to the team-film sub-grouping, Joe Kember, James Lyons and Dan North, and to Steve Neale who offered insights, read drafts, lent me obscure *noir* titles, and whose feedback on, and encouragement with, the project has been invaluable. I am also most indebted to Ashley Tauchert and Catherine O'Rawe, who read work in progress and offered extremely perceptive insights that were crucial in the final stages of the project. Conversations about feminism, women and film with Margaretta Jolly and Jess Gardner have been a most enjoyable way to work through and marshal some of my thoughts. Many thanks, too, to Karen Edwards and Mark Whalan for their friendship and cheerful support during my leave.

Friends and family have listened most patiently as I explored the ideas behind the project, and were often right on the money with their own thoughts too. I owe thanks to Hugh Adlington, Danny Westgate, Vanessa and Dominic Worrall, Jenny Harris, Lou Whitfield, Nory Meneer, Caroline Sylge, Tom Jones, Bettina Weichert and to Phil Wickham, who suggested titles, sourced articles and enthused with me about the films. My family have been a constant source of support, and this book is for all of them, but I must especially thank my sister, Liz, not only for her belief in the book, but also for her ingeniousness in finding ever new ways to encourage me on with it.

Introduction

Hollywood Heroines: Women, Feminism and Film

This book is an engagement with Hollywood heroines in two genres, *film noir* and the female gothic film, which have been commercially and critically popular over a long period. The project was born out of, and has been formed by, my own long-held interest in the narrative and generic forms that bear upon these heroines: how they are placed within their fictional worlds, what they do there, and what this 'doing' means. The term 'engagement' captures some of the diverse elements of this interest. It speaks of the way that female figures on film, and their modes of representation, can attract and hold the attention of film fans and critics, and the processes through which this attraction can be elaborated: engaging in one's own study, discussion, analysis and interpretation, and engaging with the study of others. This introduction charts some of the questions that have prompted me to engage with these genres and their heroines, and maps out some of the methods that I have used to approach them.

Hollywood's genres have always been a major originating source, and modifier, of filmic character types. The construction and marketing of character configurations by Hollywood genres intersects with audience expectations. As Barry Keith Grant argues, genre movies are 'those commercial feature films which, through repetition and variation, tell familiar stories with familiar characters in familiar situations'.[1] Across this process of repetition and variation, however, lie some key questions for the ways in which Hollywood genres are conceived, defined and categorised, both by Hollywood's industry of production, and by film historians and genre critics. Genre criticism in film studies has moved through various paradigms. The concept of it as a relatively fixed set of conventions, or structures, available to be used by film producers, directors and writers to fulfil or frustrate audience expectations,[2] has shifted through Steve Neale's work on genres as part of the cinema's apparatus,[3] to his recasting and redevelopment of this work in a model of genre that accounts for the roles of production, marketing and consumption, and the 'evolution' of generic conventions themselves.[4] Neale's work has opened up the field of genre study to reveal the interplay between the production institutions of Hollywood; that is, its studios, producers and other creative personnel. Neale's approach allows us to ask why and how particular genre formulae emerged in the studio system at particular sociocultural moments, and the ways in which characters and narrative forms were received through his attention to contemporaneous reviews. Following Luckow and Ricci, Neale conceives Hollywood genres as engaged in an 'intertextual relay'.[5]

In her process of 'rethinking genre', Christine Gledhill draws upon the notion of intertextuality as a way of understanding both genres' uses of narratives and styles, and their interactions with their socio-cultural realms:

> Genre provides the conceptual space where such questions can be pursued. In this space issues of texts and aesthetics – the traditional concerns of film theory – intersect with those of industry and institution, history and society, culture and audiences – the central concerns of political economy, sociology, and cultural studies. To understand exactly how the social and films interact we need a concept of genre capable of exploring the wider contextual culture in relationship to, rather than as the originating source of, aesthetic mutations and textual complications.[6]

These approaches to genre have shaped my engagement with *film noir* and the female gothic film. Both these genres arose in early 1940s Hollywood, though they have an older generic heritage in other literary, filmic and popular cultural forms. Both genres have been fascinating to critics studying gender and genre. They have been discussed as stylistically, narratively and socially interesting. The moment in which these genres appeared was one of significant socio-cultural changes in gender roles and identities. Both these genres, and the female figures within them, possess an interesting socio-cultural charge. The ways in which their female figures are positioned within the genres' narratives, what those narratives require them to do, and the ways in which their action is represented through the films' narrational processes, are part of a discourse about women in the period.

Existing critical discourse on both *film noir* and the female gothic film has already provided a fertile and productive arena of debate about these genres, their female figures and their socio-cultural charge. In the 1970s, second-wave feminist film criticism on *film noir* argued for the genre's complex representation of the *femme fatale* figure as condensing male anxieties about women's sexual and economic freedom coincident with shifts in gender roles in America's wartime and post-war society.[7] This work was important in forming an image of the *femme fatale* as sexually, and generically, transgressive: a female figure refusing to be defined by the socio-cultural norms of femininity, or contained by the male-addressed, generic operations of *film noir* narratives in which her fatality resulted in her ultimate destruction. In the 1980s, feminist film criticism produced an array of work on female genres, and questioned the modes and contradictions of Hollywood's address to its female audiences through melodrama and the woman's film.[8] Particular strands of this work analysed the female gothic film, finding the trials and tribulations that its heroine endured as positioning the genre as a particularly problematic one for feminism, the position of its suffering heroine constituting a victimised figure with whom female viewers identified through its female-address.[9] Given the fertility of this existent critical history, why revisit, review and re-read these genres and their female figures? What might be added to this area of debate, and what approach might be used to do so?

My impulse to revisit these genres arose from a conviction that although one story had been told about the heroines of Hollywood's *film noir* and female gothic film, this was a story with a particular focus on certain types of character and informed by certain assumptions and expectations about the agency of those characters, and their currency for feminism and for female viewers. In looking again at *film noir*, my attention was captured not by *femmes fatales* figures, fascinating though those figures still are, but by an array of alternative female characters such as working-girl investigators, who appear in a number of *films noirs* in the early to mid-1940s. I began to ask what this array of female characterisations meant for the concept of *film noir* as a male-addressed genre, and what meanings the working-girl investigator had within the socio-cultural context of the 1940s, and within feminist critical debates that had addressed the period. These questions, and their outcomes, are explored in detail in Chapter 1 of this book. My attention was also drawn to Hollywood's female gothic film. I wanted to account for the reasons why, if these films presented a picture of female suffering and victimisation, they had enjoyed such significant critical and commercial success. In accounting for this popularity I traced the heritage of the female gothic film in its literary forms. The literary female gothic has been notably deployed by female writers, and has provoked interesting feminist literary critical debate. I was interested in the ways this critical debate intersects with, and modifies, the issues and terms of film theory on the female gothic film. In tracing the heritage of the female gothic, and examining the processes of female gothic narration through detailed attention to the films' audio-visual styles, I have revisited the 1940s female gothic film to conceive it as offering a narrative trajectory as a female journey to subjectivity. This journey has a charge in relation to the socio-cultural shifts in gender relations coincident in the period. Chapter 2 of this book traces the generic heritage of the literary female gothic, locates the 1940s female gothic cycle within Hollywood of the 1940s, and explores the history of feminist critical engagements with it. Chapters 3 and 4 explore the female gothic films in detail. With a particular focus on the films' narrational styles, I examine how the gothic narrative trajectory is represented on film, and the consequences this has for the genre's female address and its politics. Chapters 5 and 6 examine the recurrence of *film noir* and the female gothic film in the period since the 1980s, in which the terms of feminist identity have been the subject of considerable debate. I examine the transformations of the heroines of *film noir* and the female gothic in relation to these debates to examine the different currency of Hollywood heroines in the era of post-feminism and New Hollywood cinema.

My engagements with these genres and their female figures across this long period have been informed by three key issues. The first issue is the categorisation of genres and its relation to gender. In my discussions of *film noir* of the 1940s, and neo-*noir* of the 1980s to the present, as well as the 1940s female gothic film and its neo-gothic revival, I have acknowledged the plethora of terms that form these films' intertextual relay. My concern has not been to tie down these generic terms, but rather to illustrate the interpenetration of industrial and critical genre discourses as they inform understandings of female characterisation. These tensions are shown to be particularly productive where I have revisited questions of gender and generic address.

The second issue is how female characterisation and agency are constituted through filmic narration within the two genres. As noted above, the processes of generic repetition construct a familiarity of character types and narrative situations received by critics and by audiences. This repetition has, within feminist critical studies of Hollywood, often been examined as revealing how Hollywood genres speak about female figures, and to female audiences. Frequently classical Hollywood texts, and their narrative operations, have been critiqued as bearing an ideological, and consequently socio-cultural, charge. Hence, generic repetition has often been understood as producing female stereotypes, or formulaic representations of what women do, and what they are like. In my examination of *film noir* and the female gothic film, I have tried to bring together an acknowledgement of generic representations and narrative repetitions with attention to the processes of narration through female characters and their actions.

Theories of narratology have analysed the interplay of character and agency in the narrative forms of fiction and film. Within these theories the formal structures of narratives constitute systems, and all fictional figures (agents, actants, personae or personages) work as functions. H Porter Abbot glosses the term 'characters' as 'any entitities involved in the action that have agency',[10] and agency as 'the capacity of an entity to cause events (that is to engage in acts)'.[11] In this formal definition of narrative, any character, male or female, has agency. Issues of gender come into play in the typical (in the sense of familiar, repeated, generic) placement of those characters within certain groups of texts. Within critiques of Hollywood genres, particularly those produced in Hollywood's classical era, agency has tended to be conflated with male characters and their generic placements. So in genres such as the Western, male–male, and importantly public, conflicts are resolved by the actions of the hero, which lead to a resolution where civilised values are established out of the chaos of the wilderness. Similarly, in the crime film, law and order are restored by male investigative action into transgression. In their most common definitions as male-addressed genres, both the Western and the crime film are understood as addressing public, hence read 'universal', concerns, and are opposed to the 'private' concerns of home, hearth and family attributed to female-addressed genres. However, it is my argument that within both *film noir* and the female gothic film, female characters are frequently placed in narrative positions that challenge assumptions of gendered agency, and which show a grasp of issues in the socio-cultural and public sphere. In examining the female characters in these texts, I have been concerned with narrative placement not as a static textual position, but as shifting within the narrativity of these genres. In her discussion of narrativity, Teresa de Lauretis illustrates the necessity to engage with the processes and particularities of different narrative structures:

> The "transhistorical" narratological view of narrative structures seems to have given way to an attempt to historicize the notion of narrative by relating it to the subject and to its implication in, or dependence on the social order, the law of meaning; or to the transformative effects produced in processes of reading and practices of writing. More often than not, however,

those efforts all but reaffirm an integrative and ultimately traditional view of narrativity. Paradoxically, in spite of the methodological shift away from the notion of structure and toward a notion of process, they end up dehistoricizing the subject and thus universalising the narrative processes as such. The problem, I believe, is that many of the current formulations of narrative process fail to see that subjectivity is engaged in the cogs of narrative and indeed constituted in the relation of narrative, meaning, and desire; so that the very work of narrativity is the engagement of the subject in certain positionalities of meaning and desire. Or else they fail to locate the relations of narrative and desire where it takes place, where that relation is materially inscribed – in a field of textual practices. Thus, finally, they fail to envisage a materially, historically, and experientially constituted subject, a subject gender, we might say, precisely by the process of its engagement in the narrative genres.[12]

The engagement with female characters in the narrative genres of *film noir* and the female gothic film form the subsequent chapters of this book. Following de Lauretis' call for attention to process, I emphasise the shifting positionalities of the heroines that I examine. Rather than thinking of these positionalities as stereotyped, and thus static, I have acknowledged these characters and their actions as speaking both from and to shifts in female identities, desires and roles in both the periods that the book examines. I have drawn upon Hilary Radner's notion of female characters as 'public femininities',[13] which arise as part of a relay between the cinema genres and their cycles of popularity and discourses on female identities that exist as part of a wider conversation about gender in the popular media. As such, this notion captures the qualities that characterise women on screen in particular eras, their transformations through narration, and the relation of these characterisations to the public world beyond it.

The third issue that informs this book comprises the histories, processes and protocols of feminist debates on Hollywood. As my encounter with these debates taught me so much about how to approach Hollywood and its genres, and prompted me to pursue my own questions and engagement, I have tried to keep feminist methodological questions at the forefront of my discussion. This is partly an attempt to acknowledge a debt of scholarship, and partly an expression of enthusiastically taking part in a shifting and developing discourse. The shifts that I trace in this ongoing debate stretch from feminist criticism of the 1970s to contemporary discussions of women and film. As such they form a bridge between my examination of genres in the 1940s and the recurrence of those genres in the more contemporary period. Feminist engagements with film were the starting point of this project, the facility of feminist debate to encompass different approaches and different views allowed the project to take shape, and the vibrancy and intellectual rigour of feminist work made me want to complete the project and to offer my own engagement with Hollywood heroines and their meanings.

Chapter One

At the Margins of Film Noir: Genre, Range and Female Representation

Introduction

Film noir has been one of the most debated, most discussed and most contested terms in studies of film history and film genre. *Film noir* has usually been talked about in terms of its historical resonances, its treatment of gender and its uses of style, and these three trends in *noir* criticism continue to inform criticism on and of *noir*, contributing to the long, unfinished, and arguably unfinishable, process of its discursive formation. This chapter looks again at the discussions and debates about *film noir*, gender and its industrial and socio-cultural contexts. It draws upon both contemporaneous and critical discourses, in order to explore the heterogeneity of *film noir*'s styles and narratives. It examines *film noir*'s historical coincidence with other forms, particularly the female gothic film cycle of the 1940s. It analyses *noir*'s relation to gender, revealing considerable variety in its characterisation of female figures and their agency by focusing upon the working-girl investigator figure. It suggests that *noir*'s 'Ur' narrative (a male investigation of a fatal female enigma) is only one strand in *noir*'s quite varied array. Finally, it retraces *noir*'s relation to its socio-cultural contexts by exploring the resonances of the working-girl investigator as a representation of female independence in the

1940s. This figure offers a different picture of gender relations than the 'gender crisis' or 'gender conflict' that is so commonly ascribed as central to *noir*'s meaning.

Noir's 'Zeitgeist' in the 1940s

Perceptions of *film noir*'s 'special' role in expressing the cultural anxieties of its time arise very early in its critical history. In 1947, producer John Houseman noted the trend for the 'tough' crime thriller in Hollywood, exemplified for him by *The Big Sleep* (Howard Hawks, 1946): 'It almost looks as if the American people, turning from the anxiety and shock of war, were afraid to face their personal problems and the painful situations of their national life.'[1] He sees the hero, Philip Marlow (Humphrey Bogart), and heroine, Vivien Sternwood (Lauren Bacall), as manifesting an amoral hopelessness paradigmatic of the national mood. Similarly, French film critics Raymonde Borde and Étienne Chaumeton, who were among the first critics to use the term '*film noir*' to describe Hollywood's 'tough' crime thriller, focus upon 'moral ambivalence … criminality, [and] … complex contradictions in motives and events'.[2] Borde and Chaumeton see viewers' experiences of these elements as central to *film noir*'s creation of 'a *specific alienation*'.[3] The national mood that Houseman identifies, and the 'specific alienation' that Borde and Chaumeton attribute to *film noir,* are key to *noir*'s relation to its socio-cultural context. The terms of *noir*'s purchase on its context has been a recurrent theme in *film noir* criticism, with questions of *noir*'s gender relations forming a central focus. However, to accurately identify this mood, and the specificity of *noir*'s alienation, is not a straightforward process. I will chart the discussion of these issues in *noir* criticism, and then illustrate some of the complexities that arise from *noir*'s heterogeneity, and its socio-cultural and industrial contexts.

As Steve Neale notes, several socio-cultural themes are recurrent in criticism charting the ideological significance of *film noir*. These themes include the wartime mobilisation of women and men, with its subsequent disruption of gender roles, and post-war cultural readjustments.[4] Much critical discussion of *film noir*'s socio-cultural meanings finds parallels in these contexts in *noir*'s representation of gender and sexuality:

> For many commentators, the principal hallmarks of *noir* include a distinctive treatment of sexual desire and sexual relationships, a distinctive array of male and female character types, and a distinctive repertoire of male and female traits, ideals, characteristics and forms of behaviour. For some these elements can be related directly to contemporary social and cultural trends and factors; they help not only to define *noir*, but also to account for its existence.[5]

Feminist work on *film noir* and gender, such as that by Christine Gledhill[6] and Janey Place,[7] typify this focus. Gledhill argues that *noir* presents 'certain highly formalised inflections of plot, character and visual style',[8] which 'offer[s] a world of action defined in male terms; the locales, situations, iconography, violence are conventions connoting the male sphere'.[9] She continues:

> Women in this world tend to split into two categories: there are those who work on the fringes of the underworld and are defined by the male criminal ambience of the thriller – bar-flies, night-club singers, expensive mistresses, *femmes fatales*, and ruthless gold-diggers who marry and murder rich old men for their money; and then there are women on the outer margins of this world, wives, long-suffering girl-friends, would-be fiancées who are victims of male crime, sometimes the objects of the hero's protection, and often points of vulnerability in his masculine armour.[10]

Janey Place's work on female character types in *film noir* also focuses upon a division into 'the two poles of female archetypes',[11] what we might understand as a 'vice–virtue' polarity between 'the dark lady ... and her sister (or alter ego) the virgin ... the redeemer',[12] in which sexuality is the terrain of both female agency and female threat:

> *Film noir* is a male fantasy, as is most of our art. Thus woman here as elsewhere is defined by her sexuality: the dark lady has

access to it and the virgin does not... women are defined *in relation to* men, and the centrality of sexuality in this definition is a key to understanding the position of women in our culture. The primary crime the 'liberated' woman is guilty of is refusing to be defined in such a way, and this refusal can be perversely seen... as an attack on men's very existence. *Film noir* is hardly 'progressive' in these terms ... but it does give us one of the few periods of film in which women are active, not static symbols, are intelligent and powerful, if destructively so, and derive power, not weakness, from their sexuality.[13]

These approaches are predicated on a definition of *film noir* as a male genre, envisaging a male sphere of action and control, where female agency is expressed in terms of trangressive desire. While the *femme fatale* figure has been an important one in initiating feminist debates about the politics of Hollywood representation, and interpretation in feminist criticism, the story of *film noir*'s women is not reducible to this vice–virtue polarity. There is a much wider range of female characterisation in the *noir* crime thriller during the 1940s, and these characters undertake roles and display agency in ways that are not solely reducible to their sexuality. The relative lack of critical engagement with these characters in the 1940s is due to the fact that the *femme fatale* has cast an imaginative shadow over the period, occluding and obscuring female roles that fit neither within the 'vice' or 'virtue' polarity of sexuality. This is partly attributable to *noir*'s identity as a discursively constructed category within genre debates, leading to a 'consequent haziness about the contours of the larger *noir* canon',[14] and partly attributable to the way that the *femme fatale* has stood as paradigmatic of socio-cultural changes in women's roles in the World War II and post-war eras. Bringing the range of female characters of the 1940s out from under this shadow means looking again at *noir*'s contemporary moment, acknowledging the heterogeneous array of films and character types that comprise it, and registering their coexistence and popularity at the time.

In 1947, replying to John Houseman, Lester Asheim disputed the 'tough' movie as expressing an American 'zeitgeist', asking: 'How popular is the tough movie? How overwhelming is the popular

preference for this kind of entertainment?'[15] Citing the trade journal *Variety*, and a Gallup poll of movie-goers' favourite films for
1946 – the year marking the all-time peak of American cinema
attendances – Asheim argues 'at least half the films listed are pure
entertainment, light and gay, preferably with music; yet no claim is
made that postwar America is a lighthearted, song-in-its-heart
haven of romance and the joys of youth'.[16] Asheim's discussion
questions the representativeness of the 'tough' film, marking a
wider spread of popular genres at the time.[17]

Other contemporary perspectives show that *film noir*'s *femme
fatale* was only one manifestation of 'tough' female characterisation during the 1940s. In October 1946, the editorial of *Picturegoer*
magazine remarks on 'ruthless women' in a range of genres,
including the costume film, the epic, the western and the 'woman's
picture'.[18] Similarly, Steve Neale shows a range of labels for 'tough'
female characterisation in the 1940s, and gives instances of
'tough' womanhood in 'psychological women's pictures', such as
The Dark Mirror (Robert Siodmak, 1946), comedies and westerns,
such as *Ball of Fire* (Howard Hawks, 1941) and *The Ox-Bow
Incident* (William Wellman, 1943), and gothic thrillers, such as *Ivy*
(Sam Wood, 1947). He concludes that '*femmes fatales* were by
no means restricted to *noir*'.[19] These perspectives show that the
category of 'the' *femme fatale* is heterogeneous and does not simply arise in one cycle (the crime film), nor serve a single function
(object of male crime quest).

Noir's distinctiveness, in terms of the specificity of its stylistic
narrative form, is also open to question in ways that challenge its
boundaries as a category. The visual style that has come to be synonymous with *noir* – camera framing, chiaroscuro lighting, editing
patterns and so on – in discussions by critics such as Janey Place
and Lowell Peterson and Foster Hirsch, were stylistic elements
commonly used across a range of film cycles in the 1940s, most
widely in the horror film and the female gothic cycle. Discussions of
style across these groups of films were occurring in the professional journals of the industry during the 1940s.[20] I will trace the
stylistic alliances between *noir* and the female gothic cycles in
more detail in Chapter 2, but it should be noted that a definitive
noir style is, as it were, less than black and white.

Gender and Narrative in *Film Noir*

Elizabeth Cowie outlines the typical critical picture of *film noir* as structured around a male-centred, male-addressed narrative. In this model of *noir*, the narrative deals with a triumph 'over a threatening and dangerous feminine element' and, often relatedly, resolves 'conflict with the law'.[21] Frank Krutnik's work, for example, locates *noir*'s specificity in the 'tough' thriller which:

> ... tends to be structured around a testing of the hero's prowess – not merely a testing of his ability as a detective or criminal, but of how he measures up to more extensive standards of masculine competence. For it is through his accomplishment of a crime-related quest that the hero consolidates his masculine identity.[22]

Other critics have focused on *noir* as presenting dangerous desire from a male perspective, with the work of James Damico, Marc Vernet and Foster Hirsch exemplifying this focus.[23] Cowie suggests that within these critical perspectives, *films noirs* 'appear to be the antithesis of the "woman's film"'.[24] But she challenges the 'tendency to characterize *film noir* as always a masculine film form'[25] by demonstrating the variety of roles women played. Female characters investigate crimes (in films such as *Phantom Lady* (Robert Siodmak, 1944), *The Dark Corner* (Henry Hathaway, 1946) and *I Wouldn't Be in Your Shoes* (Marvin Mirsch, 1948)), fall victim to the criminal underworld (*The Reckless Moment* (Max Ophuls, 1949), *The Damned Don't Cry* (Vincent Sherman, 1950) and *Too Late for Tears* (Byron Haskin, 1949)), and are sometimes tempted into relationships with duplicitous men. This is also a feature of the female gothic cycle, explored in later chapters.[26] Cowie's enumeration of female character types asks 'questions of narrative focus'[27] which challenge assumptions of *noir*'s exclusive male-address. Cowie asks:

> Whose story does the film tell? On which character does it centre? Does it centre on more than one character? Does it tell a man's or a woman's story? Finally, what does it mean to ask the last question?[28]

The famously complex or convoluted narrative structure of the *noir* crime thriller,[29] then, potentially accommodates a multiple narrative focus, and a division of narrative labour through a centring on female as well as male characters, and therefore offers a space for the telling of women's alongside men's stories.

Film Noir from the 'Woman's Angle'

Following Cowie's perspective, Angela Martin also advances a critique of *noir* as a male-addressed form. Suggesting that the term *film noir* has become 'something of a phrase *fatale*'[30] in film criticism, she argues that the discursive boundaries of *noir*'s critical canon become particularly contested regarding the categorisation of films where female characters are narratively central:

> Critical texts often deal with the genre/cycle question; the problem of style or historical moment; or that of misfitting films: films with certain crucial (generic) elements missing, or films which belong to another genre – particularly (though not always, and this is never signalled as such) when they have central female characters.[31]

Martin charts many *films noirs* that are explicitly woman-centred. Some of these are eponymously titled, indicating the important position of female stars and their ability to carry dramatic crime narratives, for example: Gene Tierney in *Laura* (Otto Preminger, 1944), Joan Crawford in *Mildred Pierce* (Michael Curtiz, 1945), Rita Hayworth in *Gilda* (Charles Vidor, 1946), Barbara Stanwyck in *The Strange Love of Martha Ivers* (Lewis Milestone, 1946) and Ann Sheridan in *Nora Prentiss* (Vincent Sherman, 1947). Martin lists a further 80 films produced between 1941 and 1959 that contain central female characters, 33 of which had women involved in the films' production, in the roles of writing source stories or novels, as adaptors or screenwriters, or as female directors or female producers.[32] Of all the many *noirs*, central or marginal, that Martin catalogues and examines, she finds only a fraction of central characters who could be unproblematically labelled as a *femme fatale*,[33] again lending weight to a widened view of *film noir* as a heterogeneous genre with a complex gendered address.

A critical perspective that takes account of female characters and their narrative agency in *film noir* is not, of course, altogether new. *Laura*,[34] *Mildred Pierce*,[35] *Gilda*[36] and *The File on Thelma Jordan* (Robert Siodmak, 1950)[37] are all films that have been discussed as advancing or portraying female points of view in complex ways that exceed and problematise the 'vice–virtue' polarity of *noir* female characterisation.[38] These instances of the textual centrality of female characters and concerns within the *noir* crime film of the 1940s are underpinned by some key contextual factors, both relating to shifts within the institutions of the Hollywood studio system, and its wider socio-cultural context.

The first of these factors is movie-going audiences in the 1940s: their volume and composition, particularly their composition by gender. As Thomas Schatz notes, in Hollywood's studio era producers had long been convinced that most movie-goers were women.[39] During the early 1940s, motion picture executives began to take advantage of powerful new public opinion polling, and other social surveying techniques. These had grown out of the advertising industry in the late 1930s, and were identified as useful techniques for gauging public opinion and morale during the war years.[40] The formation of George Gallup's Audience Research Institute (ARI) in 1940, and the data that it produced about the movie-going public, was significant in revealing both audience composition and preferences. In a poll taken in July 1941, Gallup showed that just over half (51 percent) of the audience was female, 'although that proportion could vary up to 75 percent for both sexes depending on the specific film'.[41] The 1941 Gallup poll revealed that 'women tended to prefer romance and serious drama, while men preferred action and comedy'.[42] In June 1946, noted earlier as a significant year in terms of cinema attendances, *Motion Picture Herald* reported an audience poll from *Woman's Home Companion*, in which 54 percent of (female) respondents preferred 'romantic dramas' and 29 percent 'mystery' films,[43] types of films that encompass both the *noir* crime thriller and the female gothic film. There was also a conviction in the advertising industry, and Hollywood, that women led purchase decision-making, which included entertainment choices.[44] This is particularly key in considering Hollywood's gendered address and its relationship to the production and positioning of genres through female characterisation and marketing to women.

The second contextual factor underpinning female characterisation in the *noir* crime film was the increased presence of female screenwriters in Hollywood during the war years. In her work on women screenwriters, Lizzie Francke argues that the war's impact was twofold: first, the conscription of male screenwriters opened up opportunities for the women screenwriters remaining in their jobs; and second, during the war years the homefront audience was predominantly female: 'the woman's angle' was being stressed more than ever. But this was a decade when the women's picture would begin to show some of the stresses and strains of the female experience.[45]

This is evident in writers' perspectives on their own roles. Catherine Turney, adaptor and screenwriter for Warner Bros, recalls:

> They [Warner Bros] recognised the fact that a woman could handle a story about a woman's troubles better than most men could. Anyway, you can rest assured that if the studio didn't think the woman did a better job, she wouldn't have been there for very long... One of the reasons they hired me is that the men were off at the war, and they had all these big female stars. The stars had to have roles that served them well. They themselves wanted something in which they weren't just sitting around being a simpering nobody...[their characters were women] battling against the odds.[46]

During the 1940s Turney worked on Warner's projects, bringing a vivid but realistic female 'angle' to dramas with the studio's top female stars. She worked on the Bette Davis vehicle *A Stolen Life* (Curtis Bernhardt, 1946) and *Mildred Pierce*, starring Joan Crawford. But emphasis on the 'woman's angle' in the 1940s was not confined to 'the woman's film', so often defined as the domestic melodrama. Emphases on female characters, issues and concerns were key features of 'crime' and 'mystery' films too, and the *noir* crime thriller and the female gothic film are both included under this female-influenced production trend.

The work of writer-producers Joan Harrison and Virginia Van Upp and writer Leigh Brackett illustrate a female influence on crime and mystery films in the 1940s. Van Upp produced the female-centred *noir* thriller *Gilda*.[47] Already a successful author of crime and science fiction novels, Leigh Brackett's first major screenwriting assignment was her collaboration with director Howard Hawks and writers William Faulkner and Jules Furthman on *The Big Sleep*. Hawks' films have been synonymous with distinctive characterisations of the 'independent' woman, and Brackett's collaborations were part of the Hawksian woman's formation on the screen.[48]

Joan Harrison had earned eight years of experience working with Alfred Hitchcock in Britain before moving to Hollywood as part of his team in 1939. Beginning as a secretary, her work on the Hitchcock team gradually encompassed experience working on all aspects of production, including casting and set design.[49] Harrison co-scripted five Hitchcock films, including *Rebecca* (1940), *Foreign Correspondent* (1940) and *Suspicion* (1941). She moved into the 'hyphenate' role of writer-producer at Universal, where her first assignment was as associate producer for *Dark Waters* (Andre de Toth, 1944). Later in the same year she produced *Phantom Lady* at Universal, which is discussed in detail later in this chapter. Harrison's position as a female writer-producer was exceptional enough to attract a significant amount of publicity in the movie industry and the press covering it. A *New York Times* article covers Harrison's appointment at Universal, and plays on her connection to Hitchcock, reporting 'She's going to specialise in mystery films – "from the woman's angle"'. It quotes Harrison: 'Women must have something to pull for, you know, whether it's a dog, a horse, an old beggar – or even another woman!'[50]

Harrison's career as a producer extended over 27 years and included producing for television, notably with Hitchcock again on *Alfred Hitchcock Presents*. Her work in the 1940s shows she did indeed become a successful specialist in the mystery and crime genres, co-writing the female gothic *Rebecca*, co-writing and producing the female gothic *Dark Waters*, and producing the female-centred crime film *Phantom Lady*, the crime/mysteries *The Strange Affair of*

Uncle Harry (Robert Siodmak, 1945) and *They Won't Believe Me* (Irving Pichel, 1946), and the detective/crime films *Nocturne* (Edwin L Marin, 1947) and *Ride the Pink Horse* (Robert Montgomery, 1947). Harrison was not alone in taking on production roles: in early 1945, Fred Stanley noted that 'Hollywood Bows to Ladies':

> Picture-making, like everything else, is coming more and more under feminine influence. The ladies, no longer content with being just glamorous, are invading in increasing numbers the production field, a sphere hitherto almost entirely masculine.[51]

Stanley's article covers Harrison's work at Universal and Virginia Van Upp's appointment to the role of executive producer at Columbia, as well as upcoming productions supervised by other women, and shows the increasingly visible profile of women in production roles.[52]

The importance of female audiences and the presence of women workers in Hollywood conditioned and influenced *film noir*'s heterogeneity in its treatment of gender. The audience research cited above makes clear that there were strong female audience preferences for drama and mystery films. It is also clear that women screenwriters and producers working in Hollywood in World War II, and after it, made their influence felt on a range of genres, with a particular emphasis on the 'woman's angle' of the crime and mystery genres. The cultural and institutional environment in which Hollywood *noir* was produced and consumed in the 1940s resulted not in a clear generic form, stratified absolutely by gender, but one with multiple influences and, consequently, a complex gendered address. These shifts in the working patterns and generic styles within the film industry were part of a larger context of shifts in female roles during the war years.

Independent Women and Working-Girls: Women's Pre-War and Wartime Roles

There is no doubt that the social and economic shifts inherent in America's wartime economy had a profound effect on American

11

women's lives during the 1940s. Cultural critics such as William Chafe and Betty Friedan, and social historians of film like Marjorie Rosen, have argued that women's wartime employment and the subsequent post-war 'return' to home and family life initiated a 'crisis' in women's perceptions of their identities which constituted a proto-feminist consciousness.[53] Rosen characterises America's entry into World War II as follows:

> On December 7, 1941, the Japanese bombed the hell out of Pearl Harbor, Johnny got his gun, America mobilized. And social roles shifted with a speed that would have sent Wonder Woman into paroxysms of power pride.[54]

And Sheri Chinen-Biesen argues that '… the representation of transgressive *noir* femme fatales coincided with a wartime female labour force, nationally and inside the film industry'.[55] But the ways in which women's wartime jobs are characterised and understood need some careful consideration. The working roles that women undertook in wartime employment were quite varied, and were conditioned by longer and underlying patterns in the pre- and post-war eras. Further, the concepts of 'home' and 'family' did not necessarily have stable meanings in early twentieth-century America.

Highly visible female icons of the working woman were key to wartime propaganda campaigns designed to encourage women to join the wartime workforce, particularly in heavy industries like the war plants. One of the most visible of these icons was, of course, Rosie the Riveter.[56] Rosie first appeared in 1942 in a popular song by Redd Evans and John Jacob Loeb, and recorded by big-band leader Key Keyser. She was formed into an image in posters produced by the War Production Co-Ordinating Committee, and Norman Rockwell's design for the cover of the *Saturday Evening Post* magazine, 29 May 1943.

Hollywood also had a role in cementing Rosie as a public icon. Leading man Walter Pidgeon was covered by the press when he met a production-line worker called Rosie Will Monroe on his promotional tour of the Ford Motor Company's aircraft assembly plant in Ypsilanti, Michigan.[57] Female war plant workers featured in home

War Production Co-Ordinating Committee poster.

front dramas such as *Tender Comrade* (Edward Dymtryk, 1943) and *Since You Went Away* (William Wyler, 1944), and the 'character' of Rosie (Jane Frazee) appeared in the musical *Rosie the Riveter* (Joseph Santley, 1944). The film offered a comic take on wartime

13

housing shortages in its story, which concerned four war plant workers forced to share the one vacant room in town across the different hours of their shifts.

The circulation of Rosie advanced a patriotic, 'can-do' wartime figure. She constituted an icon of feminine identity in the public sphere, showing women 'doing their bit' for America in radically new roles. As such, Rosie has become synonymous with the war era as proto-feminist. The high numbers of wartime working women were covered in the press, initiating intense public debates focused on the social effects of shifts in family and gender structures.[58] Questions circulating included: 'Were women in male roles squeezing out more "deserving" male breadwinners?', 'Would these women quit their jobs at the end of the war?' and 'What were the implications for family life?'[59] It is these debates that have underpinned the notion of a social 'crisis' in gender relations that has been central to debates on *noir*'s social purchase.

However, social historian D'Ann Campbell traces much longer patterns to female employment that underlie the war era, showing that from the depression of the 1930s onwards nearly all women leaving school sought, and found, employment.[60] It was the norm for young women to work between finishing their education and marrying, and although the war brought extra women, particularly married ones, into the workforce, 'one misconception must be cleared away immediately. Very few of the women were strangers to employment.'[61] Campbell shows that women's moving into, and out of, the labour market was a common pattern in American female employment in the early twentieth century. In fact, temporariness typified female employment, but this became particularly accented and visible during the war era.[62] Drawing on public opinion polls and social survey sources, Campbell also argues that the decade of the 1940s was marked by a transformation in the ways in which American women saw their private and public roles:

> ... the meanings of marriage and motherhood were changing for younger women. Many women still espoused the traditional view "what is good for my family is good for me"; nevertheless, younger, better-educated women were seeking less passive, more egalitarian, and more emotionally satisfying

companionate marriages. Very few women at the time claimed to want independent lives, but the younger generation wanted to adapt the old roles to new personal aspirations. They sought to transform the roles of wife and mother, and to improve the quality of personal relations in the face of disruptive forces – the draft and migration to war centers – as well as new advantages, especially the availability of well-paid jobs and the higher levels of education and personal competence of the younger generation.[63]

Campbell also provides a wider and more complete view of women's wartime roles, showing that by far the commonest roles undertaken were in the white-collar jobs associated with administering the war effort. Propaganda campaigns also visualised clerical work as 'patriotic', as the US Civil Service Commission poster in the image on page 16 shows.

In the years 1940–7, American women held an average of 41.4 percent of *all* white-collar jobs, comprising professional, managerial, clerical and sales roles. Women also held the *majority* of all clerical positions in the American white-collar workforce, forming 52.6 percent of clerical workers in 1940, rising to 70.3 percent by 1945 and dropping to 58.6 percent by 1947.[64] So that for every 'Rosie' working in a war plant, there were two women working in clerical roles, but it was 'Rosie' who tended to get more publicity. Campbell notes: 'few articles, newspaper stories, films or radio shows featured secretaries, whereas Rosie the Riveter was everywhere... perhaps part of the reason was that women were not novelties in the office. The war only amplified an existing trend that actually grew faster in the postwar era.'[65]

Secretarial roles were important in women's developing economic independence in the late nineteenth and early twentieth centuries. The urbanisation of large populations, and the modernisation of working business practices, through the development of new technologies (the typewriter, filing cabinet and the index card), brought many newly educated young women into new roles.[66] Secretarial work authorised the presence and place of young women in the city, allowing them to display competence in processing and managing information and make social connections of

The patriotic working-girl: US Civil Service Commission poster.

their own outside their family circles. The female secretary is a common character in late nineteenth- and early twentieth-century New Woman fictions,[67] and in magazine stories in the 1930s and 1940s.[68] During World War II, the training that young women received in clerical work provided many with a career in the post-war period that did not have to be sacrificed for returning veterans. As well as being more economically secure than war plant work, clerical roles were qualitatively different. Campbell analyses their advantages as follows:

> If money, glamour, and opportunity for advancement were not the main inducements for women taking clerical jobs, what were they? Job security was one key factor. Blue-collar jobs paid good wages, but only for the duration, as women rightly feared. After the war, white-collar salaries went up faster than blue-collar wages. Clerical work was more "feminine", permitted attractive clothes, encouraged good grooming, was clean, emphasized intellectual and interpersonal skills, was physically less tiring, rarely involved night hours, was located in a prestigious skyscraper or Main Street building instead of a grimy industrial estate, and involved regular contact with well-educated, well-paid colleagues who tried to be polite to one another. A secretary, furthermore, could pride herself on an individual relationship with her boss; she was not just one of the gang. All of these advantages can be summed up with one word: clerical jobs were "classy".[69]

Towards the end of the war, typewriter companies capitalised on the assumption that women workers in heavy industry or war plant work would shift into other jobs.[70] This is illustrated by a Smith-Corona advertisement, which promotes clerical work by showing a woman metal worker holding her factory identity badge and asking: 'When it becomes a souvenir ... what then? Stay at home ... do nothing? You *know* you won't! Like our fighting men, you've earned the right to choose work you enjoy and the time to prepare is ... now!'[71]

The address of the Smith-Corona to the enterprising working-girl shows the establishment of a place for women in the public sphere of work. The increase in female clerical workers coincided with distinct modifications in how Hollywood imagined female figures in the crime and mystery film. The increased emphasis on the 'woman's angle' resulted in a number of films where working-girl characters use their position in the city to investigate and solve crime enigmas. The films present female investigative action as concurrent with a negotiation of women's public and private roles, and narrative strands of the crime-enigma are intertwined with romance. The films therefore visualise women negotiating, adapting and transforming their roles in meaningful and revealing ways.

'Not (herself) Mean': The Working-girl Investigator in *Film Noir*

> ... down these mean streets a man must go who is not himself mean, who is neither tarnished nor afraid. The detective in this kind of story must be such a man. He is the hero, he is everything. He must be a complete man and a common man and yet an unusual man. He must be, to use a rather weathered phrase, a man of honour, by instinct, by inevitability, without thought of it, and certainly without saying it. He must be the best man in his world and a good enough man for any world – Raymond Chandler.[72]

A secretary, Jane (Margaret Tallichet), goes out into the city streets seeking to clear her her fiancé Michael (John McGuire) of a murder charge. She encounters the prime suspect, an unstable stranger (Peter Lorre), at a diner, and befriends him. She extracts his confession before he threatens her and she takes flight through the night-time streets. Giving chase, the 'stranger' suspect falls under a truck and confesses with his last breath. The film, *Stranger on the Third Floor* (Boris Ingster, 1940), closes with Jane and the now liberated Michael going to City Hall to get married.

A secretary, Jill (Betty Grable), outwits the police staking out her apartment by climbing over the city rooftops to join forces with murder suspect Frankie (Victor Mature) and helps free him from being framed for her sister's murder. Faking the dead woman's voice, she helps Frankie and the police extract a confession from the murderer Harry Williams (Elisha Cook Jnr) and exposes the corruption of the lead investigator, Ed Cornell (Laird Cregar). The film, *I Wake Up Screaming* (H Bruce Humberstone, 1941), closes with Jill and Frankie, now proved innocent, dancing together on their wedding day.

A secretary, Carol/'Kansas' Richman (Ella Raines), saves her boss, civil engineer Scott Henderson (Alan Curtis), from a death sentence when he is wrongfully convicted of killing his wife. When the police give up on the case, Kansas re-traces Scott's movements on the night of the murder, seeking and eventually finding the alibi that he needs. On her quest, she encounters physical jeopardy from several threatening men, ending up in the lair of the murderer Jack Marlow (Franchot Tone) who is foiled in his intention to kill her by the arrival of Inspector Burgess (Thomas Gomez). The film, *Phantom Lady* (Robert Siodmak, 1944), closes with Scott's reinstatement to his business, and his proposal to Kansas.

A secretary, Kathleen (Lucille Ball), helps her boss, private detective Brad Galt (Mark Stevens), track down the man who is trying to frame him. She goes out on the trail of a heavy 'White Suit' (William Bendix), helps Brad conceal a body in his apartment, acts as a sounding board throughout the investigation, and makes the final connection between 'White Suit' and art dealer Hardy Cathcart (Clifton Webb) which allows Brad to prove himself innocent. The film, *The Dark Corner* (Henry Hathaway, 1947), closes with Kathleen and Brad planning to marry.

These four films show distinct modifications of the *noir* crime narrative and the characters that inhabit it. They reveal a different picture of *noir* to its most frequent categorisation by genre criticism. In these films the necessities of narrative situation require the working-girl to become an investigator who is fitted for her role through her possession of intelligence, resolve and resourcefulness. Her central elucidating role also gives her the agency to forward and complete the narrative. Her character is thus both determined and determinant. *Noir* genre criticism has tended to emphasise its connection with 'hard boiled' detective and crime fictions, by writers such as Dashiell Hammett, James M Cain and Raymond Chandler, a connection that foregrounds male narrative centrality, and perceptions of male agency, particularly where the narrative is structured around a criminal investigation. Chandler's now familiar evocation of the detective-hero, cited above, makes this figure both morally and narratively central: 'he is everything'.[73]

This centrality is echoed in Krutnik's focus on the *noir* crime narrative as formative of masculine identity: 'it is through his accomplishment of a crime-related quest that the hero consolidates his masculine identity.'[74]

However, within the variety of *noir* narratives there are frequent scenarios in which male characters fail to accomplish the crime quest. Richard Maltby argues that the investigative crime narrative underwent a particular inflection in the 1940s, becoming more complex and convoluted, and containing an ambivalent hero:

> Uncertainly adrift in a world of treachery and shifting loyalties, the investigator of the *noir* movie was himself less than perfect, frequently neurotic, sometimes paranoid, and often manages to re-establish a stable world in the film only by imposing an arbitrary resolution on the other characters.[75]

This suggests that the 'completeness' of the hero might be more accurately understood as an 'ideal' narrative position for a male character, rather than a universal or essential one. The discussion of the films that follow will show how male characters become enmeshed in convoluted crime narratives, and are dependent for their liberation on the motivations and consequent actions of female figures who take on temporary investigative roles. In *Stranger on the Third Floor*, *I Wake Up Screaming*, *Phantom Lady* and *The Dark Corner*, male identity is both explored and consolidated through female investigative action, and the closure of the films in the formation of a couple constitutes the end point of the woman's exploration of her partner. The main strand of my discussion will centre on *Phantom Lady*, but I will elaborate with references to a range of other films.

The Female Sleuth in *Phantom Lady*

Phantom Lady is the story of one woman's search for another. Its drama arises from the motivation for and processes of that search. The film's opening shot shows Ann Terry (Fay Helm) wearing a highly distinctive hat and ordering a drink in Anselmo's Bar. She encounters Scott Henderson (Alan Curtis), who buys her a drink and invites her to join him at a musical revue. She agrees, on the condition that they do not exchange names or any personal information. The sequence lays out their evening together, they take a cab, attend the review where the star attraction wears an identical hat, before parting. On returning to his apartment, Scott finds the police waiting for him. His wife, Marcella, has been murdered and he is the prime suspect.

The opening narration of the film has given the audience knowledge of Scott's innocence by showing the existence of the 'Phantom Lady', but the situation and conditions of her evening with Scott – 'no names' – make his alibi, and therefore his innocent status, difficult to substantiate. Accompanied by the lead investigator, Inspector Burgess, Scott retraces his movements on the night of the murder. The bar man, Mack (Andrew Toombes Jnr), the cab driver (uncredited), and revue singer, Estela Monteiro (Aurora Miranda), all deny seeing Scott and the Phantom Lady on the night in question. Scott is tried and convicted for Marcella's murder on circumstantial evidence.

The remainder of the film concerns Carol Richman and her corroboration of Scott's story through her search for evidence. Known as 'Kansas' (Scott's nickname for her) throughout the film, she attends Scott's trial, where prominent reaction shots of her distress and disbelief show that she is convinced of his innocence and gives her the motivation to reopen the case. The trial, and Kansas' visit to Scott's jail, show her gradually picking up the lines of inquiry. Where Scott is despairing, Kansas argues: 'You've got to fight' and 'you need someone to help you who really wants to. Someone who just won't be beaten.' Kansas thus takes on the central role in exploring the crime enigma, and 'embarks on a sleuthing tour to find the woman with the hat',[76] moving into the central elucidating position in the narrative.

Working to the same pattern as Inspector Burgess has, Kansas retraces Scott's movements, and the people he encountered on that night, becoming 'a femme amateur detective'.[77] Kansas' sleuthing, though, offers new leads where Burgess' investigation had been blocked. She extracts evidence of a cover-up as she stakes out Anselmo's bar for several nights, causing the guilty

Working-girl investigator Kansas (Ella Raines) corners and confronts her quarry in *Phantom Lady* (Robert Siodmak, 1944).

barman to display his nerves, and trails him through the night-time streets. She eventually corners her quarry, insisting: 'You've got something to tell me.' Her courageous confrontation of Mack puts her in danger. Humiliated by her questions he attacks her, before fleeing and falling to his death under the wheels of a car.

Returning to her apartment after trailing Mack, she finds an ally in Inspector Burgess. He admits he also knows Scott is innocent, but that he lacks the evidence to close the case. Telling Kansas that he will help 'unofficially', he effectively appoints Kansas to the side of the law, and they collaborate on the subsequent investigation, eventually acquiring the Phantom Lady's hat as evidence.

Kansas' next assignment is undercover. Disguised as 'Jeannie', she plays a highly sexualised 'hep-kitten' to gain the attention and confidence of revue-drummer Cliff Milburn (Elisha Cook Jnr).

Meeting him after the show, Kansas/Jeannie accompanies him to a jam-session, then to his apartment where he admits he has been paid off to keep quiet about the Phantom Lady's presence at the revue with Scott. Kansas' disguise is exposed when Cliff rummages in her bag for cigarettes, and finds details of his name and address on police notepaper; he threatens Kansas, forcing her to flee.

While Kansas waits for Burgess, Cliff meets his end at the pathological hands of Marlow. Marlow, a paranoiac sculptor, is behind Marcella's murder, and the framing of his 'best friend' Scott for the crime. Marlow collaborates with Kansas and Burgess on their investigation, in order to control events. Initially neither of them suspect their prime suspect is so close. It is only after Kansas has secured the Phantom Lady's hat as evidence, and returned to Marlow's apartment, that he is exposed. Realisation dawns on Kansas when she finds 'Jeannie's' bag in a drawer, and calls for Burgess. Marlow reveals his solipsistic monomania, threatening Kansas: 'If only you'd never come to New York and met Scott. The world's full of men like him. You can buy stupid people a dime a dozen.' Kansas tries to escape, but finds the door locked. Her plight seems hopeless, until Burgess arrives and breaks down the door, at which point Marlow throws himself to his death from his apartment window. With the murder case resolved, and Scott liberated, Kansas resumes her secretarial role. The final scenes of the film show Kansas, Burgess and Scott at Scott's new offices. Scott's outlook is markedly different to the despair he displayed when imprisoned. His confidence is fully restored, so that Burgess remarks to Kansas that he is 'quite his old self', adding that 'he owes you a great deal'. Kansas recommences her work, checking papers and listening to instructions that Scott has left on the office Dictaphone. Kansas wearily notes the list of tasks, but at the end of the recording Scott surprises her, telling her: 'you know you're having dinner with me tonight? And tomorrow night? And every night!' The shifts and transformations in Kansas' role in the conclusion of *Phantom Lady* are typical of 'the woman's angle' of the *noir* crime thriller. In all the films cited the working-girls undergo shifting roles and positions in the films' narratives.

In *Stranger on the Third Floor*, Jane shifts from secretary to investigator, putting herself in physical jeopardy as she follows the 'stranger' through the streets. Throughout the film she thinks and acts as a moral centre. Her fiancé Michael is a journalist, and he is a key witness at a murder trial that wrongly convicts taxi-driver Briggs (Elisha Cook Jnr). Jane repeatedly expresses her concerns that Briggs' conviction is unsound, and as Michael himself becomes trapped as a suspect it is the justice system that is exposed as mistaken. Jane's suspicions are ratified as she tracks down the real suspect in the final sequence.

Jill, in *I Wake Up Screaming*, undertakes different roles as she comes to the aid of promoter, Frankie Christopher. When she and Frankie return to her apartment to find the police waiting for them, Jill knocks the lead investigator over the head with a statuette, and directs an accompanying officer the wrong way. She then hides out with Frankie at a cycle repair shop, and frees him by sawing through his handcuffs. Their dialogue takes on a comic tone, but also evidences the way that crime and romance strands are intertwined. When Frankie asks if she'll mind being married to a hunted man, Jill quips back 'most married men have a hunted look anyway', and Frankie promises that he's 'going to show [her] how to play hide and seek in the big city'. Jill's investigative role thus allows her to adventure in the city's urban playground, as she and Frankie become an outlaw couple. Jill has to elude the police who are watching her apartment, and she does so by clambering up a fire escape and over the night-time rooftops. Their prearranged meeting place is an all-night adult cinema showing *Flames of Passion*, and the couple are reunited, with Jill bringing a new investigative lead: florist cards from her sister's funeral flowers. She and Frankie pursue the lead by posing as reporters, to ascertain who has been sending the flowers. Pursuing this lead yields new information about the afternoon of Vicky's (Carole Landis') murder, namely it confirms Harry Williams as the prime suspect, and exposes Cornell's corrupt approach to the investigation. As noted earlier, Jill helps to extract Williams' confession as she impersonates her dead sister over the telephone. Jill thus moves through several different roles: secretary, investigator, reporter and impersonator of the victim. At times she joins Frankie on the 'wrong' side of the law, but her actions are motivated and justified by the closure of the film and in Frankie's restoration to innocence.

Similarly, in *The Dark Corner*, Kathleen shifts from being a detective's secretary to becoming Brad's investigative partner. She accompanies him in investigative peregrinations around a threatening New York city. Her character is marked by a show of determination and resolve as she helps unravel the complex net of alliances and antipathies that Brad is enmeshed in. When Brad's former partner, Tony Jardine (Kurt Kreuger), is found dead at Brad's apartment, Kathleen radiates calm and demonstrates practicality, helping to clear away the murder weapon and giving Brad refuge at her own apartment. Like Jill and Frankie, Kathleen and Brad are an outlaw couple. The bald evidence of the murder plot, Brad's past relationship with his corrupt partner Jardine, and the body at his apartment, seem to preclude his innocence. But the narration of the film has allowed the viewers to see the machinations of Hardy Cathcart and his hired heavy 'White Suit'. The audience's knowledge that Brad is being framed justifies Kathleen's investment of faith in him, and locates the film's suspense in how the investigative couple will escape their situation.

In all four of these films, the working-girl investigators are characterised by their physical activity in the films' urban spaces. They deploy an active investigative gaze, and the editing of the sequences, particularly the use of reaction shots, constructs the action from a female perspective. Endorsement of the female optical point-of-view, despite its temporariness, offers a suspension of Hollywood's politics of looking, as it has been understood in spectatorship theory.[78] These are instances of women driving the narrative in a 'male' genre, and 'male' generic space, and provide a distinctive modification of *noir* as an exclusively 'male' mode.

The ways in which these scenarios are permitted are interesting. The mobility of the female characters contrasts with the static imprisonment of the male characters who are unable to move around the city freely. In one sense, then, these women are 'deputising' in a male role. But it is not the case that the female characters become 'masculinised' in this role (the strategy which occurs with the action heroine in contemporary cinema). The key to their deputised role can be found in the motivation for their bearing of the look; that is, the woman's stake in the investigation. In all the films examined, the immobile male character is constrained by his rather ambivalent status as crime suspect. It is the conviction of the female character that he is innocent that motivates her investigation, with actions that put her in physical and moral jeopardy in the urban city spaces. By forwarding, and helping to resolve, the detection narrative, the female investigator restores the male character's position, and he shifts from potential villain to the safe central hero.

The re-establishment of a morally redeemed hero clears the narrative so that it can close in the formation of the couple. The heterosexual romance closure also serves to secure the moral status of the female investigator figure. Further, it is *through* the process of her investigation that she is able to ascertain the suitability of the hero as a marriage partner. In all four films the working-girl's investigative adventure lends her moral ambivalence. In *Stranger on the Third Floor*, Jane's trail of the stranger leads to her being mistaken for a streetwalker. In *Phantom Lady*, Kansas' impersonation of 'Jeannie' puts her in danger from Cliff's advances. Jill's hiding out in the adult cinema with Frankie leads to her censure by a patrolling police officer in *I Wake Up Screaming*. When Kathleen conceals Brad at her apartment, the milkman gives her a 'grown up' look as he delivers the milk. These scenarios all suggest that the status of the single working-girl is one of liberation – her independent position in the city – simultaneously conditioned by social codes governing appropriate feminine behaviour and identity. The shifting and conditional status of the working-girl is explored in these crime films through a process of negotiation which has important contemporaneous resonances. The films place, and move, female characters across two interrelated narrative strands: the crime strand in which the working-girl investigator actively adventures through the city, and the romance strand which permits her adventure and which closes in the formation of a companionate couple. This placement and movement has some important outcomes for the ways that gender and genre are understood.

The female investigator has been seen as a rather exceptional figure in some *noir* genre criticism. Frank Krutnik, for example, argues that 'It is rare to find female detectives in 1940s thrillers',[79] citing *Stranger on the Third Floor* and *Phantom Lady* as exceptions. He sees these films as illustrating the difference between male and female modes of investigation. In Krutnik's model, drawn from 'hard-boiled' *noir*, the male detective figure embodies 'control over the external world',[80] whereas the agency of Jane (*Stranger on the Third Floor*) is 'compromised by her femininity'[81] and Kansas (*Phantom Lady*) is 'constrained by the fact that she is "supervised" by a male figure of the law, Inspector Burgess'.[82] Krutnik also argues that the woman's investigative position is prescribed by romance.[83]

While Krutnik's perspective fits a view of *noir* as hard-boiled, extending from the Chandleresque model of gendered character cited earlier, female investigators – femme detectives, girl-sleuths, investigating school teachers, reporters and librarians – were actually staple female figures in popular detective fictions and films in the 1940s, particularly in B-pictures and series films. Girl-sleuths, such as Nancy Drew and Judy Bolton, created in novels by Carolyn Keene and Margaret Sutton respectively, enjoyed a wide readership from the late 1930s onwards, leading to Warner Bros producing a Nancy Drew cycle comprising *Nancy Drew Detective* (William Clemens, 1938), *Nancy Drew and the Hidden Staircase* (William Clemens, 1939), *Nancy Drew, Reporter* (William Clemens, 1939) and *Nancy Drew, Trouble Shooter* (William Clemens, 1939).[84] Investigating schoolmarm Miss Hildegarde Withers featured in a series of films produced at RKO in the 1930s, such as *The Penguin Pool Murder* (George Archainbaud, 1932), *Murder on the Blackboard* (George Archainbaud, 1934), *Murder on a Honeymoon* (Lloyd Corrigan, 1935, story by Robert Benchley), *Murder on a Bridle Path* (William Hamilton and Edward Killy, 1936), *The Plot Thickens* (Ben Holmes, 1936) and *Forty Naughty Girls* (Edward F Kline, 1937). Warner Bros's popular series character, female reporter Torchy Blane (Jane Wyman), worked as a female investigator in *Torchy Blane Playing with Dynamite* (Noel Smith, 1939). Wyman also co-starred as an investigative side-kick, Robbie Vance, to Jerome Cowan's detective Sam Campbell in the Warner's B-film *Crime by Night* (William Clemens, 1944). MGM's irrepressible series character Maisie Revere (Ann Sothern) joined the police force to hunt down a team of con-artists in *Undercover Maisie* (Harry Beaumont, 1947). Female investigators can also be found outside the series-film. Librarian Kay Ryan (Lynne Roberts) partnered reporter Hal McByrne (Richard Denning) to track down a ring of Nazi spies in Twentieth Century-Fox's *Quiet Please: Murder!* (John Larkin, 1942). Republic Studios cast Stephanie Bachelor as a private detective in *The Undercover Woman* (Thomas Carr, 1946), and Marsha Hunt took the title role in *Mary Ryan Detective* (Abby Berlin, 1949), a Columbia B-picture.[85]

The reason that these numerous working-girl investigators have not been acknowledged within genre criticism on the detective film is, as Neale notes, that discussions have repeatedly focused on *noir*'s alliance with the hard-boiled tradition: 'As a result, detective films made prior to the 1940s, and those which in general are considered neither as *noir* or as hardboiled, have often either been ignored or mentioned merely in passing as inauthentic counterpoints to *noir* and the hardboiled tradition.'[86] Comparisons between the female investigator and the hard-boiled detective occlude the popularity, roles and agency of the working-girl investigator, what the figure does and the contextual resonances the figure evokes. Although 'there are no female equivalents to Philip Marlowe',[87] there *are* many female investigators of all kinds in the crime film, but, as Cowie notes, they are 'usually dismissed on the grounds that the women are never shown to be "as good as" equivalent male figures in some way'.[88] She argues that this critical perspective 'privileges an implied lack of narrative dominance that the female protagonists always lack, yet which is frequently absent where the protagonist is male'.[89] Arguments that female investigators are endangered, compromised or constrained by their femininity do not sufficiently acknowledge that narration in the detective film typically operates through positioning the protagonist in dangerous, threatening or compromised scenarios. However, investigative narratives in the crime and mystery film always offer any detecting figure, male or female, several lines of inquiry. False leads, misleading witnesses, unpredictable situations and chance encounters form the detective film's generic territory of investigation. This structuring is part of the way that the detective narrative, in fiction and film, is characterised by 'gaps and retardations'[90] in narration, so that it presents both a search for knowledge and 'its suppression and restriction'.[91] Detective narratives hold the viewer by creating 'curiosity about past story events (e.g., who killed whom), suspense about upcoming events, and surprise with respect to unexpected disclosures ... to promote all three emotional states, the narration must limit the viewer's knowledge'.[92] The unfolding narration of the detective and mystery film requires investigative characters to navigate a 'maze of episodes',[93] and to endure the dangers of their quest in order to initiate narrative revelation. What is interesting is that the generic disadvantage of *all* investigative characters, vis-à-vis the unfolding narration and its situational dangers, is barely ever remarked upon where those characters are male. Of course, the presence of a female investigator can give a special cast to the curiosity, suspense and surprise of the narration, particularly through the reactions of other characters to her as a woman, but her gender does not discount her sleuthing ability. Furthermore, in *Stranger on the Third Floor*, *I Wake Up Screaming*, *Phantom Lady* and *The Dark Corner*, the female investigators' sleuthing is not at odds with their romantic desire but of a piece with it. The woman's angle and position allows both crime and romance quests to be resolved. This is significant, as 'romance' in *noir* has so often been read as playing out a crisis in gender relations: the desire of the male hero for the *femme fatale* figure muddies his thinking and threatens his investigative agency, frequently ending in death of one or both of the couple. Krutnik suggests that romance, and its closure in the heterosexual couple, represents a profound threat to the detective's independence and self-sufficiency.[94] But understanding the inter-relationship of crime and romance from the perspective of the investigating woman offers a rather different view. Through progressing the elucidation of the crime narrative, the working-girl investigator ensures the innocence of the male hero figure. And her carefully negotiated role as resourceful helper-in-exceptional-circumstance allows her to embody a female figure who is a suitable 'partner' to the man of the city.

The working-girl's eventual position as part of a couple resolves any moral jeopardy that her investigation has prompted, as well as justifying its motivation. This is not, however, the same as saying that romantic closure is straightforwardly reducible to women's containment. The negotiations of these narratives have a currency for female figures, and are evident in the intertwining of two distinct strands in these films: the crime strand in which the working-girl investigator actively adventures through the city, and the romance strand which permits her adventure and which closes in the formation of a companionate couple. These narratives can thus be seen as advancing 'masculine testing' from a different perspective than that outlined by Krutnik. The 'woman's angle' and her investigative quest, with the question of her male partner's innocence at its centre, allows her to 'test' her male counterpart before the film closes in marriage.

This distinctive modification of the crime film narrative for women is coincident with the transformation of women's private and public roles. As I have noted earlier, this transformation has been identified by several social historians such as Chafe, Friedan and Campbell. Public debates about gender identities during the World War II era focused on new identities for women; Hollywood's shifting characterisation of women drew upon these emergent identities by imagining women in new ways in screen fictions. This trend is noted by Virginia Wright Wexman who argues, as many critics have, that the 1940s in particular was an era when 'heterosexual relations were strongly marked by volatility and flux',[95] though she does not extend this to a characterisation of 'crisis' (as critics of *noir* are wont to do). Wexman finds a typical instance of companionate coupling in Howard Hawks' *The Big Sleep* (1945), arguing that 'Hawks' version of the hard-boiled-detective formula is about cooperation rather than competition, about getting together rather than getting ahead'.[96] Wexman's observations on the ways in which Hawks' film portrays the qualities of companionship between the leads is very interesting. The 'Hawksian Woman' has been understood as a visible instance of the 'independent' woman on film in the 1940s. Writing about Hawks' 'conception of woman'[97] on film, Molly Haskell suggests:

> He may not penetrate the secrets of a woman's heart and her unique dilemma the way the so-called 'woman's directors' do. But at the same time he never excludes them from the action, never even implicitly suggests that a woman occupies a fixed place – the home, society – or that she is a man's subordinate. Instinctively, he strikes a very modern note in the image of

a couple united not by the attraction of opposites but the unanimity of similarities.[98]

Naomi Wise sees Hawksian heroines as playing 'consequential roles', embodying a 'heroic heroine, who is both sexual and valuable'.[99] Screenwriter Leigh Brackett, whose collaborations with Hawks were noted earlier, characterises the Hawksian woman as 'pushing the whole plot'.[100]

The 'companionate' gender relations of *The Big Sleep* and *To Have and Have Not* (1944) are very often put down to either the mark of Hawks as auteur, and/or the currency of Bogart and Bacall as stars and their offscreen relationship. Hawksian gender relations and female characterisations, though, might be seen as part of a wider picture. The working-girl investigators of *Stranger on the Third Floor*, *I Wake Up Screaming*, *Phantom Lady* and *The Dark Corner* share common qualities with the wise-cracking romantic equal embodied by Bacall. They, too, are characterised by their energy, determination and verbal sparring with their romantic partners. A further parallel is offered by the fact that in 1942 *Phantom Lady* star, Ella Raines, had been signed as a contract player by B-H Productions, a company owned by Hawks and Charles Boyer.[101] In fact, the working-girls' actions extend further than those of Bacall's characters, as they crucially collaborate in freeing the hero from his imprisonment within the 'frame' of the crime narrative. What is interesting is that both Hawks' films, and the crime thrillers discussed in this chapter, run counter to the idea of a crisis in gender relations, so often seen as paradigmatic of *film noir* of the 1940s. These films suggest, rather, ways in which gender relations might be undergoing some careful negotiations as well as crises and conflicts. They also evidence *noir*'s heterogeneity and its complex and multiple address.

It is clear that the modifications of the crime thriller to accommodate 'the woman's angle', its female characterisation and melding of crime and romance, were identified as highly marketable. Promotional materials for the films discussed foreground their appeal to female audiences by showcasing feminine consumer tie-ins and by selling the appeal of male stars. The pressbook for *I Wake Up Screaming* (first released under the title *Hot Spot*) suggests: '*Hot Spot* has a powerful woman appeal. Hammer it home to them in every way you can' and sells 'New "it" man Victor Mature'.[102] *Phantom Lady* was positioned as 'First Mystery for Lady Fans', with a focus on the film's novelty as 'a mystery story based on feminine psychology for its essential appeal', and the draw of 'Handsome Alan Curtis ... [who] makes [a] romantic bid'.[103] Its pressbook also promotes Joan Harrison as 'Lady Producer'.[104] Twentieth Century-Fox brands Mark Stevens as 'the hard-boiled but romantic detective' in *The Dark Corner*.[105]

Conclusions

The working-girl investigator figure and her narrative agency evidence a range of female roles in the *noir* crime thriller that extends beyond the ruthless *femme fatale* and the passive, domestic redeemer figure. The working-girl investigator offers a different way of conceiving of 'women in *film noir*' in the 1940s, particularly during the war years, which locates her in the world of work, the world of crime, and the world of men. Understanding the working-girl investigators as presenting a negotiation of women's roles, in work and in the city, allows different perspectives on these crime thrillers to emerge. It could be argued that the films chosen are 'marginal' to the *film noir* canon, as it has traditionally been constituted in genre debates since the 1950s. But it is precisely at its margins that *noir*'s multiple contexts, sources, affiliations, intertexts, influences and characters become evident. Some of these contexts have been traced: women working in the Hollywood industry, patterns of female employment in 1940s America and the wider intertextual affiliations of the crime and mystery film in popular detective fictions. These contexts recast questions of *noir*'s 'zeitgeist', its gender relations, and particularly its angle on women. In the next chapter, I continue to focus on 'the woman's angle' in 1940s Hollywood by examining another investigative female figure with a purchase on female concerns: the heroine of the female gothic cycle.

Chapter Two

Reviewing the Female Gothic Heroine: Agency, Identification and Feminist Film Criticism

Introduction

In the next three chapters I turn to the female gothic cycle, one of the most popular, critically and commercially successful cycles of films in 1940s Hollywood. I will continue to address questions I have already laid out in relation to *film noir*: of generic categorisation and its relationship to gender, of female characterisation, representation and agency, issues of the feminist interpretation of these films, and the resonance that this cycle has to its contemporary socio-cultural moment.

Gothic Heritage

The gothic is an extremely promiscuous and fertile aesthetic and affective category which has proliferated across different media and cultural forms for over 200 years. Gothic is discernible as a style in forms of architecture, literature, film and television. The gothic narrative mode is characterised by stylistic excess, and by stories that thematise the transgression of boundaries and values. In its ability to express, evoke and produce fear and anxiety, the gothic mode figures the underside to the rational, the stable and the moral.[1] In its literary narrative form, the gothic reaches back to sensation fictions of the eighteenth century, texts such as Horace Walpole's *The Castle of Otranto* (1764), Clara Reeve's *The Old English Baron: A Gothic Story* (1778), and Ann Radcliffe's *The Mysteries of Udolpho* (1791) and *The Italian* (1797). The gothic shows its ability to meld with other forms in the horror fictions of Mary Shelley (*Frankenstein; or, the Modern Prometheus* (1831)) and John Polidori. In the nineteenth century it inflects the work of the Bröntes and of Edgar Allen Poe. In the twentieth and twenty-first centuries its circulation has been augmented by its presence and expression in the mass media of film and television. The gothic mode's fertile proliferation, then, is evident in the frequency with which it is revived and deployed in different media and at different historical moments.

Fred Botting outlines principal components of the gothic as follows:

> In Gothic fiction certain stock features provide the principal embodiments and evocations of cultural anxieties. Tortuous, fragmented narratives relating mysterious incidents, horrible images and life-threatening pursuits predominate in the eighteenth century. Spectres, monsters, demons, corpses, skeletons, evil aristocrats, monks and nuns, fainting heroines and bandits populate Gothic landscapes as suggestive figures of imagined and realistic threats. This list grew, in the nineteenth century, with the addition of scientists, fathers, husbands, madmen, criminals and the monstrous double signifying duplicity and evil nature. Gothic landscapes are desolate, alienating and full of menace. In the eighteenth century they were wild and mountainous locations. Later the modern city combined the natural and architectural components of Gothic grandeur and wildness, its dark, labyrinthine streets suggesting the violence and menace of Gothic castle and forest.[2]

The gothic possesses the ability constantly to renew itself, to assert its relevance in distinct socio-cultural eras, to find new expressions and outlets in evolving cultural forms and productions, while it is simultaneously, and rather paradoxically, a mode that plays on a fraught relationship to the past. The narratives of gothic literary fictions and films commonly deploy suspicions and suspense about past events. Shrouded in secrecy and ambiguity, the past is revealed in horrifying ways, accompanied by violence of an atavistic form. In its moves across the present and the past, and its tension between progress and atavism, the gothic forces witness the present as conditioned and adapted by events, knowledge or values pressing on it from the past. The gothic narrative drive, then, is more typically retrogressive than progressive, its complicated and unpredictable narration forces characters, protagonists, readers and viewers to move backwards as well as forwards, and to reprocess their present conditions and knowledge in relation to events or secrets in the past which were not known, or only partly known. It is within this retrogressive narration that the gothic embodies cultural anxiety, and it is this that mobilises its potential as social critique.

The gothic signals its potent relationship with the past through style and setting:

> Architecture, particularly medieval in form ... signalled the spatial and temporal separation of the past and its values from the present. The pleasures of horror and terror came from the reappearance of figures long gone. None the less, Gothic narratives never escaped the concerns of their own times, despite the heavy historical trappings.[3]

Botting observes that in the eighteenth century the locus was bleak and alienating: gothic castles, or ruined edifices – abbeys, churches, graveyards and ruinous estates – were common. In nineteenth-century gothic fictions, 'the castle gradually gave way to the old house: as both building and family line, it became the site where fears and anxieties returned in the present. These anxieties varied according to diverse changes: political revolution, industrialisation, urbanisation, shifts in sexual and domestic organisation, and scientific discovery.'[4]

The gothic's relation to shifts in sexual and domestic organisation will be explored in relation to the 1940s film cycle. The ways in which women writing in the gothic mode have addressed gothic sexuality, domesticity and female agency shows that the gothic as a genre has been repeatedly mobilised to highlight particular issues about gender and identity and their vicissitudes. My concerns in examining the connections between gender and the gothic mode will follow two strands. The first is to outline the ways in which the gothic mode has had a recurrent purchase upon gender and identity at different socio-cultural moments. The second is to trace the diverse feminist critical engagements with the gothic and the ways in which these engagements have impacted upon interpretations and understandings of the gothic heroine figure.

Ellen Moers' critical work on the gothic was one of the first feminist engagements with the literary form. As such, it initiated debates about the gothic's purchase on issues of gender and identity. Her *Literary Women* (1963) constructs a feminist history of women's writing as an occupation. It provides an examination of a female literary tradition, its works, its genres and its creation of distinct female figures and character types. Moers' work importantly draws attention to the authorial presence of women writers in the gothic mode. She coins the term 'Female Gothic'[5] to describe and demarcate the use of the literary gothic mode by women, and for women. In engaging with a female literary tradition, Moers identifies the presence of distinctive types of female characterisation by women writers across the eighteenth and nineteenth centuries. She suggests that the development of writing as a career for women gave a 'female self-consciousness'[6] to literary characterisation, bringing 'heroinism' to literary form. Moers defines 'heroinism' as the intent of female writers to 'create a heroic structure for the female voice in literature'.[7] She finds this heroinism in works such as Mary Wollstonecraft's *Mary: A Fiction* (1788) and George Eliot's *Middlemarch* (1871–2), through a writerly meditation on the status of female character. The preface of Wollstonecraft's *Mary* states: 'In delineating the Heroine of this Fiction, the Author attempts to portray a character different from those generally portrayed';[8] this presents, for Moers, 'the sound of literary feminism'.[9]

Moers is careful about her claims for literary feminism: 'feminism is one thing, and literary feminism ... is another'.[10] She points out that the nascent literary feminism (heroinism) in women's literary fiction of the late eighteenth and early nineteenth centuries is always complicatedly engaged in a dialogue with literature as a male tradition and pursuit: 'an order of reality perhaps more intractable than social fact'.[11] Despite her caveats, Moers persuasively traces instances of heroinism as being particularly clear in Ann Radcliffe's gothic novels, which strongly influence the 'female gothic' narrative formula drawn on by the 1940s Hollywood cycle. Moers writes: 'the Gothic fantasies of Mrs Radcliffe are a locus of heroinism which, ever since, women have turned to feminist purposes'.[12] Arguing that Radcliffe's writing comes out of the same 'heroinist' cultural moment as that of Wollstonecraft, Moers focuses upon Radcliffe's creation of 'female selfhood',[13] and sees her gothic heroine as an exploratory figure: '[a] travelling woman: [a] woman who moves, who acts, who copes with vicissitude and adventure'.[14] Moers continues:

> For Mrs Radcliffe, the Gothic novel was a device to send maidens on distant and exciting journeys without offending the proprieties [of her time]. In the power of villains, her heroines are forced to do what they could never do alone, whatever their ambitions: scurry up the top of pasteboard Alps, spy out exotic vistas, penetrate bandit-infested forests. And indoors, inside Mrs Radcliffe's castles, her heroines can scuttle miles along corridors, descend into dungeons, and explore secret chambers without a chaperone, because the Gothic castle, however much in ruins, is still an indoor and therefore freely female space. In Mrs Radcliffe's hands, the Gothic novel became a feminine substitute for the picaresque, where heroines could enjoy all the adventures and alarms that masculine heroes had long experienced, far from home, in fiction.[15]

Moers, then, defines the gothic heroine figure as one involved in navigating adventure, and change, in the course of the gothic narrative. Her interpretation bestows the agency of the adventurer on the gothic heroine, an explorer who encounters danger and threat as concomitant with her narrative positioning. Describing the figure of Emily in *The Mysteries of Udolpho*, Moers suggests that she typifies the adventurer's shifting narrative position, one always moving, acting, reacting between the threats she encounters, and her survival of them:

> As early as the 1790s, Ann Radcliffe firmly set the Gothic in one of the ways it would go ever after: a novel in which the central figure is a young woman who is simultaneously perse-cuted victim and courageous heroine.[16]

As one of the earliest second-wave feminist engagements with the gothic mode, the terms of Moers' argument, particularly her emphasis on the heroine figure and, more generally, her notion of heroinism, are enabling and useful. As noted, Moers presents fem-inist intersections with the gothic carefully, acknowledging that women's writing is not necessarily coincident with feminism, but rather that '[f]eminism and heroinism can often be seen to touch in women's literature'.[17] Many subsequent feminist engagements with the literary and filmic gothic have sounded a note of caution about the processes of gothic texts, the way they represent and position female characters narratively, the affects that arise in the gothic narration, and how these affects are both interpreted and felt by readers and viewers of the gothic. These aspects of the gothic mode have been key to feminist inquiry and interpretation, as they are embedded in larger questions about the politics of fictional texts and the ways these texts both express, and address them-selves to, women's socio-cultural contexts.

Hollywood's Female Gothic in the 1940s

The gothic's enduring popularity, and its facility for revival and pro-liferation across different media, is clearly evident from its pres-ence in literary, dramatic and filmic form in America in the 1940s. Commentator Norman Matson heralds the period of the 'Gooseflesh Special' in his *New York Times* review of an anthology of terror fiction. He writes:

> Hollywood these days is haunted as never before, and so is Broadway, and there aren't enough new ghost stories to meet

the demands of the book buyers ... For an important number of readers the American Dream begins to look more like a nightmare, a "Gothic", medieval one. It's an odd sort of escape from a world in which evil and terror are, objectively, literally, so important, but not unexpected.[18]

Also noting the vogue for the 'macabre', Donald Barr comments that:

> ... a few decades of studiously uninventive 'naturalism' have turned the minds of readers, writers and the in-between folk who collect short stories, toward the macabre and the fanciful. New selections of specters and night-sweats, werewolves, lunacy and decaying families, exquisite mental torture and forthright bloodcurdling have been frequent lately.[19]

Similarly, in a 1946 article tracing publishing trends, Howard Mumford Jones notes that novelists 'are obsessed by terror. Adjectives like "Gothic," "terrible," "macabre," "horrible," and their companions, turned up continually in the book reviews.'[20] From this he concludes that:

> In fiction of the last six months, mankind is, in Swift's words, the most odious, filthy little race of vermin that ever encumbered the earth.[21]

Hollywood reporter Fred Stanley notes the impact of the trend on Hollywood:

> Possibly as a breathing spell from war and "hate Nazi" pictures, Hollywood, temporarily at least, has all but shelved martial pictures in favor of films bulging with screams in the night, supercharged criminal phenomena and esthetic murder. Every studio has at least one such picture in production and others coming to a witching boil.[22]

It is within this wider trend in popularity for gothic and horror fictions and films that the 1940s female gothic cycle is located.

The cycle is typified by films such as *Rebecca* (Alfred Hitchcock, 1940), *Suspicion* (Alfred Hitchcock, 1941), *Shadow of a Doubt* (Alfred Hitchcock, 1943), *Dark Waters* (Andre de Toth, 1944), *Experiment Perilous* (Jacques Tourneur, 1944), *Jane Eyre* (Robert Stevenson, 1944), *Gaslight* (George Cukor, 1944), *Dragonwyck* (Joseph Mankiewicz, 1946), *The Two Mrs Carrolls* (Peter Godfrey, 1947), *The Spiral Staircase* (Robert Siodmak, 1946), *Secret Beyond the Door* (Fritz Lang, 1948), *Caught* (Max Ophuls, 1949), and *Under Capricorn* (Alfred Hitchcock, 1949). A fuller list of films included in the cycle can be found in the appendix at the end of this book.

The female gothic cycle has been defined with a variety of generic terms. In the industry and trade press the films are frequently described as 'suspenseful drama',[23] 'murder thriller',[24] 'heavy drama with femme appeal',[25] 'melodrama'[26] and 'cinematic psycho-thriller'.[27] Film critics and historians have also used different labels for the cycle. These labels indicate the multiple influences and intertexts of the cycle. Some of these labels indicate the 1940s female gothic cycle's connections to literary intertexts, whereas others suggest its affiliations with the broader generic categories of melodrama and romance, or its commonalities with *film noir*. All of the terms used in defining the female gothic cycle acknowledge its gendered specificity.

Describing the cycle as 'Freudian feminist melodrama[s]',[28] Thomas Elsaesser marks them as a particular inflection of the historically long and diverse family melodrama arising in the 1940s and deploying explicitly Freudian themes. Elsaesser sees Hitchcock's work in the cycle as advancing 'strange fantasies of persecution, rape and death – masochistic reveries and nightmares, which cast the husband into the rôle of the sadistic murderer'.[29] He sees these themes recurring across the cycle:

> This projection of sexual anxiety and its mechanisms of displacement and transfer is translated into a whole string of movies often involving hypnosis and playing on the ambiguity and suspense of whether the wife is merely imagining it or whether her husband really does have murderous designs on her.[30]

Indications of the cycle's hybridity and influences are found in Diane Waldman's use of the term '"Gothic romance" films',[31] Tania Modleski's naming of the films 'the "gaslight" genre',[32] and Guy Barefoot's examination of several films of the cycle in his *Gaslight Melodrama*.[33] Analyses of the gender politics of the cycle occur in Mary Ann Doane's reading of the films as 'paranoid woman's films',[34] and Andrew Britton's inclusion of them in 'the persecuted wife cycle'.[35]

The multiple terms used for the female gothic cycle, both in industry and trade discourses and in film criticism, raise some questions that need to be acknowledged. As Steve Neale argues, histories of genres need to distinguish between categories as they are created and circulated in critical circles and those with an industrial origin which are more clearly part of Hollywood's inter-textual relay: 'it is probably best to distinguish theoretical genres from genres proper by renaming the former "theoretical cate-gories".'[36] Neale also shows that these theoretical categories are not fixed, but are part of the circulation of terms and meanings of genre within cinema's critical, rather than its industrial, institutions. Neale cites the work of Todorov, who argues that genres also exist 'in discourse dealing with genres (metadiscursive dis-course)'.[37] So although 'genres proper' have a life outside critical constructions, there is a specific circulation of concepts of genre in 'the writings of critics and theorists, and the discourse produced by academies, universities, and other institutions of a similar kind'.[38] Attention to genre's critical metadiscourses, then, can be advantageous in that it allows a critical history of the use of terms to be traced, as well as the critical, and political, stakes of that usage, which is particularly useful in charting the identities of the woman's film.

The metadiscourses bearing on both *film noir* and the female gothic cycle become quite complex where critics have retrospec-tively charted similarities between *film noir* and the gothic woman's film cycle. The complexity arises due to the privileged position that *film noir* occupies in the canon of Hollywood genre categories, and its putative male focus, issues I have addressed at some length in the previous chapter. Murray Smith's examination of *Deception* (Irving Rapper, 1946) illustrates this complexity. *Deception* tells the story of a violent love triangle between music teacher Christine (Bette Davis), whose relationship with an older man, composer Alex Hollenius (Claude Rains), breaks down when Karel Novak (Paul Henreid) returns from the war in which she believed he had died. Smith argues that this film is special because it crosses over the boundaries between *film noir* and gothic woman's film:

> The film's interest lies in its unstable position between two popular generic forms of the Forties, two forms which are in a sense the inverse of each other – the *film noir* and the female gothic.[39]

In his summary of the features of the two generic forms, he points out common features: both feature a sexual other as an enigma to be investigated (*noir*'s duplicitous femme fatale, the gothic's mysterious husband), but delineates their difference in strategies of narrative closure. He argues the female gothic film positions female perceptions either as 'paranoid and incorrect' or, if correct, as requiring the authority of corroboration by a secondary male character.[40] Smith writes:

> From this perspective, we can see how the two forms mirror each other, *film noir* dealing with the investigation of the female, the female gothic with the investigation of the male. The reflection, though, is skewed. In *film noir*, male perception is rarely under question – there is no doubt that the woman is duplicitous. In the female gothic, female perception is as much scrutinized as enigmatic male behaviour, since frequently the woman's perception is proven erroneous.[41]

While Smith's thesis points up the fact that driving *film noir*'s narrative of investigation is not an inherently male position, nor unique to its category, the implicit placing of *film noir* as the proper (male) form *from* which the gothic woman's film diverges reinforces *noir*'s canonical position. Furthermore, as discussed in Chapter 1, *noir* male protagonists are frequently questionable, and it is actually very rarely the case that the gothic heroine's perceptions are proved to be imagined or incorrect at the close of the gothic film, as I will demonstrate in more detail in my discussion.

While *film noir* and the gothic woman's film share many stylistic visual and aural elements (chiaroscuro lighting designs, mobile camera, high contrast sound mixing and dramatic scoring), these elements have often been seen as characteristic of *noir*, and 'shared' by the gothic film, again implicitly placing *noir* as iconographically and sonographically special or innovative. However, the gothic woman's film cycle was commercially and critically very successful at the moment of its production, much more so, in fact, than *film noir*. The box-office figures, and Academy Awards and nominations for the cycle, are listed in the appendix. This evidence suggests that gothic women's films were both highly visible and influential in the industry of the time. Indeed, *Rebecca* is cited as a stylistically influential film by both Robert Carringer and James Naremore in their discussions of *Citizen Kane* (1941). They note that the opening of *Citizen Kane* draws on *Rebecca*'s use of mobile camera and mise-en-scène, which evoke mystery and suspense at the entry to a large and forbidding house. Similarly, *Rebecca*'s closing shots – tracking mobile camera framing the burning 'R' on a nightgown case – are also structurally echoed in the track and frame on the burning sled 'Rosebud' in *Citizen Kane*.[42]

A clear summation of the common elements shared by the gothic woman's film and *noir* is made by Steve Neale, who also warns of the tendency to privilege *film noir*:

> … they have, in fact, a great deal in common: they frequently centre on an element of potentially fatal sexual attraction; they stress the risks, emotional and physical, this may entail for the central protagonist; they lay a great deal of emphasis on the protagonist's perceptions, feelings, thoughts and subjective experiences; and they share the context of a culture of distrust. One of the reasons these similarities have been obscured – and why the gothic film in particular has been relegated to the margins of the *noir* canon – is that a great deal of writing on *film noir* has stressed its affiliation with the hardboiled novel rather than with the stage thriller or the gothic romance.[43]

In my own discussion of the cycle, I will be following Ellen Moers' use of the term 'female gothic' to refer to the films. While Moers' term is more 'theoretical' than industrial, it captures a particular narrative form which is recurrent across the 1940s cycle, and acknowledges the cycle's intertextual affiliations with its literary antecedents as well. In addition, Moers' focus on a female authorial presence in the gothic, and its female address, also usefully account for contemporaneous production factors in the cycle. The cycle provided central dramatic roles for major female stars of the period such as Joan Fontaine, Gene Tierney, Ingrid Bergman, Hedy Lamarr and Katharine Hepburn, and involved a relatively high proportion of women writers involved in the cycle, signalled in my appendix listing of the films.

The female gothic formula was recognised as distinctive and exploitable by producers such as David O Selznick (of Selznick International Pictures) and Darryl Zanuck (of Twentieth Century-Fox). The publication of Daphne Du Maurier's bestselling 'Modern Gothic' novel *Rebecca* in 1938 revived reading of the literary female gothic, which developed into a mass popularity in the mid- to late twentieth century.[44] The contemporaneous popularity of gothic fiction in the 1940s has been noted earlier. Within this context the specific popularity of the female gothic in the late 1930s and early 1940s needs to be acknowledged as it is instrumental in initiating and cementing the Hollywood film cycle. Three instances illustrate this: Du Maurier's *Rebecca*, Charlotte Brönte's *Jane Eyre*, and Patrick Hamilton's stage play *Gaslight: A Victorian Thriller* (1938).

Du Maurier's novel was a highly visible commercial success from the date of its publication. Shortly after the novel appeared in 1938, it was serialised in Britain and America in *The London Daily Express* and *The New York Daily Mirror*. The novel was adapted as a radio play and broadcast by Orson Welles' Mercury Theatre in December 1938, and Du Maurier herself adapted it for the London stage, where it was produced at the Queen's Theatre in April 1940 and later at the Strand Theatre in 1942.[45] Selznick can be seen as a key figure in initiating the transfer of the literary female gothic to the screen in the 1940s. Famous for his astute commercial sense, Selznick was particularly experienced in the acquisition and adaptation of popular classic literary properties, transforming them into 'prestige' productions. He produced *David Copperfield* (George Cukor, 1935) and *Anna Karenina* (Clarence Brown, 1935) at MGM studios in the 1930s, and garnered huge success with his adaptation of Margaret Mitchell's *Gone With The Wind* at his own production company in 1939. It was during the production of *Gone With The Wind* (Victor Fleming, 1939) that Selznick aquired the rights to Du Maurier's novel. It was brought to his attention by his properties assistant Kay Brown, and its acquisition for Selznick International Pictures was part of the deal that brought British director Alfred Hitchcock to Hollywood. The similarities between *Rebecca* and *Jane Eyre*, noted by literary historians such as Patsy Stoneman,[46] were evident to Selznick, who considered *Rebecca* a 'veiled adaptation of *Jane Eyre*'.[47]

As Thomas Schatz notes, Selznick had long considered *Jane Eyre* to be a desirable project. Its commercial visibility was enhanced by a successful American stage version of the play, starring Katharine Hepburn and subsequently Janet Gaynor, which toured in the late 1930s. In April 1940 the Mercury Theatre company produced a radio dramatisation of the novel, with Madeleine Carroll in the role of Jane and Orson Welles playing Rochester.[48] So, in the same period that *Rebecca* and *Suspicion* (for which Selznick influenced the casting of his contract-star Joan Fontaine) were produced and released, Selznick was simultaneously gathering research for a film production of *Jane Eyre*. In 1940, Selznick assigned his story editor, Val Lewton, to assess the popularity of Brönte's novel; Lewton's findings were that it was consistently present on lists of 'greatest' and 'most read' novels.[49] Selznick devoted considerable resources to developing his *Jane Eyre* project, capitalising on the '"Jane Eyre formula" [that] was emerging in Hollywood during the early 1940s'.[50] Selznick signed producer, playwright and Mercury Players co-founder John Houseman to adapt the story, which he intended to have Hitchcock direct.[51] He also commissioned extensive market research on the novel's readership, and on the variable potential marquee values of casting different stars in the film's major roles.[52] The research found there was 'widespread recognition of the resemblance between the situation in *Jane Eyre*, *Rebecca* and *Suspicion*', and that Joan

Fontaine's performances in *Rebecca* and *Suspicion* made her the readers' favourite for the title role of *Jane Eyre*.[53] This clearly attests to the firm establishment of the female gothic cycle with audiences early in the 1940s.

Patrick Hamilton's play *Gaslight: A Victorian Thriller*, and two adaptations of it on film in the 1940s, can also be seen as contributing to the cultural visibility of the female gothic formula in the early 1940s. Barefoot shows *Gaslight*'s 'extraordinary popularity',[54] charting the play's long and successful runs on the stage in London, Los Angeles and on Broadway, where it ran under the title *Angel Street*. It also toured the United States throughout the 1940s.[55] In 1940, Thorold Dickinson directed a film version for British National, starring Anton Wallbrook and Diane Wynard, and in 1944, MGM studios produced *Gaslight*, directed by George Cukor and starring Ingrid Bergman and Charles Boyer. Its highly visible circulation on stage position it with *Rebecca* and *Jane Eyre* as playing a part in the initiation of the female gothic cycle on film.

Promotional materials for the female gothic films exploit the popularity of their literary sources. Pressbooks for *Rebecca*, *Jane Eyre* and *Dragonwyck*, an adaptation of Anya Seton's bestselling novel, encourage exhibitors to exploit connections between book and film in activities such as reading groups and tie-ins with local bookstores. Poster designs for the films include images of the novels, and *Variety* reviews of the films namecheck their literary sources; all of these aspects reveal the film cycle's potential to cater to an already existing audience of readers.

During the 1940s every major Hollywood studio produced at least one film version of the female gothic formula. The female gothic film was often, though not always, packaged as a prestige production, cast with female stars who had strong box office appeal in the period. Joan Fontaine's audience following has been noted; other stars include Gene Tierney in *Dragonwyck*, Ingrid Bergman in *Gaslight*, *Spellbound*, *Notorious* and *Under Capricorn*, Hedy Lamarr in *Experiment Perilous*, and Katharine Hepburn in *Undercurrent*. The productions were assigned directors with known reputations as distinctive stylists, such as Alfred Hitchcock (*Rebecca*, *Suspicion*, *Shadow of a Doubt*, *Spellbound*, *Notorious* and *Under Capricorn*), Jacques Tourneur (*I Walked With a Zombie* and *Experiment Perilous*), Robert Siodmak (*The Spiral Staircase*), Orson Welles (*The Stranger*), Douglas Sirk (*Sleep My Love*), and Max Ophuls (*Caught*). The female gothic formula was also given lower-budget treatments at Columbia (*My Name is Julia Ross*) and at Eagle Lion (*Bury Me Dead*).

Given these factors – the popularity of the female gothic, its status as a highly marketable commodity, and studios' exploitation of that status – what can be said about its contemporary resonance and meanings? It can clearly be located as informed by social shifts in the position and perception of marriage. The wartime 'rush to the altar'[56] was mirrored by an increase in divorce rates in the immediate post-war era when the stresses and strains of long separations, or the necessity of accommodating a partner not well known before marriage, took their toll. D'Ann Campbell and Andrea Walsh also suggest that divorce rates are partly attributable to women's shifting expectations of marriage.[57] Walsh writes:

> The war intensified already progressing twentieth-century trends towards companionate marriage and serial monogamy. As traditional patriarchy declined, the ideal of companionate marriage arose, embodying rising expectations of love, communication and friendship. If these needs were not met, after a period of mutual effort, the marriage, in this model, should terminate. And the spouses would again search for a partner of the companionate mode. This ideal became more popular and affordable during the war.[58]

It is within this context that Tania Modleski and Diane Waldman place the female gothic cycle, suggesting that it expresses anxieties of shifting gender roles, and the social upheaval of World War II, from a female perspective:[59]

> Beginning with Alfred Hitchcock's 1940 movie version of *Rebecca* and continuing through and beyond George Cukor's *Gaslight* in 1944, the gaslight films may be seen to reflect *women's* fears about losing their unprecedented freedoms and being forced back into the homes after the men returned from fighting to take over the jobs and assume control of their

families. In many of these films, the house seems to be alive with menace, and the greedy sadistic men who rule them are often suspected of trying to drive their wives insane, or to murder them as they have murdered other women in the past. The fact that after the war years these films gradually faded from the screen probably reveals more about the changing composition of movie audiences than about the waning of women's anxieties concerning domesticity. For Gothic novels have continued to this day to enjoy a steady popularity.[60]

Modleski and Waldman uncover the female gothic's potential to function as a progressive critique of gender relations and the institution of marriage, and suggests the purchase of this cycle on women's concerns in the period.

Gothic Engagements: The Woman's Film, Feminist Film Criticism and Identification

The Hollywood woman's film has offered a privileged site for feminist discussions of identity. Common issues have included the ways in which the woman's film represents, or constructs, women within the narrative processes of the text and how these representations or constructions address and position female viewers.[61] Within this large and complex body of work, the female gothic text has been the focus of considerable debate. The processes by which it represents, advances and elaborates female experience and identity have crystallised issues relating to female agency, or its lack. Key to this focus has been the status of the female gothic heroine within the text, and how the relation of this figure to female viewers have been theoretically understood.

Diane Waldman's discussion is illustrative of a certain critical hesitation about the gothic woman's film. She writes:

> ... the central feature of the Gothics is ambiguity, the hesitation between two possible interpretations of events by the protagonist and often, in these filmic presentations, by the

spectators as well. This it shares with other filmic and literary genres, for example, the horror film and the fantastic.[62]

Waldman suggests that ambiguity provides the unstable and shifting centre of narration in the female gothic film. However, as she continues to discuss the protagonist and spectator of the film in more detail, and to identify the gender politics at stake, she marks this ambiguity as problematic for feminist criticism:

> Yet in the Gothic, this hesitation is experienced by a character (and presumably a spectator) who is female. Within a patriarchal culture, then, the resolution of the hesitation carries with it the ideological function of validation or invalidation of feminine experience.[63]

Waldman's 'yet' pulls the discussion up short and diverts her perspective from generic affect to a critique of gender relations, centred upon the validation, or not, of 'feminine experience'. This hesitation is echoed in Mary Ann Doane's work, for her the treatment of a woman's point of view in the films is directly related to issues of female spectatorship. Her discussion of the female gothic cycle in *The Desire to Desire* reads these films through spectatorship theories, with their attendant emphasis upon knowledge and identity. She posits an intimate relationship between the suffering of the heroine and her inability to see and interpret events, calling gothic women's films '"paranoid woman's films," the paranoia [is] evinced in the formulaic repetition of a scenario in which the wife invariably fears that her husband is planning to kill her – the institution of marriage is haunted by murder'.[64] The scenario that Doane outlines in these films is one in which the heroine is both despecularised and fears that she is being watched by an aggressive male figure.

For Doane the female gothic cycle's representation of paranoia 'foregrounds ... a fundamental semiotic mechanism of the cinema',[65] that is a helpless position of being observed and objectified:

> ... it is in the paranoid gothic films that the attempt to attribute the epistemological gaze to the woman results in the greatest

degree of violence. Due to the difficulty in localizing, confining, and restraining the representation of paranoid subjectivity in the cinema, the cinematic apparatus itself is activated against the woman, its aggressivity an aggressivity of the look and the voice, directed against her.[66]

Doane sees this objectified position as typical of the woman's film in classical Hollywood cinema, where female subjectivity is promised, but foreclosed by the organisation of vision beyond feminine access.[67] She sees this position as particularly intensified in the female gothic cycle, which 'lends to the films their quality of metatextuality in relation to other women's films of the 1940s'.[68] Because the way that the structures of looking are understood as constitutive of gendered identity, desire and knowledge in this paradigm, a cycle of films which recurrently focus on a heroine, theoretically categorised as passive and masochistic, are read as textually positioning a female spectator in the same victimised position. This perspective on the female gothic condenses the most antithetical aspects of the classical Hollywood textual apparatus to feminist politics. There are two issues that arise from this: the first relates to the ways in which identification for viewers is understood in relation to the theoretical subject positions offered by the classical Hollywood film in general, and the woman's film in particular; and the second, relatedly, concerns perceptions of gender and narrative agency.

'Identification' is a slippery term, suggesting both a process of identifying someone, or something (identification *of*) and a process of engagement (identification *with*). It is this second sense that has been widely discussed in film criticism, where the terms of identification *with* have come to carry an ideological weight in discussions of the relationships between viewers/readers and texts. In psychoanalytically informed film criticism it usually speaks of the ability of mainstream film texts to offer fantasies of empowerment to (male) spectators identifying with male hero figures by awarding them a 'satisfying sense of omnipotence'.[69] This empowerment is predicated on an assumption of male narrative centrality, dominance and agency. Within the same strand of criticism the identification process has been seen as less empowering for female spectators, precisely because of the 'closeness' that it seems to evoke. Mary Ann Doane articulates an anxiety about the lack of distance between woman and image in mainstream cinema, arguing that feminine genres (the woman's film, soap opera) dictate an 'over-identification' between woman and image which she sees as a 'claustrophobic closeness'.[70] This perspective is predicated on the notion that the classical Hollywood text offers male ideals, hero figures, whereas it simply reconfirms women's lack of sexual and social agency through the objectification of female stars and characters. The solution to this impasse for the female spectator is that to carry the 'look' in mainstream cinema she must assume a masculine position and 'masquerade' in order to insert a necessary distance.

Several questions, though, might be asked of the safety of male identification: what happens to this model of identification if there is a female character at the centre of the narrative, or if the male character does not fulfil the ideal of narrative dominance? Is spectatorial identification always ordered according to gender? In *Visible Fictions*, John Ellis conceptualises identification as rather more fluid, and as conditioned by the shifting processes of narration:

> Cinematic identification involves two different tendencies. First there is that of dreaming and phantasy that involve the multiple and contradictory tendencies within the construction of the individual. Second, there is the experience of narcissistic identification with the image of a human figure perceived as other. Both these processes are invoked in the conditions of entertainment cinema. The spectator does not therefore 'identify' with the hero or heroine: an identification that would, if put in its conventional sense, involve socially constructed males identifying with male heroes, and socially constructed females identifying with women heroines. The situation is more complex than this, as identification involves both the recognition of self in the image on the screen, a narcissistic identification, and the identification of self with the various positions that are involved in the fictional narration: those of hero and heroine, villain, bit-part player, active and passive character.

Identification is therefore multiple and fractured, a sense of seeing the constituent parts of the spectator's own psyche paraded before her or him.[71]

Drawing upon Ellis' work, Ian Green explores the ways that narrational shifts 'offer some kind of space to open up multiple, fluid and even contradictory identifications and phantasies',[72] whether or not the text attempts to ideologically 'regulate' identification according to gender. Green continues:

Overriding any channelling or regulating of identification in relation to *sexual division* are identifications with the vicissitudes of a particular narrative and with characters as the mechanisms of narrative ... Viewers trade off their identifications in relation to the economy of the plot.[73]

Green's argument is particularly interesting in that his focus is on identification in the woman's film. His textual reference points are *Now Voyager* (Irving Rapper, 1942) and *Mildred Pierce* (Michael Curtiz, 1945), where women 'are the main characters who motivate the narrative, however one argues their relative activity/passivity.'[74] Green suggests that the struggles the characters of Charlotte and Mildred go through can have potent meanings for *all* audience members, precisely because these characters and their struggles are central to the plot: '[t]hey are issues around which they suffer and are signs of their sensitivity and vulnerability – within the conventions of tragedy and melodrama, they are available for fashioning ideal images, even cross-gender ones.'[75] Green argues that the woman's film offers centrally involved female characters, whose perspectives are elaborated through the complexities of narration. For Green, their position and perspectives offer them as identificatory figures for men and women viewers. He argues that more importance 'needs to be attached to character as part of narrative and genre as a main channel of identification processes'.[76]

Genre is indeed a key shaping element of character perspective and audience identification, through the 'vicissitudes' of generic variations in narration. Identification in the female gothic cycle is conditioned by the long intertextual heritage of the gothic mode and its purposeful production of sensations, most typically its evocation of fear. The popularity of the literary and filmic gothic is predicated on its ability to involve its readers and viewers in powerful ways. Botting asserts that '[I]n Gothic productions imagination and emotional effects exceed reason. Passion, excitement and sensation transgress social proprieties and moral laws.'[77] He suggests that the gothic 'signified a trend towards an aesthetics based on feeling and emotion... associated primarily with the sublime.'[78] Moers cites early popular receptions of gothic 'sensation' novels which spoke of the direct effect that gothic reading provoked, arguing that the gothic has 'one definite authorial intent: to scare'.[79] Coral Ann Howells finds the felicitous title *Love, Mystery and Misery* for her study of feeling in gothic fiction in an early nineteenth-century novel, suggesting that it is 'emblematic ... for it defines the precise combination of feelings that are distinctly Gothic.'[80] Arguing that the gothic mode typically stages 'transgressive acts ... [that] are often violent, and always frightening',[81] Donna Heiland states 'gothic novels are above all about the creation of fear – fear in the characters represented, fear in the reader.'[82] And Charlene Bunnell characterises the literary and filmic gothic as participative and experiential for readers and viewers: '[a]n audience cannot merely read the Gothic story; they must experience it. Their own sensibilities must be aroused, their own values re-evaluated, and their own social codes questioned.'[83] The 1940s female gothic cycle foregrounds fear, sensation and involvement as key to the films' appeal, as many of the film titles attest: *Suspicion, Shadow of a Doubt, Spellbound, Shock, Undercurrent, Secret Beyond the Door* and *Caught*.

The production of fear is predicated upon the shifting positions of characters within the unfolding of the female gothic narration, with a particular focus upon the gothic heroine's positions and perspective. The female gothic heroine is an investigative figure and the generic situations of the gothic story require her to navigate a series of positions conditioned by her speculation about, or knowledge of, events at different moments in that story. The centrality of the heroine as protagonist means that unfolding of story events are understood in relation to her, and what the audience understands about her. This 'relation' is quite intricate in the female gothic film, where the process of narrating – the 'structure of arranging through which the reader or spectator learns of the event'[84] – is generically motivated by secrecy and concealment, a restriction of knowledge that is a common feature of the mystery narrative. I will return to explore the characteristics of female gothic narration in more detail. Before doing so, though, I want to revisit discussions of narrative and narration in order to situate these characteristics.

Elizabeth Cowie discusses the way that narrative theory has traditionally separated narrative form and content. For narrative theory, arising out of the work of Russian Formalist critics, there is a distinction between story (*fabula*) and plot (*syuzhet*): 'The *fabula* is the order of events and their causal logic referred to by the narrative, so that the story is "the action itself" while the *syuzhet* or plot is "how the reader learns of the action".'[85] She notes that subsequent discussions of how readers and viewers 'learn of the action' have modified these distinctions. In David Bordwell's work on narrative processes in film, 'narration' involves an interaction between *syuzhet* and filmic style. Bordwell suggests that although filmic style is 'typically subordinate' to plot, 'a film's systematic use of cinematic devices',[86] such as 'mise-en-scène, cinematography, editing, sound ... can also be foregrounded ... enabling sense-making.'[87] In other words, film style can make a contribution to 'how' viewers learn of the action.

Cowie proceeds to argue that the narration processes through which readers and spectators make fictional narratives meaningful involve both the 'what' and 'why' of events: motivational cause and effect:

> The narration, as a process of narrating, opens us to knowledge of events – not only knowledge of what happened but also, and for some narratives more importantly, why the events occur – that is we come to understand what motivated characters to act as they do, and this motivation, rather than the actions themselves, may become what the fictional work as a whole is 'about'.[88]

She argues that reader and spectator recognition of the meaning of any story retrospectively exceeds the events and actions of plot to include its telling too:

> The story... is the totality of signifieds, it is what the film was 'about' as a human experience for the characters and the spectator, the 'real' story lying in the transformation in the characters and the understanding given to the spectator as a result of the events and actions, and not these events and actions alone ... Reading the story becomes an act of making sense not of the 'story' but of the 'storytelling', the *syuzhet*. Considered in this way the traditional distinction between form and content must disappear in favour of analytic categories through which a narrative can be understood to come into being in its process of narration.[89]

For Cowie, then, the manner of narration – which encompasses film style – is of a piece with narrative meaningfulness. Related to this, the manner of any film's narration, and subsequently how it engages its viewers, is also conditioned by its genre. Cowie writes:

> ... how we learn of events, may also encompass an affective component so that the structure of suspense in a melodrama or thriller may give rise to emotions of anxiety or compassion as well as enabling us to cognitively anticipate the narrative outcome or to evaluate the position of characters.[90]

This affective component is, as noted above, characteristic of gothic narration. This narration is characterised by restrictions, and sometimes imbalances, in knowledge, for characters and viewers, combined with excessive and elaborate uses of filmic style. As Cowie argues, all narrative reading and viewing experiences are prompted by 'the wish to know',[91] in that narrative presents an enigma and gradually unfolds its solution.[92] The unfolding, though, is always a play between narrative revelation and delay, answers will be given, but are also 'withheld in favour of continued narration. The story is the period of delay between the setting of the enigma and the solution.'[93]

The narratives of the female gothic films foreground questions of knowledge and interpretation, a feature they share with the detective and suspense film. Outlining the female gothic plot, Diane Waldman writes:

> ... a young inexperienced woman meets a handsome older man to whom she is alternately attracted and repelled. After a whirlwind courtship ... she marries him. After returning to the ancestral mansion of one of the pair, the heroine experiences a series of bizarre and uncanny incidents, open to ambiguous interpretation, revolving around the question of whether or not the Gothic male really loves her. She begins to suspect that he may be a murderer.[94]

Waldman identifies the motivating enigma of the female gothic formula, the heroine's experience of 'bizarre incidents' and the delaying strategies of 'ambiguous interpretation' which prompt her suspicions. I would rather characterise the narratives as passing through several stages, which are: romance, suspicion, investigation/discovery, confrontation or confession, and resolution. The romance stage shows the attraction of gothic male and heroine, rapidly culminating in marriage. The stages of suspicion and investigation and discovery may vary depending on the individual plot of each film, but often there is a high degree of interrelationship. Suspicion relates to the 'repulsion' side of the relationship dichotomy that Waldman identifies, and at the point of investigation/discovery the heroine learns about the gothic male's past. In some plots it is suspicion that comes first: the unpredictable and threatening behaviour of the gothic male plants doubts about her husband in the mind of the heroine, leading her to explore her suspicions through learning about his past. Discovery occurs through various means; other characters may tell the heroine stories about her husband's past, for example, which can mislead her. In other plots the investigation and discovery stage, a key element of which is the gothic male's relationship to another woman, prompts the heroine's suspicions. Confrontation or confession involves a revelation of the gothic male's 'true' character to the heroine. In some cases the confession is made willingly by the gothic male (*Rebecca*); in others the heroine forces the confession by entering a forbidden space (for example, *Dragonwyck*,

Gaslight, The Two Mrs Carrolls, Undercurrent and *Secret Beyond the Door*). The confession or confrontation affects what happens in the resolution stage: in *Rebecca* and *Secret Beyond the Door*, the heroine and gothic male overcome the past and are united against a common enemy (Mrs Danvers in *Rebecca*; Miss Robey in *Secret Beyond the Door*). In other cases (for example, *Gaslight*, *Dragonwyck* and *The Two Mrs Carrolls*), and the heroine's suspicions are confirmed and the gothic male is revealed as a threatening murderer from whom she must escape. The resolution often has the heroine forming a couple with a secondary male character, who may have a role in helping the heroine escape from the gothic male. The progress of the narrative through these stages is portrayed from the heroine's perspective: she is the central protagonist of the story.

The female gothic narratives share common features with detecting narratives in that they distort or extend periods of delay to promote viewerly feelings of curiosity, suspicion and suspense. But although female gothic films frequently deploy suspense in discrete sequences or segments, the predominant discomforting mood is suspicion or uncertainty. This is driven by the female gothics' ambiguous knowledgibility. The heroine, and the viewer, are given distinct reasons for suspicion (the gothic husband's unpredictable behaviour, stories from other characters), but these reasons must be clearly defined for the enigma to come into focus and be resolved. Defining the enigma is the investigative process of the female gothic narrative. This constructs the female gothics' knowledge relations, and is at the centre of the way that the female gothic heroine's agency (or putative lack of it) has been interpreted within feminist film criticism. As I have noted earlier, the heroine has been understood as victimised because of her lack of access to an investigative 'look' (spectatorship theory), and, relatedly, because of a correlative lack of knowledge. To understand the knowledge relations of the female gothic films, we need to understand the ways in which these narratives borrow and mix suspicion, investigation and suspense.

Discussing knowledge relations in investigative narratives, Cowie distinguishes between the detective film, where she argues that the audience share the detective's knowledge, and the suspense thriller, where they know more than a character or characters. During the narrative stages of the female gothics the knowledge of the heroine and the viewer are, in the vast majority of instances, parallel. Where the enigma of the female gothic film differs significantly from that of the detective film is that the event causal to the investigation is unclear, shrouded in secrecy. The motivating question of the female gothic is not, then, 'who killed whom?'[95] but, crucially, 'was someone killed?'. In dealing with this motivational question the female gothics deal both with defining a crime (suspicion) and once this is clarified, its investigation.

Suspense narration involves different knowledge relations. It gives the viewer knowledge that the protagonist does not possess; this knowledge is frequently only partial. The 'master of suspense', Alfred Hitchcock, famously distinguishes between creating surprise and creating suspense by offering a scenario where a bomb is concealed under a table where two characters are talking. An audience with no knowledge that the bomb is concealed will be shocked and surprised by its explosion. An audience with the partial knowledge that a bomb is concealed, but restricted in the knowledge of whether it will explode, will endure suspense: 'the public is participating in the scene. The audience is longing to warn the characters on the screen.'[96] This participation is usually elicited at particular moments in the film's narrative, as Cowie explains:

> ... the 'hero' is displaced as site of knowledge though he or she never ceases to be the protagonist – provoking and taking action within the narrative. However a different structure of identification/implication within the narrative is established with the abandonment of the illusion that we are finding out along with/in competition with the detective and we are thrust into the insecurity of not yet knowing all but worse off than the character since we know something. As a result 'having knowledge' in the suspense film is not simply part of the pleasure of 'finding out', indeed it is associated with the thrill of unpleasure, and hence the relation of 'coming to know' is not commensurable across different types of narrative. This marks the radical divergence possible within a general strategy of delay,

and shows the importance of the narrative's construction of the positions of protagonist and viewer/reader vis-à-vis the knowledge itself. The character or protagonist in suspense becomes, in a way, the victim of the narrative – acting blindly in comparison with the audience's knowledge.[97]

Suspense sequences, then, temporarily put protagonists at a knowledge disadvantage, in order to thrill and engage the viewer by clearly defining a threat to the narrative's protagonist. What is clear from Cowie's discussion is that the victimhood of suspense is not an inherently gendered position, but the position of all protagonists at distinct moments in a suspense segment. Suspense sequences are deployed in the female gothics, but at a point in the narrative *after* which suspicion has been confirmed through investigation, discovery and, usually, the confrontation of the gothic husband/lover. These sequences also function to realise the suspicions of the female gothic heroine. By exposing the threat to her in concrete form, they corroborate, or in Waldman's terms 'validate', her experience of suspicion and uncertainty. The heroine's victimisation in the female gothic film is only one position in her adventurous narrative trajectory: she is 'a young woman who is simultaneously persecuted victim and courageous heroine'.[98]

Further, as Pam Cook suggests, victimhood in the female gothic film is a position occupied by male characters too. Taking up Doane's perspective on the films as characterised by female masochism (for characters and viewers), Cook argues that many of the films complicate gendered subject positions as follows:

[Doane's] adherence to a negative notion of female masochism, defined in terms of passive suffering, ignores the extent to which many of the films she discusses have as their backstories dramas of male masochism. That is titles such as *Rebecca* (1940), *Secret Beyond the Door* (1947), *Jane Eyre* (1943) and even, perhaps, *Now Voyager* (1942) feature damaged male characters who in the past have been punished and/or abused by dominant, powerful women who continue to exert a hold over them. In these films, then, the hero is not the only sexual aggressor, and he is also a victim. Thus, in the course of the woman's picture narrative the heroine confronts not only her own victimization, but that of the hero as well (and sometimes that of subsidiary characters). In the Gothic influenced films in particular, female pathology is matched and often outdone by male psychosis in a kind of overlapping of male and female desire.[99]

This elaborates a shifting character positionality in the female gothic, and an oscillation between the positions of victim and heroine. The typically excessive and fragmented characteristics of gothic narration mean that no character has 'mastery' of the narrative domain: as Botting argues, gothic 'ambivalence and uncertainty obscure single meaning'.[100] The female gothic heroine navigates ambiguous events, confronting her own fears, and the threat of other characters. The filmic style of the gothic narration presents this navigation in a highly affective manner, where formal elements – such as mise-en-scène, camera movement, sound effects and music – are utilised as 'an expressive code'[101] for an 'odyssey of suffering'.[102] I will discuss in detail the stylistic modes of these films' narration in Chapters 3 and 4.

Having established the female gothic's narrative stages, its relations of knowledgibility, and the shifting positions of its characters, I shall examine one final characteristic of gothic narration: its retrogressive quality, and show the ways that it informs, and revises, issues of identification. I began this chapter by arguing that retrogressive gothic narration produces a re-conditioning of knowledge, for characters and viewers. As Pam Cook also points out, a 'backstory' forms a key part of the female gothic narrative, specifically what it reveals about another woman, and her relations to the gothic husband/lover. Understanding another woman's story is at the centre of the female gothic heroine's own. Establishing her situation, and the enigma, in the narrative present requires explorations and revelations of the past.

Female predecessors abound in the female gothic: Bertha Mason (*Jane Eyre*), Rebecca De Winter (*Rebecca*), Azeald and Johanna Van Ryn (*Dragonwyck*), Alice Alquist (*Gaslight*) and the first Mrs Carroll (*The Two Mrs Carrolls*), to name but a few. As I will show in

Chapters 3 and 4, these women haunt the marital house of the heroine. They are recurrently and insistently present through half-told family stories and secrets, through images and returning memories. Here, though, I want to explore the resonance that understanding a woman's story has in relation to identification, and identity, in the woman's film.

Female identification is potentially both pleasurable and political. It is pleasurable as a concomitant of narrative engagement with character. It is simultaneously political in that fictional character attributes, offered in the narrational processes of texts, are in relay with socio-cultural expectations and codes governing gendered identity and behaviour. As discussed earlier, feminist perspectives on identification, as constituted through spectatorship theory, involve issues of textual positioning for female spectators, where 'closeness' to the fictional woman of the text signals disempowerment, through a textual relay of constructed female identity. Distance from the politics of the text are, then, key to feminist critique of the Hollywood woman's film, and distinguish the criticism from its object. This distance is a feature of criticism on the female gothic cycle, films that seem to explore dangerous disempowerment in their narratives. In tracing the moves and identities of feminist criticism, Charlotte Brunsdon conceptualises critical distance, or what she terms 'disidentity', as follows:

> Disidentity – not being like that, not being like those other women, not being like those images of women – is constitutive of feminism, and constitutive of feminism in all its generations. For if second-wave feminists were not like the housewives and sex objects they saw in the media, they were in turn othered by the postcolonial critique of the 1980s.[103]

Feminist antipathy to the female gothic expresses 'not being like that ... not being like those images of women' through its critique of identification, female subjectivity and the politics of identity, both textual and social. But feminism has also been committed to 'knowing another woman's story', and I argue that the female gothic text is interesting precisely because it explores the negotiations of 'female selfhood'.[105] And it does so textually through the female gothic heroine's identification of another woman's story, and her determination of her own fate as different. 'Not being like that' is the formation of the heroine's self image, as distinct from a woman in the past, and 'not being like that' also constitutes survival. I consider this process in more detail in the next chapter.

Chapter Three

Narrative Journeys of the Female Gothic Heroine

Introduction

As I have outlined in the previous chapter, the female gothic film cycle presents some key issues for the ways in which identification and address are understood. Where the centrality of affect and the promotion of fear to the gothic modus operandi intersects with feminist criticism, most specifically feminist theories of the visual, identification and address, the female gothic bears a political charge. The freight of fear in the female gothic, and the ways that this has been understood in relation to female consumption of the cycle, is the subject of this chapter. I go on to argue that rather than understanding the female gothic heroine as necessarily lacking independence, or narrative agency, the female gothic cycle of the 1940s circles around questions of identification, recognition, likeness and disidentity through its use of multiple (and mutable) images of femininity within the text. Drawing upon Ellen Moers' characterisation of the female gothic heroine as a 'travelling' figure, I consider the processes of the films' narration as offering shifting positions for the heroine. I also consider the role of filmic style in the female gothic narration, particularly as it relates to female images and ideals. In this chapter, I consider the role of costume and of painted portraits in the formation of female gothic selfhood. In Chapter 4, I consider the role that sound and music makes to a positioning and understanding of the gothic husband/lover.

Gothic Romantic Estrangement

In her wide-ranging examination of thematic tropes in the Hollywood woman's film, Jeanine Basinger, rather wonderfully, writes:

> Marriage hovers over the woman's film like a black cloud. It is the "after" of all those "happily ever after" movies, which end with a woman making the right choice, accepting love and the fine print of its social contract, marriage. When the film is a story about that marriage, however, plot development dictates the need for something to go terribly wrong. When the movie begins where the romance leaves off – when it starts after a woman's basic choice is made – it has to be a different story indeed. As far as movie marriages in the true woman's film go, it's a hard knocks world.[1]

Romance, as it is typically articulated in Hollywood, is very brief in female gothic cycle. It is often presented as an intense or condensed 'whirlwind courtship',[2] sealed with a wedding ceremony that is more of a passing incident than a developed event. Michael Walker suggests that it is 'deromanticis[ed]'.[3] In several instances it is only partly shown. In *Rebecca*, Maxim de Winter (Laurence Olivier) and the heroine (Joan Fontaine) are seen coming out of the room where they were married, only to find that they have forgotten the marriage certificate. In *Suspicion*, a sense of foreboding is created as Lina (Joan Fontaine) and Johnny Aysgarth (Cary Grant) are glimpsed through a rainy window. In *Undercurrent*, viewers see only the end of the ceremony at which Ann Hamilton (Katharine Hepburn) marries Alan Garroway (Robert Taylor). In *Secret Beyond the Door* (Fritz Lang, 1948), Celia's (Joan Bennett) procession up the aisle to marry Mark Lamphere (Michael Redgrave) is marked by her voice-over saying 'Suddenly I'm afraid, I'm marrying a stranger'. Celia's fears are fuelled when Mark abruptly disappears from their honeymoon in Mexico, telling her he has business to attend to. In *The Stranger* (Orson Welles, 1946), the groom, Charles Rankin (Orson Welles), disappears from the reception celebrating his union with Mary Longstreet (Loretta Young). Often the wedding ceremony is elided completely, and the action shifts to the beginning of the marriage relationship. In *Gaslight*, Paula (Ingrid Bergman) and Gregory (Charles Boyer) wake up in the Italian lakes to start planning where they will live. In *The Two Mrs Carrolls* (Peter Godfrey, 1947), the action shifts from the death of Geoffrey's (Humphrey Bogart) first wife to his new home with her successor Sally (Barbara Stanwyck). In *When Strangers Marry* (William Castle, 1944), it takes several days for the hastily married small town girl Millie Baxter (Kim Hunter) to find her new husband, Paul (Dean Jaggar), in New York. And one of the most discomfortingly inauspicious starts to a marriage occurs in *My Name is Julia Ross*. The bride, Julia (Nina Foch), wakes from a drugged stupor to find herself wearing a nightgown, monogrammed with M.H. – her 'new' name Marion Hughes – and she stares with amazement at the wedding ring she has no memory of acquiring.

In 'begin[ning] where the romance leaves off', the female gothic cycle presents a distinct take on ideas, and ideals, of romance. The presence of romance as *the* dominant narrative strand in Hollywood's output has been acknowledged by David Bordwell, Janet Staiger and Kristin Thompson. In their random sampling of 100 films from Hollywood's classical studio era, 'ninety-five involved romance in at least one line of action, while eighty-five made that the principal line of action.'[4] They continue:

> To win the love of a man or woman becomes the goal of many characters in classical films. In this emphasis upon heterosexual love, Hollywood continues traditions stemming from the chivalric romance, the bourgeois novel, and the American melodrama.[5]

Romantic closure in the formation of the heterosexual couple is synonymous with the Hollywood ending. The conflicts and delays of romance narratives are the 'quest for love',[6] their resolution being an expression that 'love conquers all'.[7] The common ending of romance in the social contract of marriage secures both narrative and social order. This, allied with its powerful expression of gender roles, and the cultural positioning of popular romance as a feminine cultural form, has been examined and widely interrogated by feminist cultural critics.[8] But the ubiquity of romance, what Lynne Pearce and Jackie Stacey call its 'pervasive textuality',[9] make it available for rewritings or 'rescriptings'.[10] So that, although a romance closure might signal stability, or the desire for it, romance itself is constantly in flux, constantly being retold.

Some of the ways that romance was rescripted during the 1940s were explored in relation to the crime film, examined in Chapter 1. In this chapter, the intersection of romance, or its impetus, with the ambiguity and unpredictability of the gothic mode will be discussed as illustrating a negotiation of the romance impetus for women. Pearce and Stacey characterise the romance quest as:

> ... a quest for another about whom the subject has very definite fantasies, investments and beliefs. This quest involves the staging of desire whose fulfillment may be realized with attainment, or, just as likely, with its loss.[11]

The female gothic cycle has a purchase on those fantasies. The cycle is positioned within the shifting socio-cultural meanings of marriage outlined in the previous two chapters. Its female authorial presence and marketing also locate it within 'a circuit of female discourse ... *by and for women*'[12] that Maria LaPlace sees as characteristic of the woman's film, and as distinct from an idea of Hollywood's dominant male view. Within these contexts, the female gothic's distinct mood of romantic estrangement allows romance to be re-explored from the woman's angle.

Prince Charming Becomes Bluebeard

The seeds of romantic estrangement are often established early in the female gothics' 'romance stage', through ways in which the gothic husband/lover acts. His moodiness and unpredictability sometimes signal potential danger to the heroine even before she marries, as the following examples suggest. In *Rebecca*, Maxim ruins a developing romantic mood between himself and the heroine. His abrupt answer to her question of why he chose her company is harsh enough to make her cry. In *Gaslight*, there are several occasions where Gregory Anton (Charles Boyer) lurks just beyond the frame. The film's first encounter between Gregory and Paula as the film's romantic couple occurs as he waits for her to emerge from the house of her music teacher. Gregory calls her from behind an ornate metal grill, which divides the screen space and signals secrecy. His urgency to marry her, conditioned by her protests, 'I don't know anything about you!', looks like romantic readiness. Paula, however, insists on time alone to think about his proposal – but Gregory breaks their bargain. When she arrives at her destination a hand silently reaches into the frame to firmly take her arm, signalling Gregory's desire to control Paula. His domination of her screen space and movement at this early stage is developed and played out vividly in the rest of the film. In *Dragonwyck*, Nicholas Van Ryn (Vincent Price) tries to develop the 'feelings' that he and Miranda (Gene Tierney) have for each other on the very night he poisons and kills his first wife Johanna (Vivienne Osborne). For him, the bell tolling for her death recalls his wedding day as an unhappy date. Although at this stage of the story Miranda does not suspect him, it is hardly an encouraging start to a love affair. Predecessors also shadow romance in *The Two Mrs Carrolls*. Sally Morton (Barbara Stanwyck) discovers that Geoffrey Carroll (Humphrey Bogart) is married when a letter to his wife falls out of his jacket. Even though he protests that the letter is to ask for a divorce, she feels betrayed. The film elides their reconciliation and marriage.

The rapid move from the romance stage of the narrative to one of suspicion and investigation shows the transition in the heroine's perception of her husband. Her whirlwind romance with a glamorous and charismatic Prince Charming gives way, as she learns more about him, to fears about what his past might conceal. The *Bluebeard* narrative is played out through the heroine's investigation into her new husband's past. The exploration of a forbidden room of his castle in his absence leads her to find evidence that he has murdered his previous wife or wives: Prince Charming may turn out to be really Bluebeard the ogre.

In her discussion of the frequent use of fairy-tale narratives in film, Marina Warner discusses the motif of marriage as a rite of passage experience for female heroines:

> ... many fairy tales, tell the story of an all-important move in women's lives: the departure from the natal or paternal house and its exchange with another man's house. The stories begin with the heroine in one place and end with her in another, and in this respect are women's stories, founded on the social principle of female exogamy or marrying-out for women.[13]

Marriage settings, houses or castles are, Warner suggests, key in both fairy tale and film as the space through which the rites of passage must be navigated: 'The Beast's castle in such tales (both on film and in print) commands as much attention and awe as the Beast himself.'[14] She notes 'a long tradition of marital cells which fairy tale brides enter in stories like *Bluebeard* or *Beauty and the Beast*, and where they have to come to terms with their husband – or flee him.'[15] Marriage, then, is associated with female transformation, both sexual and social. Marriage, as 'romantic closure', is the contractual, legal and fixing correlative of the romance's magical and transformational mutabilities.

The young female gothic heroine undergoes a phase of transition through her marriage. The narrative features her process of self-redefinition, or even reinvention, as she becomes, or tries to become, mistress of her husband's estate: Manderley in *Rebecca*, Dragonwyck in *Dragonwyck*, Middleberg in *Undercurrent*, Blaize Creek in *Secret Beyond the Door*, or sometimes the property she owns but reinhabits with her new husband, such as Thornton Square in *Gaslight*. Warner shows that the heroines' changing social status is imbricated with a change of sexual status; the transition from bride to wife involving both fear of, and fascination with, the sexual other:

> The terrors and excitements of the bride's state are metonymi-
> cally contained in the groom's house, his castle. The transfer-
> ral from one to the other constitutes the central experience of
> the fairy tale heroine, as it in turn constituted the most crucial
> event in women's lives until the present century made a
> greater degree of independence possible. Sexual initiation
> combined with a change of social identity, a new family and a
> new domicile.[16]

Learning about the new family and house that she has entered is
central to the transition process. And the telling and receiving of
stories, often in 'fairy-tale mode', structure this process.

Fairy-tale Narratives and Narration

In *Rebecca*, the heroine hears, half hears, reads and mis-reads
stories about Maxim's first wife Rebecca de Winter from nearly
every character in the film. The heroine's dominating employer,
Mrs Van Hopper (Florence Bates), makes a string of comments
about Rebecca, such as 'I suppose he just can't get over his wife's
death. They say he simply adored her'; comments that are
repeated and replayed in the heroine's dreams. Once she arrives at
Manderley, stories about Rebecca abound; they come from Maxim's
sister Beatrice (Gladys Cooper); the unfortunately named 'Barmy
Ben' (uncredited), a vagrant figure who spends time at Rebecca's
deserted cottage on the beach; Manderley's estate manager Frank
Crawley (Reginald Denny); and most potently from the keeper of
Rebecca's memory, Mrs Danvers (Judith Anderson). All the stories
that the heroine receives fuel the idealisation of Rebecca that has
already formed in her mind in Monte Carlo. It is only Maxim himself
who is conspicuously silent. Until, that is, the night that he confesses to his part in Rebecca's death, at which point his account of
his first marriage floods out.

There are also explicit references to fairy tales in the film's
screenplay. When Rebecca's former lover Jack Favell (George
Sanders) visits Manderley, the heroine overhears Mrs Danvers
warning him to leave the house quietly, to which Favell wryly replies

'(they) must be careful not to shock Cinderella'. Later in the film, at the inquest into Rebecca's death, Favell jokingly tells the heroine that he is not really 'the big bad wolf'. The heroine is thus implicitly positioned as Cinderella to Maxim's Prince Charming, and Red Riding Hood to the wolfish Favell. The structuring presence of fairy tales in *Rebecca* is also noted by François Truffaut in his interview with Hitchcock. He observes the story of *Rebecca* is quite close to 'Cinderella'.[17] To which Hitchcock replies: 'The heroine *is* Cinderella, and Mrs Danvers is one of the ugly sisters.'[18] The film's famous opening also foregrounds storytelling as a device. The heroine's voice-over begins the narration of the film:

> Last night I dreamt I went to Manderley again. It seemed to me I stood by the iron gate leading to the drive, and for a while I could not enter for the way was barred to me. Then, like all dreamers, I was possessed of sudden, supernatural powers and passed like a spirit through the barrier before me... And finally there was Manderley, Manderley secretive and silent, time could not mar the perfect symmetry of those walls... And then a cloud came upon the moon, and hovered an instant like a dark hand before a face. The illusion went with it, I looked upon a desolate shell with no whisper of the past about its staring walls. We can never go back to Manderley again, that much is certain but sometimes, in my dreams, I do go back, to the strange days of my life that began for me in the south of France.

The languorous tone to the heroine's dream-telling accompanies the first view of Manderley, its splendour already fallen into ruin. The fluid movement of the camera is made explicitly subjective and associated with the heroine as dream-subject 'possessed of supernatural powers' and 'pass[ing] like a spirit through the barrier before me'. The sequence is strongly marked by interiority; Manderley is produced by and through the heroine's dream, conditioned by her memories. The preface importantly sets the mood and offers the thematic markers of the female gothic, desire for, and dread of, the past expressed through the uncanny setting of the house.

The preface dissolves into flashback, a flashback in which the entirety of the film is told. As it opens from the heroine's dream the main events of the film are subjectively marked, she is the organiser of the gothic's fragmented narration, and she is permitted to shift from the teller of the tale to a character within it. This shift in subjectivity often typifies the narratives or scenarios produced by the dreaming and fantasising subject where the subject dreams/fantasises herself into a range of positions. Warner discusses the use of a dreaming protagonist in films that draw on fairy tales as follows:

> The gateway to fantasy (and especially erotic fantasy) when translated to screen is opened in sleep or dreams. The dreaming woman becomes a key figure in fairy tale movies. It is through fantasy, through the uses of enchantment, that she achieves her passage from one state to another, that she manages to tame or otherwise come to terms with the Beast ... We are shown her terror from her point of view by entering a dream state ... The dreaming heroine, often considered a mere passive victim, shouldn't be underestimated. There is a sense that she is voyaging, and that the film we are watching (or the story we are hearing) emerge from her fantasy.[19]

Warner's emphasis on the process of fantasy as a 'voyag[e]'[20] for the female protagonist who is not a 'mere passive victim'[21] suggests ways of conceiving the shifting narrative, and narrational positions, of the heroine as a journey in subjectivity.

Dreaming protagonists, fairy-tale elements, and the telling and receiving of stories are also important in other films in the cycle. In *Undercurrent*, Ann's fears and suspicions about her husband keep her between sleep and wakefulness as she journeys by train to Alan's estate, Middleberg, for the 'second honeymoon' that he intends will save their marriage. Her fears and suspicions about Alan's past, specifically focused on the disappearance of his brother Michael (Robert Mitchum), are presented in the subjectively marked auditory flashback. This mixes repetitions of Alan's 'I love you Ann' with the words of another character, Sylvia (Jayne Meadows), asking 'What happened to Michael?' These repetitions are overlaid by the insistent rhythmic sounds of the train wheels, bearing her to her destination, and the sound of its whistle expressing her distress.

Sleep My Love (Douglas Sirk, 1948) opens with its heroine, Alison (Claudette Colbert), waking in confusion as she finds herself on a train journey from New York to Boston. In this portrayal of an unhappy marriage, her husband Dick (Don Ameche) attempts to systematically drive her mad by drugging her to sleep and hypnotising her. His motive is his affair with another woman, and he seeks to dispossess Alison of her fortune. This is expressed, as in many of the female gothic films, in a ruthless male control over the marital home, and an attempt to discredit the heroine's sanity.

Fairy-tale elements and the power of dreaming are present in *Secret Beyond the Door*. At their first meeting, Mark tells Celia she is 'a twentieth-century sleeping beauty', a line that elicits a wry reception from Celia's companion, Edith (Natalie Schafer): 'I suppose you, Prince Charming, will kill the dragon, hack through the hedge, and give her the magic kiss?' But Celia herself is fascinated with dreams and their meaning. The film begins with Celia musing in voice-over: 'I remember long ago I read a book that told the meaning of dreams', subjectively marking the concerns of *Secret Beyond the Door* as dreams and fantasies, and their interpretation. She continues: 'It said that if a girl dreams of a ship or a boat she will reach a safe harbour, but if she dreams of daffodils she is in great danger', explicitly foregrounding the symbolism that is characteristic to the film's subsequent unfolding. The symbolic meaning of flowers recurs later. Celia notices that the lilacs that grow around Blaize Creek have a past connection for Mark. When the couple are reunited (after Mark's departure from their honeymoon) their romantic reunion is interrupted as he recoils from the lilac in her buttonhole. Later in the film, Celia purposely takes lilacs into Blaize Creek's 'marital cell', the forbidden space of the house. Mark's passion, related to his work as an architect, is collecting 'felicitous rooms'. Felicitous, he tells Celia, in the sense of 'fitting', in the marriage of the structures and objects of the space and the events that occur there. At Blaize Creek, Mark has reconstructed a series of seven rooms in which famous murders have occurred with an obsessive attention to detail. During a party to celebrate the couple's marriage, Mark takes his guests on a tour, showing them all the rooms, except number seven. The centrality of Bluebeard is clear here, and has been noted by Cowie in her discussion of the film.[22] It marks room seven as the space of the house that Celia must enter to clarify the film's enigma, and Mark's relation to it. Like the curious, resourceful wife in the Bluebeard tale, Celia acquires the key by deceiving her husband, taking an impression in wax from a candle in her bedroom while Mark showers. Further parallels to the tale occur as Celia elicits help from other characters, sending the key's wax impression to her friend Edith who gets a replica key made. When Celia enters room seven she initially thinks it reproduces the room of Mark's first wife, Eleanor, the room that she now occupies at Blaize Creek. Eleanor's death, typically, has been presented hazily, its ambiguity playing into Celia's suspicions about Mark. Room seven, as Eleanor's room, signals Celia's journey into the past, the retrogressive move into backstory. But as a clock on the mantelpiece chimes, Celia is brought back into the present. Seeing that one of the candles on the mantelpiece has been shortened, Celia realises it is her own room, its 'props' telling that Mark knows she has made the key, and signalling her fate: 'It's my room! It's waiting for me!' She flees from the room, through the house and out into the misty grounds.

At this point the narration becomes ambiguous. Celia sees a shadowy figure approaching, screams and the screen fades to black. The narration transfers to Mark. In a highly expressionistic imagined courtroom, he 'tries' himself. His psychological instability is suggested by his dividedness as Redgrave performs both roles of prosecutor and defendant, exploring his impulse to kill. The narration seems to have confirmed Celia's fate, while life in the house seems, oddly, to go on as usual, and viewers' expectations are of her body being discovered. But Celia returns, explaining that she married Mark 'for better of worse', and that she intends to stay. Now it is Mark, fearing himself, who flees. However, when the moment comes for him to board his train from Levender Falls he is drawn back to Blaize Creek, and to room seven, where Celia is waiting to 'come to terms with her husband'. As she initiates an unlocking of his memories, Celia is 'both courageous heroine and persecuted victim'. Confronting him with the symbolic blocks of his repression –

lilacs and locked doors – she draws out the source of his conflict, his childhood fury prompted by being locked in his room by, he thinks, his mother. Celia helps him put the story together by revealing that it was his sister, Carrie (Anne Revere), who locked him in there as a childish prank. Mark is thus freed from the past, and from internal torments. But he and Celia have to endure a final trial, their escape from an inferno at the significantly named Blaize Creek, started by the avenging Miss Robey, before they can be properly reunited.

Bluebeard motifs emerge in *Gaslight* as Paula encounters a fellow passenger, the busybody gossip Miss Thwaites (Dame May Whitty), on her train journey to the Italian lakes, referred to earlier. Miss Thwaites is reading a lurid gothic novel based on the Bluebeard story, and gasping with delighted horror, she remarks: 'It's a wonderful story, I enjoy a good murder.' As well as being a metatextual moment, and marking readerly investments in popular mystery fictions, Miss Thwaites' reading matter forms a bridge, as it leads her to reflect on the 'real life murder' of Thornton Square, where Miss Thwaites lives. She relates the events of Alice Alquist's murder to Paula, not realising Paula's centrality in that story, nor Paula's increasing discomfort. Similarly, Paula retells her version of her aunt's murder to Gregory on their first visit to Thornton Square, relating her discovery of her aunt's body while not realising Gregory's role as character: the murderer. Both these versions of the story offer the murder story from different perspectives, and putting the story together and resolving the mystery occurs when Paula retells it to the detective Brian Cameron (Joseph Cotten). Having studied the Alquist murder case, Brian fills in missing parts of the story with Paula's help. Brian gains Paula's trust by deploying a symbolic prop: a glove given to him by Alice Alquist when he was a boy. Paula has the other glove, and reuniting the pair evokes the Cinderella story.

In *Dragonwyck*, family stories are told and received about the Van Ryn ancestors. They are wealthy Dutch Patroons, owners of a large estate on Hudson River in the nineteenth century. It is Azeald, the great-grandmother of the current patron, Nicholas Van Ryn (Vincent Price), who is the subject of stories. It is the arrival of Nicholas' distant cousin, Miranda (Gene Tierney), that initiates the telling of stories. Miranda comes to Dragonwyck to work as a governess to Nicholas' daughter Katrine (Connie Marshall), and is amazed and impressed at its grandeur and difference to her own upbringing.

Azeald's portrait hangs above a harpsichord in Dragonwyck's 'red room', suggesting *Jane Eyre* as an intertext, as does Miranda's employment as a governess. Azeald's backstory is unhappy: she died soon after she bore a son, and is said, by the servants, to haunt the red room by playing her beloved harpsichord. While Nicholas dismisses these 'superstitions', Miranda's fascination is fed by Dragonwyck's housekeeper, Magda (Spring Byington). Magda relates Azeald's disastrous marriage to her Patroon. She killed herself, cursing Dragonwyck, and vowing to haunt the house with her singing when disaster comes to the family. The shakiness of the gothic family is elaborated further as Magda tells Miranda that only those with Van Ryn blood can hear Azeald's ghostly voice and music.

As part of the family estate, Magda plays a role common to housekeeper characters in the female gothic: to mark the heroine as an outsider (she is not born to the estate, and may lack the social graces of aristocratic 'class') and to act as keeper of knowledge about the family. Mrs Danvers (Judith Anderson), of course, plays this role most potently in *Rebecca*, as it is she, rather than Maxim, who controls the space of Manderley.[23]

Miranda, though, receives Magda's warning story as filtered through her romantic preconceptions: it is clear she identifies with the idea of filling the role of 'mistress of Dragonwyck'. It is only later, when her own experience begins to repeat that of Azeald and that of Nicholas' first wife Johanna, that she sees the Patroon's pattern of punishment.

Storytelling patterns also feature in *The Two Mrs Carrolls*. The realisation that her artist husband Geoffrey is slowly poisoning her hits Sally when she learns details about the death of his first wife. The insight is innocently offered by Bea (Ann Carter), Geoffrey's daughter from his first marriage. Sally had understood from Geoffrey that his first wife was an invalid, but Bea describes her mother as energetic and capable, 'wonderful at sports', and relates that she was 'in perfect health' until Geoffrey returned from a Scottish fishing trip (on which Sally had met him). Sally listens with dawning horror as Bea describes her father's ministrations of care to her invalid mother: 'he insisted on bringing her milk himself', eliciting a shock of recognition in Sally as she sees a repeating pattern emerging between Geoffrey's murder of his first wife, and his intention to murder her.

The telling and receiving of stories in the female gothics illustrates the process of becoming knowledgeable for the heroine. The ways in which she comes to know and understand another woman's story, and her husband's backstory, is central to the formation of female gothic selfhood and survival. In *Rebecca* and *The Two Mrs Carrolls*, the woman in the past is the gothic male's first wife, while in *Gaslight* she is the heroine's aunt, who was involved with Gregory Anton/Sergis Bauer. *Dragonwyck* is haunted by two women in the past: the first is Azeald, Nicholas' unhappy female ancestor; the second is Nicholas' wife, Johanna, who is poisoned by him so that he can marry the heroine, Miranda.

The presence of another woman, and her backstory, is underlined in several female gothic films by the prominent presence of a portrait in the family house. They mark women who preceded the heroine, or were in the place she inhabits through her marriage. As Botting notes, portraits and their haunting presence are part of a representational trope which includes 'doubles, alter egos, mirrors and animated representations of the disturbing parts of human identity became stock devices',[24] through which gothic fictions explore 'the murky recesses of human subjectivity'.[25] Portraits encountered by the heroine in films such as *Rebecca*, *Gaslight*, *Dragonwyck* and *The Two Mrs Carrolls* play an important role in her investigation and navigation of family histories and stories. The determination of the gothic heroine's own story, her self determination, thus includes an encounter with these portrait images which signal 'the family [as a] place rendered threatening and uncanny by the haunting return of past transgressions and attendant guilt on an everyday world shrouded in strangeness.'[26] The female gothic heroine's self-determination occurs as she distinguishes her own image as distinct from the image of 'the woman in the past'.

A relay of feminine images for female characters and female viewers is typical of the woman's film. The woman's film offers feminine ideals through its use of stars and the transformational narrative trajectories of female character. It extends, or offers, these to female viewers in the circulation of these ideals in marketing and promotional materials, which constitute part of the 'circuit of female discourse' of feminine culture. Hollywood's production of idealised images of feminine glamour has been discussed as part of its social conditioning and construction of women. In her examination of glamour photography of stars in the studio era of the 1930s and 1940s, Annette Kuhn writes:

> A good deal of the groomed beauty of the women of the glamour portraits comes from the fact that they are 'made-up', in the immediate sense that cosmetics have been applied to their bodies in order to enhance their existing qualities. But they are also 'made-up' in the sense that the images, rather than the women, are put together, constructed, even fabricated or falsified in the sense that we might say a story is made up if it is a fiction.[27]

What is significant and distinct about the female gothic cycle is the foregrounding of this process, and its negotiation, both within the text and often in its promotional materials too. In this way the female gothic cycle exposes and explores the currency of feminine ideals, the way that they are understood by women, and their role in identity formation.

Gothic Portraits: Image and Self-Image

'What was Rebecca *really* like?'

In *Rebecca* there is a play around the revealing and concealing of the woman in the past – Rebecca – that is perpetuated through a tantalising trail of visual clues. The strong 'R' of her signature begins the credit sequence of the film, and it is found on many domestic items that the heroine touches. It also ends the film, the final shot featuring the camera tracking in to frame the 'R' on the embroidered nightgown case (made for Rebecca by Mrs Danvers) as it is engulfed in flames. In the scene where the heroine visits

Rebecca's bedroom, the dead woman's personal possessions are ceremoniously displayed before her by Mrs Danvers, who even re-animates Rebecca's empty clothes with her hands. However, despite the prevalence of Rebecca's signature, possessions and the frequency with which she is mentioned by other characters, there is no visual representation of her in the film. Tania Modleski attributes much of Rebecca's power to haunt Manderley and its inhabitants to her invisibility. She notes that the system of suture, where 'typically, a shot of a woman is followed by a shot of a man – a surrogate for the male spectator – looking at her',[28] does not function in the usual way to contain Rebecca:

> ... in *Rebecca* the beautiful, desirable woman is not only never sutured in as object of the look, not only never made a part of the film's field of vision, she is actually posited within the diegesis as all-seeing – as for example when Mrs Danvers asks the terrified heroine if she thinks the dead come back to watch the living and says that she sometimes thinks Rebecca comes back to watch the new couple together.[29]

If Rebecca is never fully present in the film, then equally she is never fully absent either; she 'lurks in the blind space of the film'.[30] In fact, her narrative presence is overdetermined by the recurrent discussion of her by other characters, and a theme of the unsuccessful repression of the past runs strongly through the film. Rebecca's uncanny return to haunt the living is explicitly signalled by Mrs Danvers' comment, mentioned by Modleski above, and the rediscovery of Rebecca's boat, named *Je Reviens*, which prompts Frank Crawley (Reginald Denny) to remark: 'It's going to bring it all back again ... and worse than before.'

Although Rebecca is never actually pictured in the film, the possibility of her return is emphasised through the play of nearly revealing her. There are two episodes in the film that contribute to this play around revealing and concealing, and both are also concerned with the heroine's attempt at determining her own image. The first episode begins as the heroine gathers information about her predecessor from Frank Crawley in the estate office. She tells him of the difficulties that she is having settling into life at

Manderley, feeling that everyone is comparing her with Rebecca: 'Everyday I realised things that she had and that I lacked, beauty and wit and intelligence, and – oh – all the things that are so important in a woman.' She asks Crawley directly: 'What was Rebecca *really* like?', to which he replies: 'I suppose she was the most beautiful creature I ever saw.'

The edit at the end of this scene takes us to the heroine looking at a magazine entitled *Beauty: The Magazine for Smart Women*. The image she has selected is a fashion plate of a sophisticated woman in a black dress, drawn with a frame around it. Dress, and its part in signalling female social and sexual identity, are indicated early in *Rebecca*. Fontaine uses gestures of shy nervousness, fiddling with her dowdy costume, repeatedly tucking back her hair, to portray her character's alienation from the polished, classy social circle that she finds herself part of in Monte Carlo and at Manderley. Her entrée to the great hall at Manderley is marred by her fumbled dropping of her gloves, which are haughtily retrieved by Mrs Danvers. And when she first meets Maxim's sister, Beatrice (Gladys Cooper) looks her up and down, swiftly and directly summarising her dress: 'I can tell you don't care a bit how you look.' As Jane Gaines argues, costume has a privileged position in the woman's film mise-en-scène: 'it is the woman's story that is told in dress.'[31] She notes that from the early teens a discourse of costume had developed in Hollywood, in which costume was equivalent with the social, moral and psychological 'typing' of characters:

> The dowd dresses dowdily, the woman of spirit and originality dresses that way, the business woman dresses in simple tailor-made things, and the adventuress dresses to lure.[32]

But Gaines also argues that in certain genres, particularly melodrama, costuming exceeds its typing function and comes to the fore in what she calls a 'vestural code' which acts as an exteriorisation of interior identities and emotions.[33] The frequent occurrence of transformational narratives in the female gothic films is signalled in just such moments. Costuming in the female gothic cycle often 'types' the heroine as young and inexperienced early in the film. For example, Joan Fontaine's girlish tweed skirts and twin sets in *Rebecca*. In *Gaslight*, Ingrid Bergman wears her hair unbound and uncoiffed in the film's early scenes. In *Undercurrent*, Katharine Hepburn is characterised by her sweater and slacks as a tomboyish bookworm at the beginning of the film, and is chided by her family's bossy housekeeper Lucy (Marjorie Main) for not taking more care over her appearance. Costume comes to the fore in moments where the heroine's social and emotional transformation is signalled by her change in dress styles.

In *Rebecca*, the heroine's attention to the sophisticated woman of the magazine fashion plate dissolves to show her trying on a transformed 'look' as she self consciously makes her way down the hall steps and into the library where Maxim has set up a projector to view their honeymoon home movie. His reaction to her costume is surprisingly unfavourable: 'Do you think that sort of thing is right for you? It doesn't seem your type at all.' When he realises that the heroine is trying to please him, he clumsily forces a compliment, but the cut to the reaction shot of the heroine shows that the damage has been done, she looks deflated and hurt.

The sophisticated style that the heroine has adopted is very similar to the image of an unidentified woman in the publicity materials in the film's pressbook. The film's posters offer this woman as a visualisation of Rebecca. Her figure towers over a close-up two shot of the faces of Joan Fontaine and Laurence Olivier, one hand on her hip and with her face, significantly, in shadow. The tag-lines of the posters, 'The shadow of this woman darkened our love' and 'A lonely man, a lovely girl, struggling against the secret of Manderley',[34] place Rebecca as a haunting presence to be uncovered. Suggested exploitation campaigns for the film focus on the ways in which a woman from the past can figure romantic conflict for a new bride. *Rebecca*'s pressbook offers ideas for a viewer letter contest on themes such as 'Would you marry a man you knew little about?', 'Should a girl marry outside her social class?' and 'Should a first wife be forgotten?'[35] These materials tie the instability of female gothic romance to the heroine's social transformation, and to the shifts in the status of marriage occurring in the 1940s. Thus, Fontaine's experimentation with feminine images and style can be understood not as a 'deficiency in her [own] image',[36] as in Doane's reading, but as a

'The shadow of this woman darkened our love': poster designs for *Rebecca* (Alfred Hitchcock, 1940).

negotiation of different feminine images and roles generically conditioned by the female gothic-romance and with resonances for the film's social–cultural contexts.

Tania Modleski reads the film as dramatising the story of a woman's entry into the social and Symbolic order, seeing it as a female oedipal drama. In this approach she differentiates her position from critics who have seen Hollywood narratives as primarily concerned with the development of male social and sexual identity:

> I am taking exception to the notion of the influential French film theorist Raymond Bellour that all Hollywood narratives are dramatisations of the male oedipal story, of man's entry into the social and Symbolic order. In rejecting Bellour's thesis and arguing that there is at least one film dealing with woman's "incorporation" into the social order ... I do not mean to suggest that *Rebecca* is thereby a "progressive" film for women; the social order is, after all, a patriarchal order. I do, however, maintain that all kinds of interesting differences arise when a film features a woman's trajectory and directly solicits the interest of a female audience.[37]

Modleski makes clear that a central part of this trajectory involves the heroine's attempts to detach herself from a powerful female figure, symbolising her mother, in order to attach herself to a man:[38] '*Rebecca* is the story of a woman's maturation, a woman who must come to terms with a powerful father figure and assorted mother substitutes (Mrs Van Hopper, Rebecca and Mrs Danvers).'[39] She suggests that for this transition to be successfully achieved, the heroine 'must try to make her desire mirror the man's desire'.[40] However, this is not a simple process; Modleski continues: 'the film makes us experience the difficulties involved *for the woman* in this enterprise. In order for her to mold her image according to the man's desire, she must first ascertain what that desire *is*.'[41] Modleski shows that a key part of the female oedipal trajectory in *Rebecca* is an investigation of the mystery of the male character by the heroine:

... given the complex and contradictory nature of male desire, it is no wonder that women become baffled, confused ... From the woman's point of view, then, man becomes an enigma, his desire difficult to know. Although women have not had the chance to articulate the problem as directly as men have, they could easily ask Freud's question of the opposite sex: what is it men want?[42]

It is the gothic husband's unknowability, and the unpredictability of his desire, that upsets the stability of romantic union in the female gothic cycle. In her work on the structures and reception of popular romance narratives, Janice Radway suggests that one of the key moments of the 'ideal' romance is an open declaration of love for the heroine by the hero.[43] Where the ideal romantic hero offers a transparent communication of desire, the secretiveness of the gothic anti-hero means his desire is opaque, and prompts suspicions that initiate an unravelling of romantic stability.

In trying on and masquerading in different identities, the heroine of *Rebecca* experiments with the effect of different images of femininity on Maxim's desire. Having persuaded Maxim to hold a costume ball, she is tricked into impersonating Rebecca, or more precisely in inhabiting one of Rebecca's disguises, dressing up as Lady Caroline de Winter. The portrait of Lady Caroline de Winter, one of Maxim's ancestors, hangs prominently on Manderley's staircase, and Mrs Danvers tells the heroine the picture is one of Maxim's favourites. The heroine expects Maxim's delighted reaction to her costume, but instead experiences what Modleski describes as 'a cruel reversal of the Cinderella myth',[44] as Maxim tells her to change her dress. It is only after his horrified reaction that she is told by Mrs Danvers that Rebecca wore the same costume at a previous ball, and that she has unwittingly brought Rebecca back in Maxim's memory and that of his horrified guests.

The portrait of Lady Caroline is a feminine image that both reveals and conceals. Its position as a likeness of one of Maxim's ancestors, a former great Lady of Manderley, is reinflected by Rebecca's adoption of it, and, secondarily, by its imposition on the heroine. There is an uncanny tension between the portrait's representation of Maxim's illustrious family history, and its subsequent mutability, suggestive of 'the Gothic device of portraits assuming life'[45] and indicating the instability of gothic family dynasties. A similar tension marks the portraits in *Gaslight* and *Dragonwyck*. In *Gaslight*, the subject of the portrait is Alice Alquist, the heroine's aunt, but its introduction into the film indicates a tension around its function as representative likeness. The portrait is revealed in the scene that shows Paula and Gregory entering Thornton Square for the first time as a married couple; but unknown to Paula, Gregory has actually been there before as the murderer, Sergis Bauer.

Paula's re-entry into Thornton Square, and the presence of her aunt's possessions, elicits her memory of Alice Alquist's fame, when the house was full of people and music. Now the house is shrouded with dust covers and redolent of death. Paula unveils Alice's portrait, and a crescendo of music marks her action. A close up of the portrait reveals Paula's resemblance to her aunt, a likeness that Gregory remarks upon, and which has been pointed out by Paula's singing teacher, Signor Guardi (Emil Rameau), earlier in the film. Gregory's alignment of Paula with the portrait is chilling as it indicates his Bluebeardian intentions.

Alice Alquist's portrait captures her in the process of performing what Paula calls 'her greatest role', that of the Empress Theodora. The gorgeously ornate costume that she wears in the painting, and which is hidden in the attic of Thornton Square, has priceless Russian imperial jewels sewn into it. The jewels were the secret gift of Alice's lover, the Tzar, who watched her every performance in the role. It is these jewels that Gregory covets, and for which he murdered Alice Alquist. As *Gaslight*'s detective Brian Cameron notes, the jewels have been hidden in plain sight: 'Alice Alquist hid them where all the world could see them and yet no-one would know where they were except the man who gave them to her, watching from the royal box.' The portrait thus condenses family secrets and conceals murder clues that only become clear to the heroine as she discovers more about her husband's past.

As discussed earlier, the portrait of Azeald in *Dragonwyck* represents a figure from the Van Ryn's family history, a great Lady from the past. The portrait of Azeald reappears several times during the film, and in each appearance it is evident that the family history is threatened by secrets in its past. On the night that Nicholas' first

Paula (Ingrid Bergman) unveils the portrait of her aunt, Alice Alquist, in *Gaslight* (George Cukor, 1944).

wife Johanna falls ill and dies, the portrait is shown lit by a flash of lightning coming through the gothic mullioned windows. Nicholas has staged events so that the doctor attending his wife, Jeff Turner (Glenn Langan), stays the night at Dragonwyck. After taking his wife the fatally poisoned cake, Nicholas escorts Miranda and Jeff to dinner. The camera pans to follow the three characters from the red room, but as they walk out of the frame it remains on Azeald's portrait, and a tracking shot reframes a closer view of it as Azeald's musical theme wells up on the sound track.

This unmotivated shot is unusual in its dislocation from a diegetic character. The narrating camera 'waits' for the exit of the three characters in order to present an unmediated view of the portrait accompanied by its subject's musical theme, reminding the audience of Azeald's curse on Dragonwyck. The storm outside, which motivates the high contrast lighting of the space, creates a strong sense of impending doom.

This mood builds in the following scene, in which the portrait of Azeald is strongly associated with the film score. The use of distinctive sonic styles in the female gothic film is an issue I pursue in more detail in Chapter 4. I mention it here as the scene also illustrates the function of portraits in gothic family histories. The scene begins with a dissolve, taking the action to the deserted red room in the middle of the night. The Van Ryn curse is rendered as Nicholas' daughter Katrine is lured down the stairs and into the red room by the sound of Azeald singing and the harpsichord playing. She is followed by Miranda. The music is audible to the audience, which hear it from Katrine's perspective, but Katrine has to describe the sound to Miranda. At first the music is soft, but becomes louder, more insistent and more discordant as Katrine's fear grows. In this uncanny moment the dead mistress of Dragonwyck fulfils her promise to sing and play whenever disaster comes to the Van Ryns. The division in audibility between the two characters is a clear indication of the Van Ryn family pathology, and Miranda is a witness to its effect on Katrine. Miranda observes Katrine's possession by the music that she herself cannot hear, and uses this knowledge to decode Nicholas' behaviour later in the film.

Thus, the status of family relationships are indicated through the portraits mentioned in *Rebecca*, *Gaslight* and *Dragonwyck*, and

The portrait of female ancestor Azeald Van Ryn hangs prominently above her harpsichord in the red room at Dragonwyck.

this is an issue that is explored in detail in *The Two Mrs Carrolls*, where the gothic male character is an artist.

Family Portraits: *The Two Mrs Carrolls* and 'The Angel of Death'

There are several female portraits in *The Two Mrs Carrolls*, and Geoffrey Carroll's career as artist foregrounds the status of portraiture as a representative tradition. The first painting that is shown in the film is a work in progress, portraying Geoffrey's first wife, who is very ill. It is seen during a discussion that Geoffrey has with his daughter Bea about his career as an artist; he complains that the 'definite promise' he is reputed to have does not translate into financial success. As they stand and look at the painting, Bea says that she thinks that this painting will put him on the map. The painting is entitled 'The Angel of Death', and Bea comments that the painting is 'frightening of course' and that it makes her 'shiver', but 'it's so definitely mother'. The brief shot of the picture shows its gothic style. The woman, dressed in a low-cut black dress, is surrounded by symbolic harbingers of death, and stares upwards in terror. It is quite distinct from the more naturalistic style of the portraits in *Rebecca*, *Gaslight* and *Dragonwyck*, though it has parallels in that it is the only visual trace of a female figure that is otherwise visually absent from the film. Rebecca, and Lady Caroline, Alice Alquist and Azeald bear upon their family dynasties through their portrait traces.

Bea's exposition of the painting is disturbingly mature for a child of her age. She not only reads her mother as the 'Angel of Death', but calmly discusses her mother's imminent death with her father: 'We both want her to live because we love her so much, but that

Artist Geoffrey Carroll (Humphrey Bogart) and his daughter Bea (Ann Carter) look at his death-portrait of his first wife in *The Two Mrs Carrolls* (Peter Godfrey, 1947).

doesn't mean she will live does it?' The painting is thus strongly identified with her mother and as she has been kept visually absent; in 'the blind space'[46] of the film that is associated with the past, and with death. A strange triangular relationship is set up between Bea, Geoffrey and the painting. The 'Angel of Death' ('so definitely mother') stands in for her in the Carroll family structure. Her husband and daughter converse about the state of the painting in parallel with a discussion about the state of her health. The way that the 'Angel of Death' painting is a representation for a character in the family structure has parallels with other female gothic films, and shows the ambiguous relation of the gothic mode to family structures through its defamiliarisation of stable representations of subjectivity.

Joanna Woodall suggests that, as a tradition, representing the human subject portraiture has had a key role in supporting and disseminating European aristocratic ideology since the sixteenth century:

> Portraiture ... articulated the patriarchal principle of genealogy upon which aristocratic ideology was built. The authorising relationship between the living model and its imaged likeness was analogous to that between father and son, and processes of emulation presumed identity to be produced through resemblance to a potent prototype ... Their uses included arranging dynastic marital alliances, disseminating the image of sovereign power, commemorating and characterising different events and stages of a reign, eliciting the love and reverence due to one's lord, ancestor or relative.[47]

She also points out that the possession of a collection of portraits authorised membership in a noble culture: 'the identity of the owner was produced through identification with authoritative pre-decessors.'[48] The patriarchal genealogy, the line of inheritance from 'father to son',[49] is troubled and destabilised by the portraits of female ancestors in the female gothic. Instead of authorising and stabilising the families' aristocratic or noble identities, the gothic cinematic portraits lead to the revelation of family secrets evidencing the fragility of the patriarchal line. The female gothic portraits therefore do not guarantee patriarchal authority, but threaten it.

The notion that images of femininity threaten masculine authority is central to theories of cinematic spectatorship, which draw on Freud's concept of the castration anxiety that the female body represents to the male. In gothic women's films the portrait images are doubly threatening, representing dead women from the past. 'The Angel of Death' in *The Two Mrs Carrolls* fuses the threat that both death and femininity pose to masculinity as its theme. In Elisabeth Bronfen's influential work on death, representation and femininity, she explains how the twin impulses of desire and anxiety are evident in art portraying death. Bronfen suggests that the enduring fascination with images of feminine death is rooted in their portrayal as other, as an alterity away from the self:

> The aesthetic representation of death lets us repress our knowledge of the reality of death precisely because here death occurs *at* someone else's body and *as* an image.
>
> Given, then, that representations of death both articulate an anxiety about and a desire for death, they function like a symptom... any symptom articulates something that is so dangerous to the health of the psyche that it must be repressed and yet so strong in its desire for articulation that it can't be. In a gesture of compromise, the psychic apparatus represents this dangerous and fascinating thing by virtue of a substitution, just as the aesthetic enactment represents death, but at the body of another person and at another site; in the realm of art.[50]

Bronfen shows the fetishistic function of deathly artistic images in covering over and disavowing not just the castrated female body, but death itself as the ultimate castration. But though disavowed, this repressed is always threatening to return through the very representation that structures it. In the first brief view that we get of 'The Angel of Death', we can see the process of substitution has begun. Geoffrey has painted his first wife as a figure who threatens death to him, and so in his art he draws a correlation between Mrs Carroll in the process of dying and the work of art in progress. The painting disturbingly freezes his wife in the throes of a terrifying and sexualised death; and although it is not yet finished, the destination of both the picture and the woman are chillingly clear.

Likeness and Re-presentation

The second view of 'The Angel of Death' is motivated by the look of Charles 'Penny' Pennington (Pat O'Moore), an old friend of Sally's who was in love with her before she married Geoffrey. Penny comes to visit Sally, and as he waits for her in the living room his attention is drawn by the picture. The picture is now finished, and the first Mrs Carroll is dead; Penny's look allows us to resolve our earlier brief impression into a clearer image. The late Mrs Carroll is composed centrally, looking up at two large vultures that are swooping over her, the background shows the ruins of a gothic-style building, and in the left foreground a skull is present. The audience watches Penny looking at the painting, but there is another unknown observer in the room: Bea is concealed in a large armchair, and she comments on his reception of the picture. When Penny remarks that the painting is 'slightly creepy', Bea replies that 'you get accustomed to it, then you think it's wonderful'. She analyses its style: 'It isn't exactly like mother because it isn't a portrait. Yet it is like her too. Father says it's representational.'

Bea's discussion of the painting as a likeness becomes a discussion of its status as art. Likeness is one of the defining characteristics of portraiture; Woodall defines naturalistic portraiture as 'a physiognomic likeness which is seen to refer to the identity of the living or once-living person depicted'.[51] She cites classical and neo-classical understandings of the way that portraiture can re-present an absent subject:

> The desire which lies at the heart of naturalistic portraiture is to overcome separation: to render a subject distant in time, space, spirit, eternally present. It is assumed that a 'good' likeness will perpetually unite the identities to which it refers. This imperative has been appreciated since antiquity. For Aristotle, portraiture epitomised representation in its

literal and definitive sense of making present again: re-presentation.... For him, a proper illusion of the bodily self necessarily entailed a sense of the presence of the person depicted.[52]

In all four of the female gothic films examined, the portraits' function as a likeness for the woman in the past is complicated by the fact that the portrait is also like the gothic heroine; it is a double representation. It is also complicated by the portraits' com-memoration of female ancestor figures that recall a secret in the past that has been repressed. In the power of a portrait to re-present the subject filtered through the gothic narrative, what is 'ma[de] present again'[53] is not (in terms of the gothic family dynasty headed by the gothic male) a stable heritage, but one undermined by a retrogression into the past.

The power to re-present a subject, considered a desirable fea-ture of the classical portrait, is, then, framed differently in the way that portraits are seen in the female gothic cycle. In these films the gothic theme of a past that intrudes on the present is exploited through an ambivalent attitude to imagistic representation. The commemoration or even preservation of the dead through images is traced by art historian David Piper back to ancient Egyptian beliefs 'that if the physical identity could be preserved after death, the spirit might enter back into it'.[54] He elaborates:

> The very ancient Egyptian tradition is clearly rooted in magic and religion; in the belief specifically that the spirit of the dead would be in need of a lasting physical identity, to which it could return, and re-inhabit. For this it would need a familiar home, so the necessity for a likeness if not a facsimile (or the actual body mummified) was paramount.[55]

The themes of the dead returning to a 'familiar home',[56] and the double's relationship to death, are themes that are tackled in Freud's work *The Uncanny*. Freud suggests that the theme of the double in literature often indicates an ambivalent relationship of subjects to themselves, and to death. He refers to Otto Rank's work on the double,[57] and suggests that 'the "double" was originally an insurance against the destruction of the ego, an "energetic denial of the power of death", as Rank says; and probably the "immortal" soul was the first "double" of the body.'[58] Freud refers to ancient Egyptian practices of image-making as a way of 'denying' death, and draws a parallel with childhood concepts of immortality: 'such ideas ... have sprung from the soil of unbounded self-love, from the primary narcissism which dominates the mind of the child and of primitive [*sic*] man.'[59] However, the ambivalence of this relationship comes into play later in the child's development: 'when this stage has been surmounted, the "double" reverses its aspect. From having been an assurance of immortality, it becomes the uncanny harbinger of death.'[60]

The shift that Freud identifies as occurring between the double as reassuring and the double as threatening is relevant to the use of portraits in the female gothic films. As I indicated with reference to Woodall's work, portraiture has been perceived as a guarantee against separation, but its power to make-present-again is, in the gothic context, an uncanny and disturbing power. Generic elements of the gothic narrative allow this shift to take place; they frame the representative functions of portraiture in an uncanny light. The double is of the same order as the 'substitution' that Bronfen finds commonly used in aesthetic representations of death, so that the double is similar to the fetish object in that it provides a 'cover' which allows the subject to disavow a terrible prospect: in the case of the fetishist the disavowal is of female castration; in the case of artistic representations of death the disavowal is of the subject's own death. However, the process of disavowal is always accompanied by an element of danger; the very presence of the 'cover', as fetish object or deathly artistic representation insistently signals the possibility of revealing or returning the subject to what 'he' has repressed. Bronfen discusses this return as follows, and she illustrates that death and femininity have been interconnected as central symbols of what is disavowed, because 'both involve the uncanny return of the repressed, the excess beyond the text'.[61] This excess is stabilised through representation, and Bronfen explores the double meaning of the term, which is both metaphorical in the sense that 'a symptom, a dream or an artistic image ... stands for, by making present again, another concept',[62] and metonymic 'in the political sense of standing in for, in lieu of, someone or something else'.[63] Bronfen continues:

> The threat that death and femininity pose is recuperated by representation, staging absence as a form of re-presence, or return, even if or rather precisely because this means appeasing the threat of real mortality, of sexual insufficiency, of lack of plenitude and wholeness. And yet the 're' of return, repetition or recuperation suggests that the end point is not the same as the point of departure.[64]

The work of Bronfen and Piper suggests that the return of the repressed in the female gothic films begins at the site/sight of the paintings. In *The Two Mrs Carrolls*, this return is acutely defined through the style of the pictures of the first Mrs Carroll, and a later picture that Geoffrey paints of Sally. Carroll's representations of his wives are portraits, but their inexact likeness to their subjects functions to allow Carroll to represent death 'at the body of another person and at another site; in the realm of art'.[65] His wives' deaths are directly related to his life as a painter, the 'life' in his work.

In the progress of the film, the heroine, Sally, discovers Geoffrey is poisoning her in a Bluebeardian repetition of his murder of his first wife. Geoffrey has found a new lover, wealthy socialite Cecily Latham (Alexis Smith). Sally confronts her husband, pleading for her life and offering Carroll 'anything (he) wants'. But he defines his actions in the light of his creativity, telling her: 'You must understand, it happened before, then I found you and you made my work live again. But now there's nothing more from you so I must find someone new.' Carroll's wives must die, their deaths represented in paint, for Carroll's work to 'live again'. It is when Sally has visited his studio, the film's marital and secret cell, and seen his new painting of her that his pattern of portraying and murdering becomes clear.

The paintings curiously reverse the usual process of having a memorial painted to remember the loved dead person *after* their death, prefiguring the deaths of the two Mrs Carrolls. These are not paintings as memorials (looking back), but as anticipations

94

(looking forward). Carroll is longing to be rid of Sally so he can travel to South America with his new love Cecily. But he is looking forward to *forgetting* his previous wives. This is indicated in his representation of both women as gaunt, wasting figures suffering a kind of living death, their bodily decay (the decay of Geoffrey's love for them) already occurring in the portrait-double before their real deaths in the narrative. A similar relation is evident in the 1940s film *The Picture of Dorian Gray* (Albert Lewin, USA, 1945), where the picture anticipates (takes on) Dorian's physical decay. A further notable parallel is found in the B production *Bluebeard* (Edgar Ulmer, 1944), in which Parisian artist and puppeteer Gaston Morrell (John Carradine) strangles his models after he has painted their portraits.

In *The Two Mrs Carrolls*, Geoffrey is hastening the deaths of his wives as his process of painting them, and poisoning them, progress at the same time; they die for his art. Here his art is not preservative, but destructive. As well as the evident contemporaneous parallels with *The Picture of Dorian Gray* and *Bluebeard*, *The Two Mrs Carrolls* bears resonance with the literary gothic, chiefly Edgar Allan Poe's story 'The Oval Portrait'. Poe's story tells of an artist who is married to his art, to the extent that when he undertakes to paint a portrait of his new bride his absorption in her recreation in paint completely takes him over, and his 'real' wife pines away.[66] Bronfen gives a fascinating reading of the paradoxical shifts that occur in Poe's story between the artist as creator and destroyer:

> Poe's story comes to express the tragic paradox that the resulting portrait alternates between destruction and preservation. The woman, representative of natural materiality, simultaneously figures as an aesthetic risk, as a presence endangering the artwork, so that as the portrait's double she must be removed. She is after all his second, not his first bride. At the same time it is the woman's material body upon which the effect of the aesthetic risk is carried through. A form of creation which seeks to recede from the ephemerality and death of bodily materiality can achieve this only by deanimating the organic body. For the masculine artist, incorporating

the feminine power of creation engenders and requires the decorporealisation of the woman who had inspired the artist as model and whose capacities to give birth are what the painting sessions imitate.[67]

The two Mrs Carrolls are similarly both created and destroyed in the image of their portraits. Instead of a portrait being a likeness taken from a living subject, the portraits become more lifelike as the subjects that they represent enter into death. The representation of them as in the throes of a sexualised death, both terrified and terrifying, suggests the function of the pictures as symptoms; Geoffrey paints his wives as embodiments of death (their own), but also symbolically as the threat they pose to his artistic and masculine authority. The dominance of the picture of the first Mrs Carroll in the mise-en-scène suggests this threat, and the way that symptoms insistently signal the repressed: 'any symptom articulates something that is so dangerous to the health of the psyche that it must be repressed and yet so strong in its desire for articulation that it can't be.'[68]

In gothic women's films the issue of the portraits as a likeness of the woman in the past is complicated by the fact that the portrait is also a likeness of the heroine. The return of the woman in the past takes place through the heroine, who is in her place. The image of the woman in the past threatens to overtake and obliterate the heroine's own image. The living woman is thus shaped towards the portrait image, as evident in *Rebecca*, and in a more sinister way in *The Two Mrs Carrolls*. Further, the gothic male often has murderous plans to put the heroine in the present into the place of the women in the past, to make her suffer the same fate, as in *Gaslight*, *Dragonwyck* and *The Two Mrs Carrolls*. In encountering the portrait of her predecessor, or in the case of *The Two Mrs Carrolls* her own portrait, the gothic heroine is engaged in a bitter struggle for self-determination, a struggle to differentiate herself from the woman in the past, and that woman's fate. She survives this struggle and breaks the pattern that her husband threatens to repeat with her by determining his relationship to the woman in the past, and this occurs through scenarios of confronting masculinity as a threat, examined in the next chapter.

Chapter Four

Men in the Woman's Film:
The Gothic Male, Representation
and Female Discourse

Introduction

I ended the previous chapter by examining the trope of the returning past in the gothic woman's film. A secret from the past is signalled to the gothic heroine through the presence of portraits of a woman who has a significant role in the past of her husband, either directly in his sexual past or more indirectly as a figure representing family scandal. In this chapter, I continue to examine the way that the gothic heroine uncovers her husband's past by examining scenes of confrontation and confession. The previous chapter analysed the heroine's encounter with feminine images as central to the formation of female selfhood. This chapter will examine how auditory codes and styles bear upon revelations of the gothic male's past for the heroine. Film sounds and music constitute important expressive elements in the female gothic film, elements which disclose and dramatise the gender conflicts and dynamics at the heart of the film cycle.

In his work on melodrama and film, Thomas Elsaesser argues for the centrality of film style in articulating the strongly opposed moral codes and externalising the personal crises and dramas at the heart of melodramatic narratives. He revisits the dictionary definition of melodrama as 'a dramatic narrative in which musical accompaniment marks the emotional effects'.[1] He goes on to elaborate the ways in which filmic styles, including music and speech styles, form melodrama's mode of expression:

> Considered as an expressive code, melodrama might ... be described as a particular form of dramatic *mise-en-scène*, characterised by a dynamic use of spatial and musical categories, as opposed to intellectual or literary ones. Dramatic situations are given an orchestration which will allow for complex aesthetic patterns: indeed, orchestration is fundamental to the American cinema as a whole (being essentially based on a broad appeal) because it has drawn the aesthetic consequences of having the spoken word more as an additional 'melodic' dimension than as an autonomous semantic discourse. Sound, whether musical or verbal, acts first of all to give the illusion of depth to the moving image, and by helping to create the third dimension of the spectacle, dialogue becomes a scenic element, along with more directly visual means of the *mise-en-scène*.[2]

It is how speech, sounds and music become part of the female gothic's 'expressive code' that is discussed below.

Confession and Confrontation: Sounding Out the Gothic Male

'Bringing it all back again' Recalling Rebecca
In *Rebecca*, the masquerade ball forms the moment of Rebecca's return. The event is interrupted by a ship running aground on rocks near Manderley. When divers go down to recover the ship they find Rebecca's boat with her body in it. Rebecca, though, does not only return through her image (the heroine's inappropriate costume), and stories told by others, she haunts the film through sound and music. Her sonic presence is most potently felt in a

sequence at her cottage, in which Maxim confesses to the heroine about Rebecca's death.

The scene moves the film through the stages of revelation and confession, crucial to the female gothic heroine's knowledge of the past. It is structured around Maxim's story of his marriage to Rebecca, in which he reveals that contrary to the heroine's perceptions, he didn't love Rebecca, but hated her. He describes her as a demanding, promiscuous woman, a figure with whom he was initially 'enchanted', but with whom he 'never had a moment's happiness'. On their honeymoon, Maxim says, they struck a bargain. Rebecca agreed to pose as 'the devoted wife, mistress of [his] precious Manderley', and Maxim agreed not to expose her love affairs with a divorce case. This unhappy story forms the backdrop to Maxim's confession of his part in her death, and his narration reveals both Rebecca's duplicitous nature and his suffering at her hands.

Rebecca's death provides a culmination to the larger story of the marriage, but it also works as a discrete narrative on its own, with a marked opening 'One night'. It is divided off from the rest of the scene in its narrational and cinematographic style: Maxim's very dramatic voice-over is combined with a long tracking shot, which replays Rebecca's movements, but without an embodied character in the frame. The narration is given an immediacy through Maxim's immersion and investment in his story. He moves around the space, partly acting out events through gesture. Olivier plays Maxim in parts of the scene as though he is almost in a trance, his eyes darting around, and with frequent catches in his breathing and voice. As he relates every word and movement of his confrontation with Rebecca, eyeline matches to different parts of the cottage space position the heroine centrally in the reception of Maxim's confession. As the frame moves around the room, Maxim recalls that Rebecca taunted him with the revelation that she was carrying a child, one not his, that will usurp the proper line of succession to Manderley:

> I'll be the perfect mother just as I've been the perfect wife, no-one will ever know. It ought to give you the thrill of your life Max to watch my son grow bigger day by day and to know that when you die Manderley will be his!

99

In the course of Maxim's narration the camera traces Rebecca's movements in a full circle, and returns to frame Maxim in the doorway. He relates the climax of the story: 'I suppose I went mad for a moment, I must have struck her. She stood staring at me, she looked almost triumphant, then she started toward me again, smiling, suddenly she stumbled and fell.' The mobile camera mimics Rebecca's fall with a rapid downward swoop, and the shot structure uses an eyeline match to show the heroine's attention to the spot where her predecessor fell. Maxim ends his story by telling how he realised Rebecca had fallen, fatally striking her head on some ship's tackle, and how he placed her in her boat and scuttled it.

This sequence has been of interest to feminist critics discussing the female gothic film. Tania Modleski points out Hitchcock's unusual break with the conventions of flashback narration, which allows him to retain Rebecca's power as a haunting offscreen referent. Modleski suggests that the mobile camera 'pointedly dynamizes Rebecca's absence',[3] but that this is not so much an 'absence' (or lack), but an absence the audience is 'made to experience … as an active force'.[4] Our attention is drawn to the camera-as-performer, but the tracking of the absent character of Rebecca gives a strong sense of uncanniness not only because we are being asked to visualise an absence, but because we are hearing it through Maxim's replaying of Rebecca's speech as well. Although Rebecca may be spectacularly absent, she asserts an insistent auricular presence. The 'active force of absence' makes itself felt through the combination of the sound and image; I want to consider some of the critical implications of this tension between image and sound, absence and presence, and the ways in which it relates to issues of gender, narration and gothic subjectivities.

Narration and the Voice

In Maxim's narrated reminiscence, image and sound work together to build suspense. The camera becomes animated around Rebecca's movement, and the score plays a role in marking movement and significant moments of dialogue in Maxim's retelling. Rebecca's theme, a character motif that frequently recurs in Franz

Waxman's score for the film, 'enters' near the beginning of the sequence. A low vibrating tremolo of strings, which creates tense expectation at the beginning of Maxim's story, increases in pitch and volume, and develops fully into Rebecca's theme; its signature – the distinctive quavering timbre of an organ – is just audible.

Maxim's dialogue narration, and its accompaniment of the moving images, forms a break with the usual structures of flashback narration in some interesting ways. The film sound theorist Michel Chion points to the privileged relationship that voice-over has, privileged in its relationship to image narration and to its ability to foster audience identification. He terms the voice that opens a voice-over sequence as the 'I-voice',[5] noting that it is commonly reflective in tone and usually belongs to a character central to the cinematic narrative:

> Often in a movie the action will come to a standstill as someone, serene and reflective, will start to tell a story. The character's voice separates from the body, and returns as an acousmêtre to haunt the past-tense images conjured by its words. The voice speaks from a point where time is suspended. What makes this an "I-voice" is not just the use of the first person singular, but its placement – a certain sound quality, a way of occupying space, a sense of proximity to the spectator's ear, and a particular manner of engaging the spectator's identification.[6]

Chion emphasises the way in which the voice-over that is connected to a flashback controls the images which it introduces – it 'conjure[s]' them. In not giving over to flashback, the cottage sequence does not accord Maxim as narrator the power to call up images to illustrate his memories. This prevents a close relationship between spectator and character: the 'proximity to the spectator's ear', which Chion positions within transitions to subjective flashback, does not occur here. Instead Maxim's narration is channelled *through* his wife as listener, it is her point-of-view that the camera takes on starting its movement around the cottage, and it is through her listening 'ears' that the audience receives the story. The cottage sequence, then, contrasts with the film's opening, which I have argued positions the heroine as a subjective narrator who commands the camera movement, and calls forth images of Manderley and its moonlit setting. In the cottage sequence the story revelation can only come to light through her reception of it, and audience identification, auditory as well as visual, stays with her as mediator of the story. The offscreen quality of Maxim's voice during the cottage sequence also introduces some instabilities of sound and its source, which contribute to Rebecca's haunting of the sequence.

Spatial Relationships: Sounds and their Sources

Rick Altman points out that cinematic sounds have a distinct relationship to narrative space. The spatial coordinates of hearing, namely sound's permeability of boundaries, being heard around corners, or through walls, lends them the ability to evoke tension in two distinct ways:

> ... 1) sound's ability to be heard around a corner makes it the ideal method of introducing the invisible, the mysterious, the supernatural (given that image = visible = real); 2) this very power of sound carries with it a concomitant danger – sound will always carry with it the tension of the unknown until it is anchored by sight.[7]

The 'tension of the unknown'[8] that sound can carry with it means that sounds with visibly absent sources or unknown sources can be exploited to great effect in cinematic narratives, creating a range of expectant emotions in film audiences: suspense, intrigue, unease and even dread. It is through the interrelationship of sound and image that these effects can be created, and this gives the lie to the idea that cinematic sound merely 'goes along with' the image, and is inflected by an inherent redundancy. Altman characterises the relationship between sound and image in cinema as being one of question and answer:

> Far from ever being redundant, sound has a fundamental enigmatic quality which confers on the image the quality of a

response... *The image, in terms of sound, always has the basic nature of a question*. Fundamental to the cinema experience, therefore, is a process – which we might call the *sound hermeneutic* – whereby the sound asks *where?* and the image responds *here!*[9]

Where the source of a sound is concealed, the answer to the question that sound asks of the image is withheld from the audience, producing suspense. A sound heard without the audience seeing the source is termed 'acousmatic sound' by Michel Chion, and he distinguishes this from '*visualized* sound': sound heard and source seen synchronously.[10] Chion points out the effect of uncertainty that can be produced if a question hovers over the source of the sound, and its location:

> A sound or voice that remains acousmatic creates a mystery of the nature of its source, its properties and its powers, given that causal listening cannot supply complete information about the sound's nature and the events taking place.[11]

Critical emphases thus focus on the desire of listeners to locate a sound in its source, to tie down the sound made to the object making it. This desire is more pronounced if the sound that is encountered is a voice, and the source of the voice is an unseen or unknown body. Chion has coined a special term to refer to a voice that comes from an unseen body, which he elaborates as follows:

> When the acousmatic presence is a voice, and especially when this voice has not yet been visualized – that is, when we cannot yet connect it to a face – we get a special being, a kind of talking and acting shadow to which we attach the name *acousmêtre*.[12]

Chion maintains that the voice is accorded a special place by the human listener: 'in the torrent of sounds our attention fastens first onto this other *us* that is the voice of another. Call this *vococentrism* if you will. Human listening is naturally vococentrist, and so is the talking cinema by and large.'[13] This sets up what Chion calls a 'hierarchy of perception'[14] in relation to the cinematic sound mix, with the voice usually privileged over sound effects and film music. Calling attention to the way this vococentrism has affected the development of production practices in the classical cinema, Chion remarks that 'everything is mobilized implicitly ... to favour the voice and the text it carries, and to offer it to the spectator on a silver platter.'[15] Chion suggests that voices are primary sounds that act as indices to subjective identities; they indicate the human subject, and are sought out by audiences of cinematic narratives over and above other sounds. According to this construction, the instabilities of voices, sounds and music in the female gothic cycle inflect their character-subjects in particular ways; and in those inflections they ask questions about the representation of subjectivities.

The Source of the Voice is a Body ...

If, as Chion suggests, the voice occupies a particularly potent place in film sound, then voices that are acousmatic (voice heard, source unseen) will be able to create a strong effect on the listener. To assert that the body is the source of the voice seems like a redundant statement, until we consider how often films in the gothic and horror genres separate the voice and the body, and the uncanny effect that this separation has on the audience. It is the interrelationship of body and voice that makes this separation at once so intriguing and so dreadful. But it is not only that we *see* bodies produce voices, we also *hear* voices produce bodies. Roland Barthes' work *The Grain of the Voice* examines the voice/body relation as one that is reciprocal. Voices contain the materiality of the bodies from which they have emanated; they are marked by these bodies and voices can produce, or re-produce, the bodies from which they came. The evidence of the body in the voice is what Barthes terms its 'grain': 'The "grain" is the body in the voice.'[16] Barthes considers listening to recordings of singing voices, and he lays a stress on the way that the voices can carry the very particular qualities of a singer's body to the ears of a listener:

Listen to a Russian bass ... : something is there, manifest and stubborn... beyond (or before) the meaning of the words, their form (the litany), the melisma, and even the style of execution: something which is directly the cantor's body, brought to your ears in one and the same movement from deep down in the cavities, the muscles, the membranes, the cartilages, and from deep down in the Slavonic language, as though a single skin lined the inner flesh of the performer and the music he sings.[17]

The close tying together of body and voice that Barthes finds in recordings of singing voices can be inflected rather differently in the recording of voices in the cinema. When listening to a recording of a singing voice there is no expectation of tying up an image with the voice, but the classical cinematic convention of synchronising speech with an image of the speaker creates an assumption that the voice heard 'naturally' belongs to the body that is seen. However, Chion maintains that this 'natural' relation of voice to body has actually always been arbitrary, and he refers to subject formation:

We are often given to believe, implicitly or explicitly, that the body and voice cohere in some self-evident, natural way, that becoming human consists for the child of "coming to consciousness," and that's just how it is. All the child has to do is put together the elements given to him (sic) separately and out of order. The voice, smell, and sight of "the other" the idea is firmly established that all these form a whole, that the child needs only to reconstitute it by calling on his (sic) "reality principle." But in truth, what we have here is an entirely *structural operation* (related to the structuring of the subject in language) of grafting the non-localized voice onto a particular body that is assigned symbolically to the voice as its source. This operation leaves a scar, and the talking film marks the place of that scar, since by presenting itself as a reconstituted totality, it places all the greater emphasis on the original non-coincidence.[18]

Identifying the 'grafting' of voices onto their 'symbolic' source speaks to the talking cinema's ability to compose the combination of voice and image in particular ways. Chion suggests that the talking picture is 'a form that reunites and reassembles',[19] and once this is recognised we can begin to investigate the assumptions that shape these compositions or reassemblages.

One of these assumptions is that an image of a gendered body should be accompanied with an appropriately gendered voice, an assumption that profoundly shapes the way that such gendered body images are read. At the beginning of her work on masculinity and the voice, Gill Branston points out that whereas critics have become accustomed to critically investigating gendered images in cinema, voices have been more elusive:

> For cinema, the voice in both sexes seems to be more naturalised than, say, the face which is more readily seen as coded, as "made-up" but in both there are of course systematic codes at work, often inherited from theatrical melodrama, and often in relationship with assumptions about appropriate male and female voices in the rest of our social lives. The "evidentiality" of masculinity is often signified by a deep voice, and this in itself supports and recreates cultural over-emphases on real biological differences between men and women.[20]

The issue of what kinds of voice become coded as 'appropriate' to the gendered bodies from which they emanate is a fascinating one, and I will explore it in relation to the cottage sequence in *Rebecca*. Before we can deal with this question, however, we have to investigate the specific voice or voices that we are hearing in the sequence. As I have indicated, Maxim's voice in the sequence is acousmatic, but what we hear in the sequence is not simply Maxim relating what happened in the moments before Rebecca's death. He actually replays their whole conversation and speaks Rebecca's words in direct speech, inflecting his voice to perform and reproduce hers.

The way that Maxim/Laurence Olivier distinctly produces Rebecca's voice as different to his own frustrates a clear and canny tie up of masculine voice and male body: Rebecca's voice occupies, invades and talks *through* Maxim. If we also acknowledge the visual absence of Rebecca throughout the film, the speaking of her voice by Maxim is the most potent presence that is experienced of her. Rebecca's voice has much in common with Chion's definition of an acousmêtre, a voice that 'we cannot yet connect ... to a face ... a kind of talking and acting shadow',[21] and it is her absence from the image, her invisibility, that makes her voice function so powerfully here, as Pascal Bonitzer suggests: 'The point of horror resides in the blind space.'[22] Chion writes that 'everything hangs on whether or not the acousmêtre has been seen',[23] and the mystery that the acousmêtre creates can dominate the drive of the narrative: 'An entire image, an entire story, an entire film can thus hang on the epiphany of the acousmêtre. Everything can boil down to a quest to bring the acousmêtre into the light.'[24]

The process of revealing the acousmêtre is one by which a voice is put into a body, and the longer the film withholds the sight of the acousmêtre's body the more tension is created in the audio-viewer. As Chion and Altman's theories suggest, a sound without a visible source leads the audio-viewer to search and to speculate on the source of the sound. In *Rebecca*, we do not have a 'classic' example of an acousmêtre, but we do encounter a situation where Rebecca's voice is spoken by Maxim acousmatically, and I suggest that a search for Rebecca's body, which has been so clearly foregrounded as a gothic narrative thread, is dramatised by the tracking camera in the cottage sequence. The questing camera does find a body to house Rebecca's voice, coming back to rest on Maxim, and rather than a resolution that de-acousmatises Rebecca in her own body, what is heard is her voice possessing and speaking through Maxim. Rebecca's voice is put into a body, but instead of a flashback that reunites and reassembles female body and feminine voice, we *see* Maxim but *hear* Rebecca. Maxim's reminiscence returns us to the traumatic event of Rebecca's death, preceded by their conversation, which makes clear how fully he was in Rebecca's power. Maxim killed Rebecca to rid himself of her possession of him, but as he retells the events he 'bring[s] it all back again, and worse than before', and she re-possesses him, making him speak *for* her.

Vocal performance and the return of Rebecca suggest that close attention to sound styles in the female gothic film can advance different understandings of gender and subjectivity. Mary Ann Doane's reading of this sequence argues that Rebecca's absence is an instance of Maxim 'appropriating' narrational control.[25] But I would argue that the sequence demonstrates a splitting of vocal subjectivity, and the return of the woman from the past through the telling of her story. Rebecca returns at the site of the gothic male body, which is invaded, possessed and ventriloquised.

The ventriloquism of Maxim by Rebecca's voice disturbs normative gendered subjectivity because this is a possession not just across the division separating male and female, but also across that separating living from dead; it is an acousmêtre doubly marked by its own impossibility. In fact, impossibility is central to the way that an acousmêtre can produce tension: if a voice is heard, the supposition is that someone *must be* making the sound. In his discussion of Mrs Bates' voice in *Psycho* (Alfred Hitchcock, USA, 1960), Chion analyses a situation of acousmêtric possession that has similarities in *Rebecca*. He makes an analogy between the putting of a voice into a body, and an act of burial, remarking that 'in French, the term *embodiment* (mise-en-corps) is reminiscent of *entombment* (mise en bière) and also in *interment* (mise en terre)'.[26] Chion continues:

> Burial is marked by rituals and signs such as the gravestone, the cross, and the epitaph, which say to the departed, "You must stay here," so that he won't haunt the living as a soul in torment. In some traditions, ghosts are those who are unburied or improperly buried. Precisely the same applies to the acousmêtre, when we speak of a yet-unseen voice, one that can neither enter the image to attach itself to a visible body, nor occupy the removed position of the image presenter. The voice is condemned to wander the surface. This is what *Psycho* is all about.[27]

Here, Chion posits the acousmêtre as a kind of homeless presence, a sound with no 'home' in the image, a voice with no body. The rituals around burial of the dead and ideas of a wandering soul, he emphasises, have strong resonances with the ways that portraiture functions to symbolically locate and preserve the dead. As I suggested in the previous chapter, portraits in the female gothic allow an uncanny return of their subjects, through the gothic's mobilisation of unstable and doubled subjectivities. The realm of sound is also expressive of this instability: Rebecca is not absent, but hauntingly and insistently present. In the cinematic gothic narratives examined, the framing mechanisms only partly perform this function. Hearing a (dead) female voice in and through a (living) male body in *Rebecca* offers a profoundly uncanny 'reassemblage' of the cinematic subject through sound and image.

The way that Rebecca's voice is produced *in and through* Maxim's body in the cottage sequence demonstrates the uncanny effects of this reassemblage. Earlier I noted that voices can produce or re-produce the bodies that they emanate from, the 'grain' of the voice being its audible bodily trace. The sonic qualities of Rebecca's voice, as it is produced by Maxim's body, and Olivier's vocal performance, are interesting. Maxim/Olivier progressively produces a difference in tone, timbre and accent between his words and voice, and his articulation of Rebecca's voice. Maxim renders Rebecca's voice as flat and rather thin, the tone that he uses to speak her words is a commanding one, and he does not raise the pitch of his voice to signal her femininity. His interpretation of Rebecca's voice portrays her as mean and ruthless, which contrasts with his own voice-style; when Maxim speaks the filling in parts of the story, 'she walked towards me' and 'she was face to face with me now', his voice is softer and denser, quite breathy and resonating with emotion.

In reading/hearing Maxim's rendering of Rebecca's voice, we confront assumptions of the appropriateness of certain voice styles in relation to both gender and to genre. Branston refers to discourses about the qualities of the male star which arose with the coming of sound. She cites Alan Williams on the star voices of John Gilbert and others, as follows:

> ... the 'bad voices' of the most notorious Hollywood stars were probably in part a product of their association with melodramatic *sensibilité*.

> It was, most notably, certain of the men who suffered, those whose acting was most expressive, whose screen personas were somehow feminised ... It is, for example, around the time of the transition to sound that male characters begin to cry far less frequently – and that crying begins to signify, not admirable sensitivity, but hysteria and sexual ambiguity.[28]

Branston points out that it is not only the sonic qualities of the voice that are informed by assumptions about gender appropriateness, but also the subject matter of what is talked about: that is, we are dealing with both voice and speech styles. She explores the way that different masculine voice-styles have evolved in relation to cinematic genres.[29] Her discussion tackles the voice and speech styles of Clint Eastwood, and she suggests that he brings certain elements of voice and speech styles of the western to *In the Line of Fire* (Wolfgang Petersen, USA, 1993).[30] Branston finds that the generic iconography of the western can be found in a continuum that includes landscape, masculine body and voice: '[Jane Tompkins] suggests that men in westerns often look like the hard landscape – and I'd suggest, have voices which are also constructed and/or come to sound like it: hard, parched and strained.'[31] She continues to suggest that voices of male stars often have a 'perceived status as evidence of the body',[32] a body/voice connection that I explored earlier in relation to bodies as 'housing' voices. Branston also considers male voice and speech styles in the thriller genre: 'The male voice in thrillers has often had at least the kind of mobility which allows a deadpan wit to be delivered, and it will often work in a brilliant, equal play with the deadly wit of the femme fatale.'[33]

These perspectives on the masculine voice and genre can inform the dual voices produced by Maxim in the cottage sequence. Alan Williams' discussion of the shifting perception of what is an 'appropriate' male voice in melodrama is revealing of the mutability of voice and speech styles used by Olivier/Maxim as he tells the story of his terrible suffering at the hands of Rebecca. The difference that is produced between his voice and the voice that is 'Rebecca's' is important here. Branston suggests that the 'tough' masculinity found in genres such as the western speaks in a restricted vocal range, and controls what is revealed of emotion. We encounter a different sound to Maxim's masculinity in *Rebecca*. As he tells of his marital despair, Maxim's voice, which has been very full of emotion and has quavered almost on the verge of tears, becomes very mobile. He begs the heroine for her understanding, saying: 'You despise me don't you, as I despise myself. You can't imagine what my feelings were ... Can you?' Maxim's abject self-pity is fully fleshed out in his voice, and his last phrase is delivered as a plea for forgiveness, which Olivier emotes through a sliding upward intonation. The edit to the heroine, lit so that her eyes brimming with tears glitter prominently, supplies the visual emotional response which partners her unhesitating and soothing murmur to Maxim that she does understand and forgive him. In contrast, Rebecca's voice, as styled by Maxim, is rigid and immobile, and seems to be on the verge of cracking into triumphant laughter, particularly as she revels in the prospect of Maxim raising an heir to Manderley who was not fathered by him.[34] Branston notes the importance of vocal but non-verbal sounds that are contained in the voice, but often ignored in the analysis of speech:

> One fascinating possibility for further research might be the construction, within cinematic and other voices, of a distance from or closeness to vocal but non-verbal releases of the body such as laughter, and what they are perceived to reveal of character. Does a particular voice seem to be often close to or far away from a chuckle, a sneer, a full or a thin laugh?[35]

Other such releases could include the vocal sounds produced when characters suffer grief, or the sighs and groans of pain, or indeed of pleasure.

In the contrasting voice styles that are heard through Maxim, we can see a curious reversal being played out; Maxim's voice, marked by the qualities of mobility and emotion, and his speech style of confessing his wrongs and exposing his suffering, is much closer to what is considered an appropriate *feminine* style. Rebecca's voice and speech, on the other hand, are characterised by their control of range and lack of emotion. The paradoxical situation that we hear is that Maxim is much more feminised when he presents his own words than he is when he produces those of Rebecca. Through his uncanny occupation by Rebecca's voice, Maxim is 'one [who] possesses knowledge, feelings and experience in common with the other ... [he] identifies himself with someone else, so that he is in doubt as to which his self is'.[36] His suffering is multiplied by the pervasive quality of sound, and the interrelationship between speaking and listening.

When we speak we are always also listeners to our own voices, and Chion describes the 'I-Voice' as a reassuring confirmation of identity, having the quality of being both 'completely internal and invading the entire universe ... the voice owes its special status to the fact that it is the original, definitive sound that both fills us and comes from us'.[37] In Maxim's case, this pervasiveness is experienced as a haunting possession, and one that is occurring across gender. As he is both speaker and auditor of his own persecution, it can be seen that in this case the gendering of sound and the voice is put into question. Maxim's vivid recounting of the scene, and Rebecca's possession of him, through her voice ends with the replaying of her death. Maxim's eyes flit upwards, as if he is going to swoon as he says: 'I suppose I went mad for a moment. I must have struck her'. And he repeats his step backwards to avoid the still moving Rebecca, even reproducing the clattering fall of her body as a sound effect. Both Maxim and the heroine stare transfixed at the place where Rebecca fell, and after Maxim moves out of the doorway he stands in the room staring back at it. It is then not (or not only) the female body that is the site of invasion, possession and paranoia in the gothic woman's film, but the male body too.

The situation discussed for *Rebecca*, where the gothic male is subjected to a kind of punishment through sound that brings back the woman in the past, is also found in the other female gothic films. In *Rebecca*, the suffering occurs as Maxim is forced to speak in Rebecca's voice. In other female gothic films, similar scenarios demonstrate the splitting and problematising of subjectivities through a range of sound, music and voice effects. In *The Two Mrs Carrolls* and *Dragonwyck*, the woman in the past symbolically returns through distinct interrelationships created between portrait images and sonic and musical motifs.

112

The Two Mrs Carrolls: Musical and Aural Motifs

In *The Two Mrs Carrolls*, a particular musical theme is heard the first time 'The Angel of Death' painting is seen. As Geoffrey Carroll's daughter Bea introduces the painting, a swell of music is heard which might be called a 'mystery' theme. This theme indicates narrative information to the film's audience because of the conventions of film scoring. As film musicologist Claudia Gorbman puts it, music signifies 'not only according to pure musical codes, but also according to *cultural* musical codes and *cinematic* musical codes'.[38] She elaborates:

> Any music bears cultural associations, and most of these associations have been further codified and exploited by the music industry. Properties of instrumentation, rhythm, melody, and harmony form a veritable language. We all know what "Indian music," battle music, and romance music sound like in the movies; we know that a standard forties film will choose to introduce its seductress on the screen by means of a sultry saxophone playing a Gershwinesque melody. As for cinematic codes: music is codified by the filmic context itself, and assumes meaning by virtue of its placement in the film. Beginning and end-title music, and musical themes, are major examples of this music-film interaction. Based on the Wagnerian principles of motifs and leitmotifs, a theme in a film becomes associated with a character, a place, a situation, or an emotion. It may have a fixed and static designation, or it can evolve and contribute to the dynamic flow of the narrative by carrying its meaning into a new realm of signification.[39]

The mystery theme can be identified as such through cultural musical codes; the 'properties of instrumentation, rhythm, melody, and harmony form a veritable language',[40] the musical phrase 'says' mystery. The motif also contributes to the 'dynamic flow of the narrative'[41] by its specific association with the portrait, heard not only when the portrait is visible on-screen but when it is mentioned within the film's dialogue. The score of *The Two Mrs Carrolls*, also composed by Franz Waxman, blends with other sound effects to form a whole web of aural motifs, which are given as much prominence as visual ones. On-screen and off-screen sound effects also perform important functions in structuring the diegetic space of the film.

The most dominant aural motif of the film is the sound of bells, associated with Geoffrey from early scenes in the film. As he leaves Blagdon's chemists, where he buys the poison to slowly despatch his first wife, the shop bell jangles loudly. Later in the film, Blagdon (Barry Bernard) blackmails Geoffrey about the poison, which leads Geoffrey to murder him. In the murder scene the shop bell jangles loudly again. In another early scene an alarm bell rings to remind Bea and Geoffrey that it is 'time for mother's milk'. These alarm bells are both literal and metaphorical, given Geoffrey's method of poisoning his wives while seeming to minister care with the milk he takes to them. When Geoffrey marries his second wife, Sally, he moves to her house, which is near the cathedral in Ashton. The transition of Geoffrey's life from London to Ashton is marked by a montage, which introduces the town as a provincial idyll. The rest of the film takes place in Ashton and the cathedral bells are a constant motif in the sonic background. The bells punctuate moments of the plot, and the distinct cultural associations that they carry contribute to narrative development. Bells mark the wedding ceremony of Celia to Mark, which opens the female gothic *Secret Beyond the Door*, and form a backdrop for Celia's anxious voice-over 'I'm marrying a stranger'.[42] Bells mark times and ceremonies, such as christenings, weddings and funerals. But they can also connote psychical instability, particularly when subjectively heard. Both these allusions are mobilised in *The Two Mrs Carrolls*: at the beginning of Geoffrey and Sally's marriage, Ashton is presented as a sunny, happy location and the bells ring joyfully in celebration of their union; but as events from the past start to catch up with Geoffrey – Blagdon's blackmailing of him, his affair with Ashton socialite Cecily – pressures on his character mount. At various moments his mental turmoil is marked by a distinct throbbing chime, a sound effect only ever associated with Geoffrey and consequently subjectively marked.

The interrelationship between the portrait, the music and sound effects in two scenes between Cecily and Geoffrey take place in the room where 'The Angel of Death' portrait presides. In the first scene, Cecily is introduced to Geoffrey and Sally by Sally's old friend Penny. Intrigued by Ashton's new artist in residence, Cecily flirts with Geoffrey, asking to see his work. Moving inside, Geoffrey shows her his notorious 'Angel of Death' painting. The mystery theme swells as Geoffrey moves towards the picture and fades as he moves farther away, linking the theme and the portrait, and marking Geoffrey's absorption with it and its secrets. In the second scene, from later in the film, Cecily delivers an ultimatum to her lover: Geoffrey must leave Sally or she will go away to South America. By this point in the film Geoffrey has begun poisoning Sally, and spends hours in his attic studio working on a portrait of her as a death figure, which he refuses to show to anyone. The mises-en-scène of both scenes are very similar: both are set in the daytime living room, and revolve around the portrait. The mood of the second scene, though, is much more troubled. There is a stronger division of interior and exterior spaces, congruent with a feeling of entrapment. In the first scene, the bright summer garden, from which Geoffrey and Cecily entered the house, was made to seem accessible through open windows and doors. In the second extract, the winter setting and the howling wind outside emphasise the confinement of the characters to the house, and the cooling down of Geoffrey's marriage to Sally.

Sound and music also contribute to the mood of the space, and the action therein. At the beginning of this extract the film music works to indicate emotion, and there is even a musical joke. Cecily's announcement that she is soon leaving for Rio is initially scored with melancholic violins, but they briefly give way to a Latin flourish to suggest the atmosphere of her destination. Geoffrey's violent anger at her plans is anticipated by a lower, more menacing instrumentation of cello and horns, and a 'darker' variation on the predominant theme of the scene. Where the use of music becomes more unconventional is in a dissonant theme associated directly with Geoffrey's increasing psychological instability. As Cecily suggests he accompany her to South America, a high-pitched repeated chiming sound throbs on the sound track. Geoffrey puts his hand to his temple, suggesting the sound reflects and represents his mental state. Geoffrey's theme is further externalised as Cecily

115

leaves abruptly through the French windows. The room is invaded by the sound of the wind and of bells chiming, as Geoffrey stares intently at the 'The Angel of Death' painting. It is only after his intense look at his picture that he seems to register the sound of bells that is coming through the door from outside. As Geoffrey stands in the doorway, holding his head in his hands, the correspondence between his internal mental instability and the wind and bells outside the house make it unclear whether the sound is emanating from him or painfully invading him. His attempts at escaping the sound by closing the door and leaning his body against it are of little use; he continues to be invaded and victimised by the sounds and their connotations: memory, death and his retreating grasp on his own sanity. Claudia Gorbman has noted that although critical discussions of film music tend to categorise it according to divisions between either diegetic (source seen, sound heard by characters) or non-diegetic (source outside the film, sound not

Geoffrey Carroll (Humphrey Bogart) is possessed by the sound of the bells in *The Two Mrs Carrolls* (Peter Godfrey, 1947).

heard by the characters), there are expressive uses of music that cut across these divisions through particular thematic associations with a character's inner life.[43] She terms this 'metadiegetic' music, which she suggests is particularly allied with musical themes or variations that mark character memory. Her hypothetical example is a character remembering a lost love, marked by a swell on the film score:

> On which narrative level do we read this music? It is certainly not diegetic, for the forty-piece orchestra that plays is nowhere to be seen, or inferred, in the filmic space ... In a certain sense, we may hear it as both nondiegetic – for its lack of a narrative source – and metadiegetic – since the scene's conversation seems to trigger X's memory of the romance and the song that went with it; wordlessly, he "takes over" part of the film's narration and we are privileged to read his musical thoughts.[44]

Sally Carroll (Barbara Stanwyck) journeys to Geoffrey's attic to find her portrait double in *The Two Mrs Carrolls* (Peter Godfrey, 1947).

The complex interrelationship of metadiegetic musical strands with diegetic sonic motifs portray both mood and Geoffrey's disturbed 'musical thoughts'. This evidences the female gothic films' 'particular form of dramatic *mise-en-scène*, characterised by a dynamic use of spatial and musical categories'.[45] Sound and music, then, contribute to the ways that the domestic space of the female gothics' settings are mapped as fraught with secrets, and are subject to a battle for control between the female gothic heroine and her husband. In *The Two Mrs Carrolls*, Sally finally realises Geoffrey's murderous intentions when she enters the forbidden space of his studio, accompanied by Bea, to see her deathly portrait. Suspense, and a feeling of dread, are evoked by the framing of their approach and the high-contrast lighting. In the final scenes of the film, Sally directly confronts Geoffrey, resulting in a fatal struggle.

The Musical Curse of *Dragonwyck*

In *Dragonwyck*, the plucky heroine Miranda also has to enter a forbidden space to confront and 'come to terms' with her husband, Nicholas. Miranda and Nicholas have married after the death of Johanna, the longed-for heir that Miranda bears has died, and Nicholas begins to spend weeks at a time in his tower room. One evening, tiring of her husband's absence, Miranda journeys up to confront him. As in *The Two Mrs Carrolls*, cinematographic style marks her penetration of the space as dangerous.

The sound and speech styles of the confrontation between Miranda and Nicholas orchestrate its crisis. The curse of Dragonwyck is replayed through Azeald's theme, which is arranged in a slow tempo as Miranda moves up the stairs. Threat is suggested through instrumentation: low woodwind tones create unease, and these are mixed with sparse and discordant sounds of a harpsichord, the instrument that narratively signals Azeald, and the secrets of the Dragonwyck dynasty. The score's dynamics develop as Miranda approaches the entrance to the tower room. The instrumentation shifts to accommodate strings, and lower, discomforting tones of an oboe. These two distinct areas of

Miranda (Gene Tierney) makes the passage to confront her husband Nicholas (Vincent Price) in *Dragonwyck* (Joseph Mankiewicz, 1946).

instrumentation are important during the confrontation that follows. The strings are more closely allied with Miranda and the romance theme of the score, while the wind instruments and harpsichord are associated with Nicholas.

Entering the tower room, Miranda finds a dishevelled and unshaven Nicholas, a sharp contrast to his earlier appearances in the film as the immaculate master of the house. In the dialogue exchange that follows, the characters use strongly contrasting voice and speech styles. Nicholas is initially, and oddly, formal, using a language of courtesy signalling his aristocratic class: 'This is an unlooked for pleasure, I wasn't expecting you.' He compliments Miranda's pluckiness: 'You have courage Miranda, I like that about you. It must have taken a great deal to make this pilgrimage up to the mysterious tower room ...', and moves to parody: 'I'm sure you expected velvet drapes and heathen idols, an altar for human sacrifice at least', drawing attention to a gothic narrative that marks this a self-reflexive display of generic conventions.

When Miranda punctures his posture by asking what he does in the tower, Nicholas expresses his troubled fantasies of omnipotence, which are fuelled by his addiction to drugs:

> I live! ... I will not live by ordinary standards. I will not run with the pack! I will not be chained into a routine of living which is the same for others. I will not look to the ground and move on the ground with the rest, not so long as there are those mountain tops and clouds, and limitless space!

Where Nicholas indulges in this purple prose, and explains his resort to drugs as a response to the death of his heir, Miranda adopts a calm and pragmatic tone. The highly emotive vocal performance that Vincent Price gives in the scene is marked by a similar mobility to that of Maxim/Olivier discussed earlier. In contrast, Miranda's tone is much more stable, and her speech style is direct and sincere, rather than dramatic and sarcastic. She gives Nicholas

Nicholas (Vincent Price) is possessed by the haunting singing of his female ancestor, Azeald, in *Dragonwyck* (Joseph Mankiewicz, 1946).

an old-fashioned talking to: 'I know you better than you think ... I couldn't follow everything you said, but I think its pretty simple you're just plain running away.' Her speech is underscored with the romance theme instrumented in strings, as she begs Nicholas to give their marriage another chance. But Nicholas is not listening, and summarily dismisses her. An extended reaction shot bestows the moral triumph on Miranda before she turns and leaves.

Music continues to be a key element in foregrounding the disintegration of Miranda's union with Nicholas, and his increasing instability. After her trip to the tower room, Miranda becomes ill as Nicholas begins to poison her, repeating his slow murder of Johanna. After a visit to Miranda's sick room, Nicholas becomes agitated and distressed, and he is lured down to the red room where he stares at Azeald's portrait as he is possessed by her singing and playing. In a gesture identical to that of Geoffrey in *The Two Mrs Carrolls*, Nicholas holds his hands over his ears to try to block out the sound that is invading him.

Uncanny Voices: Musical Motifs, Aural Unpleasure and Narrative Cinema

In the previous chapter, I demonstrated the contradictory representational relationships that accrue to portraits in the female gothic film. Themes of memory, death and family secrecy are centred upon these images that commemorate women the gothic male wishes to forget, providing a 'home' to which this repressed can return. As Elisabeth Bronfen points out, visual representations of death function like the failed repression of a symptom: 'In the same displaced manner in which art enacts the reality of death we wish to disavow, any symptom articulates something that is so dangerous to the health of the psyche that it must be repressed and yet so strong in its desire for articulation that it can't be.'[46] Bronfen's use of 'articulation' to describe tensions between denial and acknowledgement also has a distinct resonance for the female gothics' uses of sonic and aural motifs. Just as the inclusion of portrait images, and their interpretation in the space of the gothic house, constitute negotiations of female subjectivity (and survival) for the gothic heroine, so the associations of sound, music and memory, discussed above, form part of a haunting female discourse which challenges stable male subjectivity and dynastic control.

In *Rebecca*, *The Two Mrs Carrolls* and *Dragonwyck*, this female discourse, and the crisis it precipitates, is 'articulated' through voice and themes of the film score narratively associated with the past. The suffering that Maxim, Geoffrey and Nicholas experience is played out in their possession and invasion by sound. The musical motifs connected with the pictures of 'The Angel of Death' and Azeald uncannily restore a voice to images of the dead; the women in the past 'speak' in voices which signify the gothic males' imminent disintegration. In these films, then, music exceeds a notion of being simply supporting 'underscore' to take on a key role in articulating, and prompting, the female gothics' retrogressive narration, in laying out the stories, and secrets of the past.

Film music has frequently been theorised as one of cinema's seductive pleasures. Claudia Gorbman, tracing the history of film music, discusses how its role was understood in accompanying silent film:

> The argument runs that sound, in the form of music, gave back to those "dead" photographic images some of the life they lost in the process of mechanical reproduction. Words such as three-dimensionality, immediacy, reality, and of course, life recur throughout film music criticism in its attempt to describe the effect and purpose of film music: "the very liveliness of the action in the primitive silent films appeared unnatural and ghostly without some form of sound corresponding to such visual vitality." Music seemed to help flesh out the shadows on the screen.[47]

Gorbman suggests that 'music permitted a deeper psychic investment in the grey, wordless, two dimensional world of the silent film'.[48] She argues this investment continued after the introduction of synchronised sound. Film music sutures audiences seamlessly into the diegetic world of the film, contributing to strategies of cinematic construction, such as shot reverse-shot editing, which take on fetishistic functions to 'restore belief (or suspend disbelief) in the immediacy and wholeness of the film events'.[49] In this model film sound and music is seen as supporting and contributing to the structure of a safe space for film audiences.

She also discusses theories that model the auditory pleasures of sound and music as paralleling theories of subject formation. The pleasures of musical immersion are, Gorbman argues, similar to the pleasures of a nostalgic fantasy of regression to an infantile state: 'The infant is born into a sort of "sonorous envelope", and is yet unaware of distinctions between self and other, inside-outside the body.'[50] Gorbman draws upon the work of Didier Anzieu, which describes the 'auditory imaginary' as a phase that precedes the Lacanian mirror phase, which signals the child's entry into language and the symbolic:

> ... the melodic bath (the mother's voice, her songs, the music she plays to the infant) provides... a first auditory mirror which it first uses with its cries. The imaginary longing for bodily fusion with the mother is never erased; and ... the terms of this original illusion are defined in large part by the voice.[51]

Gorbman also cites the work of Francis Hofstein, who suggests the relationship between the mother's voice and music which exists for the child in its pre-verbal stage: 'Speech from which, if you take away the signified, you get *music* ... holds there the acoustical image, before language restores in the universal [the child's] function of subject.'[52] Gorbman continues:

> The mother's voice is central in constituting the auditory imaginary, before and also after the child's entry into the symbolic. From this – and from even earlier auditory perceptions and hallucinations – musical pleasure may be explained. Of course, music is subsequently a highly coded and organised discourse; but its freedom from linguistic signification and from representation of any kind preserve it as a more desirable, or less unpleasurable discourse ... Rosolato ... suggests that the pleasure of musical harmony is itself a nostalgia for the original imaginary fusion with the mother's body. "It is

therefore the entire dramatization of separated bodies and their reunion which harmony supports."[53]

Two aspects of Gorbman's discussion bear upon the female gothics' uses of sound and music. The association of specific musical themes with the portraits and their secrets integrate the still and silent painted images into the moving speaking narration of the films. The themes of Azeald and 'The Angel of Death' 'flesh out the shadows on the screen',[54] but in the music's uncanny articulation of the returning past the 'entire dramatization of separated bodies and their reunion' constitutes not a pleasurable sensation of pre-subjective nostalgia, but a terrifying regression into the past.

In the scenarios discussed above, the female gothic films generically rework auditory pleasure through their musical motif associations with memory. Instead of the feminine voice belonging to a beloved mother (a 'good' ancestor), it belongs to a reviled female predecessor (a 'bad' ancestor). The invasion of the gothic male by the musical 'voice' of the woman in his past relegates him to helplessness and depossesses him of his patriarchal power over the gothic estate. He is occupied and overtaken through sound, and his grip on his ancestral position is threatened by his increasing psychical instability.

Gaslight: From Persecuted Wife to 'Goddess of Vengeance'[55]

In *Gaslight*, the confrontation scene shows the heroine, Paula, finding her voice and forcing her husband to listen to her and acknowledge his treatment of her. Despite the very powerful emotional catharsis that this scene offers, *Gaslight* has been critically interpreted as crystallising some of the problematic issues of female agency in the female gothic discussed in previous chapters. Doane argues that although the heroine penetrates the film's forbidden space – the attic where gothic male Gregory searches for Alice Alquist's jewels – Paula's investigative agency is 'delegat[ed to] the detecting gaze to another male figure who is on the side of the law'.[56] This secondary male figure is detective Brian Cameron, who pursues the unsolved Alice Alquist murder case. However, Cameron serves an important function. In Diane Waldman's reading he offers corroboration of Paula's experience.[57] The space of Thornton Square becomes nightmarish for Paula; every time that Gregory leaves the house at night she hears strange sounds, and the gaslights of the house dim and flare unpredictably as Gregory moves around in the attic above. Gregory insidiously convinces Paula that this is all her hallucination, systematically persuading her that she is losing a grip on her sanity, just as her mother did. It is only when Cameron visits Paula, and he too sees the gaslights dim, that she begins to trust her own perceptions. Although it is Cameron that helps Paula work through the mystery of Alice Alquist's death and Gregory's part in it, the full resolution of the film cannot come about until Paula has confronted her husband herself.

By entering the attic, where Gregory is bound to a chair, Paula traverses the boundary that has so emphatically divided the spaces of the house. Her confrontation of Gregory shows Paula's transition from a figure of suffering to one who avenges her aunt's murder and her treatment throughout their marriage. The scene is characterised by distinct voice and speech styles which carry the drama in similar ways to the earlier examples discussed. Gregory's loss of control is signalled by his dishevelled appearance. His disarray contrasts with his groomed appearance in the rest of the film. As soon as Paula enters the attic, Gregory tries to manipulate her into helping him. The shifting voice styles that Charles Boyer brings to his performance use registers of accusation and sarcasm, as he tries to counter the evidence that Cameron has presented to Paula. This controlled and controlling tone is the register he has used to Paula throughout much of the film. Gregory then tries to appeal to her by talking of the happy 'first days' of their marriage; his voice becomes deeper and more resonant as he essays a tone of intimacy. He begs for 'another chance', and shifts to a quieter, whispering, hissing tone as he directs Paula to get a knife in a nearby drawer to cut him free: 'Be quick Paula ... Will you get it for me?' The range of tones and sonic qualities to Boyer's/Gregory's voice here are very effective; through a delicate but deadly shifting between intimacy, persuasion and veiled threat, Gregory tries to hypnotise Paula into carrying out his wishes.

Paula (Ingrid Bergman) shifts from persecuted wife to 'goddess of vengence' as she confronts her husband Gregory (Charles Boyer) in *Gaslight* (George Cukor, 1944).

Initially, Paula seems to be under his spell as she begins to search anxiously for the knife, as she has for numerous 'lost' objects in the house which Gregory has hidden to simulate her loss of sanity. As Paula turns on Gregory, holding the knife, she 'pantomimes' her forgetfulness, 'Are you suggesting that this is a knife that I hold in my hand? Have you gone mad, my husband? Or is it I that am mad? Yes of course, that's it. *I* am mad!', and takes her vengeance:

> If I were not mad I could have helped you. Whatever you had done I could have pitied and protected you. But because I am mad I hate you, because I am mad I have betrayed you and because I am mad I am rejoicing in my heart without a shred of pity, without a shred of regret watching you go with glory in my heart.

Paula's speech and voice styles become increasingly confident, and harden into anger as she performs and parodies her former role as persecuted wife, giving a performance of 'the madwoman in the attic'.[58] At the end of the scene, Paula effectively dismisses Gregory, commanding Cameron to 'take this man away!'.

The confrontation sequences discussed in this chapter are a key stage in the unfolding of the female gothic films' narration, which is divided into distinct narrative stages: romance, suspicion, investigation/discovery, confrontation or confession, and resolution. These stages, organised as they are around the trajectory of the female gothic heroine's journey, allow the formation of female subjectivity through her shifting narrative positions and actions. As I have argued, the confrontation sequences provide insights into male subjectivity too. These sequences illuminate the gothic male's backstory, and provide the moment that, as Pam Cook notes, the female gothic heroine 'confronts not only her own victimization, but that of the hero as well'.[59] The sequences are part of the female gothic heroine's rite of passage through the narration, and constitute her coming-to-knowledge. This knowledge precipitates distinct outcomes in the resolutions of these films, resolutions that offer some questions about the grip and drive of romance in the Hollywood woman's film, and, relatedly, about shifting ideals of masculinity in the 1940s and the ways they are embodied on screen.

The gothic male character bears with him an interesting heritage of representation in the literary gothic. Fred Botting sees the writings of Romanticism as constructing a manifestation of the gothic hero as a tormented, and tormenting, figure:

> gloomy, isolated, sovereign, they are wanderers, outcasts and rebels condemned to roam the borders of social worlds, bearers of a dark truth or horrible knowledge ... [they] are transgressors who represent the extremes of individual passion and consciousness.[60]

The excessive quality of literary Romanticism's sublime settings 'mirrors the internal world of the heroic sufferer, [and] the magnificence of his suffering'.[61] Although this literary heritage is, of course, highly filtered within Hollywood's 1940s female gothic cycle, its affiliations with the literary gothic allow it to encompass elements of this male sensibility. A plethora of moody, enigmatic, unpredictable and troubled male figures populate the cycle. As well as the figures discussed earlier, they are embodied by Johnny Aysgarth (Cary Grant in *Suspicion*), Uncle Charlie (Joseph Cotten in *Shadow of a Doubt*), Rochester (Orson Welles in *Jane Eyre*), Nick Bederaux (Paul Lukas in *Experiment Perilous*), Ralph Hughes (George Macready in *My Name is Julia Ross*), Charles Rankin (Orson Welles in *The Stranger*), Professor Warren (George Brent in *The Spiral Staircase*), Alan Garroway (Robert Taylor in *Undercurrent*), Mark Lamphere (Michael Redgrave in *Secret Beyond the Door*) and Richard Courtland (Don Ameche in *Sleep My Love*).

Although these male figures were forged according to the generic demands of the female gothic cycle, they were part of a wider shift in male character types in the period that was noted by Hollywood commentator Florett Robinson. Writing in the *New York Times*, Robinson describes 'a novel kind of bad man – the *sympathetic villain*. More sinned against than sinning, this new menace is not cast in shades of black, but in the more human, indeterminate grays of a real-life character ... kindness and cruelty make up the strange personality of the lovable bad man.'[62] Barbara Deming, in her work on male character types and their socio-cultural currency in the 1940s Hollywood film, charts the occurrence of the charming villain.[63] Deming examines the characters of Alan Garroway (*Undercurrent*) and Nicholas Van Ryn (*Dragonwyck*) as particularly illustrative of male figures who suffer because they are in thrall to their emotions and fantasies. In *Dragonwyck*, the Van Ryn family is cursed and, further, Nicholas refuses to acknowledge the anti-rent movement that will give his tenant farmers' more autonomy, preferring to maintain his outdated feudal control. In *Undercurrent*, Alan drives his wife away as he is consumed with envy, convinced she is in love with his brother Michael, even though they have never met. Deming analyses scenes from both films where 'the villain approaches the heroine as a frantic suppliant ... he ... wants her to restore to him a life that has somehow eluded him, a belief in himself that fails.'[64] Similarly, Kaja Silverman observes that a 'crisis of male subjectivity'[65] is played out 'with unusual candour'[66] in several

Hollywood films of the post-war period. The titles Silverman cites include a range of genres, encompassing war, or the returning veteran, films such as *Pride of the Marines* (Delmar Daves, 1945), *Hail the Conquering Hero* (Preston Sturges, 1944) and *The Best Years of Our Lives* (William Wyler, 1946), as well as dramas with troubled men at the centre of the film: *The Lost Weekend* (Billy Wilder, 1945) and *Spellbound*. Silverman attributes this crisis to male experience of war, and to the concomitant shifts in domestic and social life. As I have suggested, the female gothic cycle also plays out these shifts, but in its position as a female-centred and female-addressed cycle, it does so by advancing some interesting negotiations in narrative outcomes and gendered identities. It maps elements of the excessive Romantic hero onto a landscape of shifting and troubled masculine subjectivity in the post-war period, which is contrasted with the female gothic films' female rite of passage.

Resolutions in Disintegration: The Female Gothics' Dissolving Dynasties

The resolutions of the female gothic cycle demonstrate the heroine's escape from the grip of her gothic husband or lover. Confrontation sequences corroborate her suspicions and expose the danger from which she must escape to determine her survival. In several female gothic films the heroine is aided by a secondary male character, such as Dr Bailey (George Brent) in *Experiment Perilous*, Charles Pennington in *The Two Mrs Carrolls*, Jeff Turner in *Dragonwyck*, Brian Cameron in *Gaslight*, Bruce Elcott (Robert Cummings) in *Sleep My Love*, and Larry Quinada (James Mason) in *Caught*.

The presence, and function, of this secondary male character, though, in no way discounts or compromises the agency of the heroine. Andrea Walsh points out that the secondary male actually plays a relatively unimportant role, the real drama of these films being what takes place between husband and wife:

... the male rescuer is relatively peripheral to the emotional intensity of the narrative. ... The roots of female madness lie not within, but without – in the identity of threatening men. "Exorcism" is not the answer. Rather, these women must escape or terminate dangerous relationships.[67]

The drama of the narrative hinges on the relationship of the heroine to the gothic male; in Marina Warner's words, the heroine must 'come to terms with [her] husband – or flee him'.[68] Although he is 'peripheral', the secondary male character offers a contrasting foil to the gothic male. The characters cited above offer a more understanding and nurturing model of masculinity than the excessive and tyrannical gothic males.[69] In some films, such as *Rebecca*, *Suspicion* and *Secret Beyond the Door*, both masculine modes are embodied in a single, divided character. These examples are relatively rare in the cycle, and the narratives show how the heroine 'mends' her husband's rifts. In *Suspicion*, Johnny Aysgarth's (Cary Grant) troubled characterisation is sustained to the final scene of the film. In a rather incoherent reversal, he declares that he 'really does' love the heroine Lina (Joan Fontaine), and that he had not been plotting her murder but his own suicide. As several critics have noted, this reversal was required by the film's studio, RKO, which resisted casting its leading man, Cary Grant, as a wife-murderer.[70] Even within these exceptions, it is the rifts within male subjectivity that are experienced by the heroine, and undeniably and powerfully played out.

Female gothic resolution, then, involves the disintegration of the gothic male and the dissolution of his dynasty. In *Rebecca*, for example, the ancestral house, Manderley, goes up in flames, as does Blaize Creek in *Secret Beyond the Door*. In *Dragonwyck*, Nicholas is shot dead while sitting on the ancient stone throne of the Patroon. In many other examples from the cycle the gothic male's hold on the heroine, dramatised through his control of the gothic house, is countered by his imprisonment, or death, at the end of the film. The dynamics of the gender relationships in these films can be understood as critiquing tyrannical patriarchal values which the gothic male embodies. The Hollywood woman's film, and the female gothic cycle in particular, is therefore not under a patriarchal stranglehold, but foregrounds the problems of the patriarchal system from the heroine's point of view.

The presence of the secondary male figure has a structural function in signalling the possibilities of romance, beyond the gothic nightmare that the heroine endures. As Waldman suggests, the power of patriarchy is 'diffused through the narrative overthrow of the patriarchal tyrant and his replacement by a gentler, more democratic type'.[71] But this character's 'peripheral' status only serves to emphasise the centrality of the main battle. The contrasting models of masculinity – the alluring but threatening gothic male figure, and a secondary male character who is understanding and nurturing – within a female-addressed cycle of films is significant. The shifting between two male character types opens up the terms of romance, and issues of romantic choice, which coincides with a period in which gender relations, and the meanings of marriage, were under scrutiny. The female gothics' fusing of a romance strand with the ambivalence and ambiguity of the gothic mode allow the tensions, fractures and feelings of marital stress to be explored, albeit in coded and filtered ways. In analysing the forms of the 'ideal' romance, Janice Radway argues that one of its most accented moments is the hero's open and transparent declaration of his feelings for the heroine, that he 'loves her for who she really is'.[72] In their fusion of romance with opacity – the gothic male's secrecy and concealment – and the emphasis on horrific, rather than romantic revelation, through sound and music, the female gothic films fuse romance with anxiety. In exploring marriage as the attendant 'black cloud'[73] of romance, and in the films' resolutions with the central couple broken apart, the estrangement of the central couple in the female gothic cycle reworks, and perhaps even unworks, romance, even as its notorious ambiguities leave the door open for new 'rescriptings' through the presence of a more companionate mate. In this cycle of films at least, the stability of the heterosexual couple is no longer assured, linked with the cycle's focus upon a female subjective journey, through strange and ambiguous narrative conflicts which allow the terms of romance to be reconsidered, and its dark underside exposed, from the woman's angle.

Chapter Five

Professional Investigators and Femmes Fatales *in Neo*-Noir

Introduction

This chapter and the next pick up questions of women's relationship to the crime and gothic thrillers in the period from the early 1980s onwards. The two chapters map the generic transformations of *film noir* and the female-addressed gothic thriller in relation to the films' styles, their narrative strands and strategies, and their placement of female characters. In doing so they trace questions of generic categorisation and its relationship to gender, female characterisation, representation and agency, and the modes and shifts in feminist critical interpretation concurrent with the period.

Genres, Contexts and the New Hollywood

The category of *film noir* was never an industrial one, emerging as it did out of film criticism that engaged with the crime film in Hollywood's late studio era. Neo-*noir*, however, which emerged in the 1980s, drew on a dark dream of *noir* as cinephile filmmakers reworked and recycled past styles, narratives and characters within the crime film. Between the decline of the production of *films noirs* in the late 1950s and the re-emergence of neo-*noir* as both a self-defined genre and a highly successful commodity in the 1980s, *film noir* was never wholly absent. The intervening period, in which the study of film established itself in the academy and interacted with popular discussions of film, was marked by intense debates about *noir*'s ontology, reaching, in Noel Carroll's terms, 'the proportions of a popular sport'.[1]

The release of Lawrence Kasdan's *Body Heat*, in 1981, marked the extent to which a filmmaker could rely on audiences being acquainted with the styles, narratives and characters of *films noirs* from the studio era, while appreciating the remobilisation, or repackaging, of these elements for a different historical moment. In neo-*noir* genre became a concept, or a product. As Geoffrey O'Brien suggests:

> *Noir* might more realistically be considered not so much a "universe" or a "sensibility" – and certainly not the "movement" that one writer calls it – as a particular sheen, a slick new variety of packaging, faddish at the time and subsequently much prized by connoisseurs: a nexus of fashions in hair, fashions in lighting, fashions in interior decoration, fashions in motivation.[2]

Noel Carroll sees *Body Heat* as typifying a stylistic move in film-making, which he terms 'allusionism', a 'tendency ... that distinguishes the seventies and eighties from every other decade in Hollywood's past.'[3] He argues that 'allusion, specifically allusion to film history, has become a major expressive device'[4] which encompasses:

> ... a mixed lot of practices including quotations, the memorialization of past genres, the reworking of past genres, *homages*, and the recreation of "classic" scenes, shots, plot motifs, lines of dialogue, themes, gestures, and so forth from film history, especially as that history was crystallized and codified in the sixties and early seventies.[5]

The shifts that Hollywood's industrial landscape had undergone by the early 1980s had a distinct impact upon the ways in which generic markers were understood by movie audiences. As Thomas Schatz argues, the much-touted predictions of the 'death of Hollywood' in the early 1950s proved to be 'greatly exaggerated'.[6] Although there were profound changes in the ways in which Hollywood production and exhibition had been organised during the classical studio era, the period that spans the early 1950s to the late 1970s might be understood as one of transition and adaptation, rather than a single break or decline.

The corporate structures of the studio system underwent reorganisations due to the anti-trust legislation epitomised by the Supreme Court's 1948 *Paramount* decree, under which the vertically integrated studios sold off their exhibition chains.[7] This impacted upon the rosters of studio personnel, as stars, writers, directors and producers no longer had the stability of long-term contracts, and studios leased their production facilities under a shift to 'one-film deals' and more emphasis upon independent productions.[8] In the 1950s, traditional modes of movie-going shifted, and the increasingly suburbanised audiences were provided with competing entertainment in the form of television, with which major Hollywood studios competed in the production of distinctive spectacle films, westerns, historical and biblical epics such as *The Robe* (Henry Koster, 1953) and *The Ten Commandments* (Cecil B DeMille, 1956). By the middle of the 1950s, some of Hollywood's major studios had diversified into television production, as well as recognising the exploitability of their back catalogues as products that could be syndicated for television exhibition.[9] Notable in the studios' shifts to television production was the use of a long-established and tried-and-tested strategy of drawing upon existent audiences for specific genres, such as the crime thriller.

During the 1930s and 1940s, studios frequently tested the potential of horror, crime and gothic narratives through radio productions, as noted in the discussion of female gothic productions such as *Jane Eyre* and *Rebecca* by Orson Welles in Chapter 2. During the 1950s, Entertainment Comics (EC) specialised in horror and crime for an adolescent readership, with series such as *Tales from the Crypt* and *The Vault of Horror*.[10] EC also initiated several series of crime comics for adults, including *Crime Illustrated: Adult Suspense Stories*, which were widely read in the 1950s and which resurfaced in the 1980s in nostalgia reprints.[11] Titles from the EC series influenced the cable TV series *Tales from the Crypt*, and were directed by 'baby boomer' directors such as John Frankenheimer, Walter Hill and Robert Zemeckis.[12]

During the 1940s, CBS radio produced radio crime dramas in their *Suspense* series, frequently adapting pulp crime stories by writers such as Cornell Woolrich and James M Cain.[13] The *Suspense* radio series was a forerunner of Alfred Hitchcock's television work in the 1950s and 1960s. Cornell Woolrich's novel, *The Black Curtain*, was adapted for television by *The Alfred Hitchcock Hour* in 1962, directed by Sydney Pollack, who later went on to direct episodes of the television crime series *The Fugitive*, and for the cinema the legal thriller *The Firm* (1993). Pollack also produced thrillers such as the neo-*noir Presumed Innocent* (Alan J Pakula, 1990) and the neo-*noir*/neo-gothic hybrid *Dead Again* (Kenneth Branagh, 1991). As James Naremore argues, the hard-boiled private-eye figure, the character type most associated with *films noirs* of the studio era, 'remained a staple of entertainment programs on both radio and television from the 1940s to the 1980s'.[14] Dashiell Hammett's Sam Spade adventures were the source for *Charlie Wild, Private Eye* (1950–2).[15] Other *noir*-influenced television series were *Richard Diamond, Private Eye* (1957–60), starring David Janssen, Philip Carey as *Philip Marlowe* (1959–60), Darren McGavin as *Mickey Spillane's Mike Hammer* (1957–60) and *Peter Gunn* (1958–61), starring Craig Stevens. One of the most popular police series on US radio and television from the late 1940s to the 1970s was *Dragnet*, which used 'noirlike photography and performance conventions'.[16] Other television crime productions, such as *Naked City* (1958–63) and the BBC's *Third Man* (1959–64), as well as *The Fugitive* (1963–7), later adapted for the screen by Andrew Davis in 1993, and *Miami Vice* (1984–9), also derived their styles and narratives from classic studio era *films noirs*.[17] All of these examples illustrate the continuity of *film noir* styles and conventions across Hollywood's transitional era. They also show the interactions between film and other entertainment forms, which had always been a way for Hollywood to test and establish audiences for certain formulae, but which became a more main-stream strategy as studios integrated television and later video production as a commercial activity.

Several critics have noted shifts in the composition of audiences in the 1950s and 1960s. Schatz argues that these decades were characterised by 'diversified, segmented movie-going trends', under the distinct influence of an emergent 'youth market'.[18] The 'baby boom' generation, born in the post-war years, came of age and developed 'distinctive interests and tastes',[19] catered for by low-budget 'teenpics' and 'exploitation' films.[20] The spaces and modes of film viewing outside the home underwent changes in the 1950s and 1960s. The boom for drive-in movie theatres, which marked a shift away from the movie palaces of urban centres, was subsequently overtaken by the rise of multiplex shopping centre cinemas, beginning in the mid-1960s, and which provided a fuller access to America's suburban youth market.[21]

The 1960s also marked the end of three decades in which the Production Code Administration (PCA) had regulated film content. Set up in 1930, the PCA vetted film scripts in the pre-production phase, advising studios on scenes or narrative strands that were considered inappropriate, or which were likely to be censored by state boards or other censorship bodies on release. This system allowed studios to avoid costly alterations to their films after shooting was completed. As Linda Ruth Williams and Michael Hammond note, by the late 1950s socio-cultural attitudes towards sex and violence were undergoing transformations. The Kinsey reports of 1948 and 1953 reshaped the public understandings of sexual mores and behaviour that had informed the Production Code since the 1930s.[22] Increasingly, films which 'tested' the code by repre-senting 'adult' themes, such as *A Summer Place* (Delmar Daves, 1959) and *Imitation of Life* (Douglas Sirk, 1959) which explored sexual desire and premarital sex, gained release in the late 1950s.[23] European films such as *À Bout de Souffle* (Jean-Luc Godard, 1960) and *Jules et Jim* (François Truffaut, 1962) which circulated on American screens but which were not bound by the code, as well as American-made films depicting sequences of explosive violence such as *Bonnie and Clyde* (Arthur Penn, 1967), were gradually illustrating the code's obsolence. In 1966, Jack

Valenti was appointed head of the Motion Picture Association of America (MPAA), and in November 1968 he instituted the MPAA Ratings System through which films were designated 'G' for general audiences, 'M' for mature audiences, 'R' for audiences over the age of 17 only, and 'X' for adults only.[24] This is, of course, not to simplistically imply that audiences since the 1960s have become more 'permissive'. The ways in which mainstream film fictions have depicted sex on screen have continued to be the subject of debate. The interventions of a feminist politics analysing media depictions of women have been particularly important since the 1970s, and will be examined later in relation to sex and violence in the neo-*noir* crime film.

The effective de-regulation of content might have opened up the potential of certain genres of film production to more 'adult' content, which was taken up by the films and filmmakers associated with the late 1960s moment of the 'Hollywood Renaissance', such as *Bonnie and Clyde* (Arthur Penn, 1967), *The Conversation* (Francis Ford Coppola, 1974) and *The Graduate* (Mike Nichols, 1967). However, the period of the mid-1970s has been identified as key to the rise of the blockbuster phenomenon and cinema's appeal to a wide audience constituency, which included families as well as 'teen' viewers. Films such as Steven Spielberg's *Jaws* (1975) and George Lucas' *Star Wars* (1977) 'recalibrated the profit potential of the Hollywood hit, and redefined its status as a marketable commodity and cultural phenomenon'.[25] These films used established narrative formulae of action adventure, presented them with an emphasis on new audiovisual technologies, and were marketed by 'front loading' the audience through saturation bookings and a big spend on advertising. This maximised their status as 'event' movies.[26] Further earnings were garnered from commercial tie-in products, such as toys, as well as the licensing of the films as reissues both at film theatres, on video and on both pay-cable and network television.[27] After their success with *Jaws* and *Star Wars*, Spielberg and Lucas collaborated on *Raiders of the Lost Ark* (1981), directed by Spielberg, with Lucas as writer and executive producer. The Indiana Jones franchise was established, worth billions of dollars, and capitalised upon the different audience constituencies of teenagers and family audiences.

Schatz argues that the rise of the super-blockbuster 'event' movie had a distinct and transformative impact upon both theatrical and video markets for Hollywood. From a position in which theatrical revenues were declining in the period up to 1975, 'the rapidly expanding global entertainment market went into overdrive in the 1980s'.[28] During the 1980s, a growth in the theatrical market was outstripped by the ancillary markets of pay-cable and home video. In the decade of the 1980s, US households owning video cassette recorders increased from 2.5 to around 66 percent. The sales of pre-recorded video cassettes increased by a staggering 6,500 percent, and the number of cable households nearly tripled in the period between 1980 and 1990, with subscriptions to pay-cable increasing from 9 million to 42 million in the decade.[29] Schatz argues that these ancillary markets fed rather than competed with the theatrical market: '[t]hrough all the changes during the 1980s, domestic theatrical release remained the launching pad for blockbuster hits, and it established a movie's value in virtually all other secondary or ancillary markets.'[30]

The rise of the blockbuster and its attendant marketing strategies have been seen as modifying film aesthetics and narrative form into a 'high concept' filmmaking system.[31] Critics such as Mark Crispin Miller and Richard Schickel have argued that the blockbuster's style marked a blurring between the movies and advertising, with the artful complexities of narrative and character development being sacrificed to the selling of tie-in products (Miller) or the refining of 'concepts' (Schickel).[32]

What lies behind the perspectives of Miller and Schickel is a perception of the 'New Hollywood' blockbuster as a departure from the clarity of classical Hollywood's narrative system. Its aggressive marketing and address to an adolescent audience also inform a sense that the blockbuster trend makes mainstream film less complex, and less able to be critically addressed through the lens of a criticism which seeks to grasp the socio-cultural politics of the medium. But as Schatz goes on to argue, there are two key issues to be considered in coming to terms with the aesthetic shifts of 'New Hollywood'. The first is that the pre-selling of films through other popular culture products, such as popular music, comic books or TV movies, means that 'younger, media-literate viewers encounter a movie in an already-activated narrative process'.[33] The second is that the activation and consumption of narratives across a range of products and media, which are simultaneously embedded in discourses about the cinema, is a situation that favors texts strategically "open" to multiple readings and multimedia reiteration'.[34] Further, Schatz points out that although the blockbuster dominates New Hollywood production most visibly, the system of New Hollywood comprises three different classes of movie: 'the calculated blockbuster designed for the mainstream market place and franchise status in mind, the mainstream A-class star vehicle with sleeper-hit potential, and the low-cost independent feature targeted for a specific market and with little chance of anything more than "cult film" status.'[35] New Hollywood production broadly operates across these three different strands, which, Schatz suggests, exist in 'dynamic tension with one another and constantly intermingle'.[36]

Hollywood's industrial shifts form a backdrop for my examination of the neo-*noir* and neo-gothic thrillers discussed in this chapter and the next. The films belong, predominantly, to Schatz's category of the mainstream A-class star vehicle. They have high production values and are narratively and stylistically inventive. They rework the crime genre in interesting ways, particularly in their placement of female characters. Although several titles enjoyed significant box office success, their production and address are distinct from the blockbuster category. They were targeted predominantly at adult audiences, and some key neo-*noir* thrillers are addressed to women, specifically titles that centre upon women working in the legal and crime spheres as lawyers and police officers. Their female-address raises interesting issues about women's sociocultural place in the 1980s and 1990s. Some of the titles, however, achieved significant success, and as Linda Ruth Williams shows, the neo-*noir* erotic thriller comprises a group of films characterised by their presence on both mainstream cinema and home video screens through the success of direct-to-video (DTV) formats.[37]

Within the shifting industrial contexts that have shaped New Hollywood, the development of the blockbuster and the spread of movie consumption across different media, genre has remained a reference point. Noel Carroll argues that after the experimentation of the late 1960s and early 1970s (the 'Hollywood Renaissance'), 'genres have once again become Hollywood's bread and butter... the viability of genres is what makes allusionism a practical option'.[38] Neo-*noir* encompasses many strands in its allusion to its 1940s antecedents. The 'memorialisation' of the past occurs in remakes of hard-boiled films, and re-adaptations of hard-boiled films and fictions, such as *Marlowe* (Paul Bogart, 1969), *The Long Goodbye* (Robert Altman, 1973), *Farewell My Lovely* (Dick Richards, 1975), *The Big Sleep* (Michael Winner, 1978) and *The Postman Always Rings Twice* (Bob Rafelson, 1981). It includes 'retro' *noirs* such as *Devil in a Blue Dress* (Carl Franklin, 1995) and Curtis Hanson's adaptation of James Ellroy's *noir* nostalgia novel *LA Confidential* (1997). Todd Erickson suggests that '[i]n 1995 thanks to contemporary cinema's flourishing cycle of self-conscious *noir*, the term is rapidly being absorbed into everyday American life'.[39] He points to Showtime Network's cable television series *Fallen Angels* and Fox Network's *X-Files* as texts that have introduced 'millions of viewers ... to the stylistic decorum of the *noir* milieu'.[40] As I have suggested above, *noir* formulae have always proliferated across different media, and *films noirs* of the 1940s constituted a wide array of films with promiscuous connections and affiliations with mystery, crime and gothic fiction, and with stylistic connections to horror and the gothic film. In earlier chapters, I have also argued *films noirs* of the 1940s have a complex and multiple-gendered address, evident in the figure of the working-girl investigator. What this chapter seeks to do is to examine the 'viability' of the neo-*noir* crime thriller in relation both to gender and key feminist, and post-feminist, discourses on women and film that arise in the same period. Against the different industrial and socio-cultural contexts of the 1980s and 1990s, and within the variety that constitutes neo-*noir*'s different strands, there are two particular modifications that illustrate the generic transformations of *film noir* in relation to gender through a focus upon two different public femininities: the investigative woman of neo-*noir* and the neo-*femme fatale*.

Neo-*noir* thrillers that centre upon investigative female characters working in the criminal and legal systems include films such as *Compromising Positions* (Frank Perry, 1985), *Jagged Edge*

(Richard Marquand, 1985), *The Morning After* (Sidney Lumet, 1986), *Black Widow* (Bob Rafelson, 1987), *Suspect* (Peter Yates, 1987), *Betrayed* (Costa-Gavras, 1988), *Music Box* (Costa-Gavras, 1989), *Blue Steel* (Kathryn Bigelow, 1990), *Impulse* (Sondra Locke, 1990), *Defenseless* (Martin Campbell, 1991), *Class Action* (Michael Apted, 1991), *Love Crimes* (Lizzie Borden, 1992), *Twisted* (Philip Kaufman, 2004) and *Taking Lives* (D J Caruso, 2004). The films centre upon women, work and crime in diverse ways. They include women protagonists in the police procedural/cop film (*Impulse*, *Blue Steel*), the legal thriller (*Jagged Edge*, *Suspect*), and occasionally women drawn into temporary investigative roles from the necessity of their narrative situation (*Compromising Positions*, *The Morning After*). These films show that the neo-*noir* thriller retains a multiple narrative focus, having a distinct currency for female as well as male viewers through telling of women's as well as men's stories.

Body Heat's narrative of fatal desire and its commodification of fatal femininity are also part of neo-*noir*'s reworking of previous film narratives and styles in the 1980s and 1990s. Other films that include and rework a *femme fatale* figure in the more contemporary period include *Fatal Attraction* (Adrian Lyne, 1987), *Black Widow* (Bob Rafelson, 1987), *Someone to Watch Over Me* (Ridley Scott, 1987), *Sea of Love* (Harold Becker, 1989), *Kill Me Again* (John Dahl, 1989), *Presumed Innocent* (Alan Pakula, 1990), *Basic Instinct* (Paul Verhoeven, 1992), *The Last Seduction* (John Dahl, 1994), *Disclosure* (Barry Levinson, 1994), *Jade* (William Friedkin, 1995) and *Femme Fatale* (Brian De Palma, 2002).

Both these forms of the neo-*noir* thriller show distinct modifications of the *film noir* crime film as it existed in the 1940s, and both interestingly intersect with ideas of female agency as advanced by second-wave and post-second-wave feminist debates in the 1980s and 1990s. This intersection illustrates some of the transformations of the crime genre and its socio-cultural charge in relation to gender.

Both forms advance key questions about female liberation and identity in relation to sexuality. The ways in which these strands dramatise and play out these questions are distinct in relation to their female characters. The neo-*noir* crime thriller narratives

142

anxiously fuse sex and crime, and present different narrative journeys for their female characters. Where the neo-*noir* crime thriller
centres upon a female investigator, issues of the sexuality and the
sexual conduct of the investigative woman arise within the sphere
of work and career. Where the female character is herself the criminal enigma, an instance of the neo-*femme fatale*, sex and crime
fuse onto the figure of the feminine. These two strands suggest two
different ways in which *film noir* is reworked in the 1980s and
1990s. Genre debates on *film noir* have always had such a distinct
grasp upon gender politics, and neo-*noir*'s reworking of its 1940s
antecedents enters into those politics and makes them explicit.

Feminism, Post-Feminism and the *Noir*-Thriller

By the early 1980s, the ways that the neo-*noir* thriller and its quite
diverse narrative strategies deployed female characters as centrally
acting heroines, or centrally acting anti-heroines, were interacting
with a complex and quite diffuse set of debates about women's
socio-cultural place, and its representation within mainstream
media and film. This interaction produces several questions about
the meanings of public femininities: the placement of female characters within the narrative forms of the crime film, female agency
and representation. Central to those meanings are debates arising
in second-wave and post-second-wave feminist discourses in the
late 1970s and early 1980s. There are some key moments and key
themes in these debates that need to be charted to show their
impact upon understandings of female figures in film, and how
these representations relate to different film genres and their
gendered address.

Rosalind Coward argues that 'unlike previous political movements, the sort of demands which emerged with the women's
movement were never exclusively political or economic. They also
involved questions about forms of organisation of sexuality.'[41]
Coward shows that whereas the activism of the women's movement
identified specific ways in which female sexuality were presented
and circulated in mainstream culture, notable examples being the
1968 protests against the Miss America contest and the National

Abortion Campaign, the period of the 1970s was also marked by an increasing fluidity and exchange between radical activist feminist discourses on women's place and more popular, commodified images of the 'liberated woman'.[42] In the same period that sexualised representations of women were coming increasingly into focus through feminist debates on the mainstream media and film, media addressed to women, such as women's magazines like *Cosmopolitan* and *Honey*, were offering 'representations of the active self-definition of female sexuality [that became] as widely diffused as the traditional definitions of woman as either housewife of mother'.[43] These female-addressed discourses partly cemented and circulated the image of the 'liberated woman' as one popular version, or popular understanding, of how feminism interacted with the changing socio-cultural position of women, with an emphasis upon notions of female choice and lifestyle through consumerism. As Coward shows, this interaction of discourses is complex. In her analysis of a single issue of *Cosmopolitan* magazine, she illustrates that whereas the magazine's content articles focus on questions of women's careers, sexual and emotional satisfaction and independence, the magazine's advertisements commercialise access to female sexuality through product consumption.[44] She therefore shows the increasing coincidence of discourses about women that are both feminist (career, sexuality, independence) and feminine (alluring self-presentation and self-image achieved through consumption). Coward thus identifies the emergence of 'new definitions of women's sexuality' outside the private sphere of home and family and in the public sphere of work,[45] which arise in the period and configure a new 'liberated' woman associated with feminism.

Similarly, Hilary Radner and Charlotte Brunsdon trace the increasing instances of women's place as represented across both private and public spheres. Radner, as Coward does, focuses upon the emergence of the popular persona of the 'Single Girl', in relation to the commodification of female sexuality for women. She notes that this figure can be traced as partly constructed in the consumerist discourses that arise in the 1920s and 1930s, with the movies as an entertainment form for women and their concomitant marketing strategies. This is analogous with Maria LaPlace's notion of a 'circuit of female discourse'[46] discussed in relation to the female gothic film cycle in Chapter 3. Thus, Radner traces the emergence of this persona, and modifications that occurred to it, as part of 'a significant intertextuality'[47] between film, consumer culture and historical cultural change. I have examined the resonances of this figure within the crime film of the 1940s. Radner suggests that from the 1960s to the 1990s the 'Single Girl' persona is increasingly inflected by intertexts that are quite diverse. She identifies the relaunch of *Cosmopolitan* magazine, under the editorship of Helen Gurley Brown, as a particularly clear instance of how cultural changes in heterosexuality become commodified into the public sphere, and become consumable 'choices' for women:

> In an era in which more than fifty percent of all women work outside the home, the 1980s and 1990s have seen the intensification of this new femininity that identifies itself within a public sphere. This new femininity defines itself and its pleasures (its libidinal economy) on a marketplace in which her capital is constituted by her body and her sexual expertise, which she herself exchanges. She is not exchanged by men, but acts as her own agent – as a "free" agent within a grid of relationships defined by office hierarchy and the "deal". Women's magazines, self-help books, women's novels, not to mention Lifetime television, are all eager to offer women a new paradigm for feminine behavior modelled on the principles originally set forth by Helen Gurley Brown.[48]

Suggesting that 'Gurley Brown rewrote venture capitalism for a specifically feminine subject',[49] Radner sees this shift in sexual mores and identities as transforming the meanings of heterosexual romance and marriage. Where the 'classical marriage plot' required the heroine's possession of chastity as central to her exchange value within the patriarchal system of exogamy, the sexual liberation of the 1960s, and the increasing emphasis on feminine sexual literacy, shifted sexual feminine values and subsequently the meaning of sexual value in the period that followed. Radner's specific focus in her essay is the romantic comedy *Pretty Woman* (Garry Marshall, 1990), but her argument is highly relevant to a more general context of female generic personae in the 1980s and 1990s, a period in which, she argues, 'new categories and structures of femininity and its attendant virtues emerged and new stories ... came to be told in which the heterosexual contract was of necessity figured differently'.[50] Transformations in the meanings of romance and marriage for women have been shown to be a key theme in the female-addressed crime film and female gothic cycles of the 1940s. I have shown that narratives in which the working-girl investigator and the female gothic heroine undertake narrative journeys in films of the 1940s play out key issues about female identities, roles and desires in the shifting socio-cultural contexts of wartime and post-war America. It is evident that the neo-*noir* crime thriller, and the neo-gothic thriller examined in the next chapter, also play out negotiations of private and public female roles. In the neo-*noir* crime thriller, female agency is negotiated in relation to work, whereas the neo-gothic thriller allows exploration of female agency, and often victimisation, in relation to contemporary marriage and domesticity. Female agency is examined in these different spheres, in order to trace how the negotiations of narrative and character show contemporary feminine identities being explored.

Charlotte Brunsdon also takes up questions of the increasing interpenetration of feminist discourses with the popular. She shows that the identities and attributes of several female personae in popular film and television since the 1970s reveal a dialogue with the question of what feminist and feminine identities are, or what they can encompass. She pinpoints three aspects informing these identities: the first is the idea of women's '*right* to fulfilment ... outside the domestic sphere'; the second is female financial independence: 'the idea of the woman worker who earns more than pin-money'; and the third is 'the separation of ideas of female sexuality from the necessary consequences of maternity and domesticity'.[51]

Each of these ideas points to a more autonomous, self-defined idea of feminine destiny, which ... did gain a wider currency in this period. In narrative terms, what was posed was the existence of female characters who were more like a hero than a heroine. Perhaps female characters could go out and have adventures?[52]

As Brunsdon continues to illustrate, the terms and processes through which female self-definition took place in the 1980s and 1990s, that is in the period after the activism and interventions of second-wave feminism into understandings of female roles, identities and desires, were, and continue to be, complex. Arising in the popular media of the 1980s, questions were raised as to the currency or relevance of second-wave feminism for women. The term 'post-feminism' originated in the popular media, and has been the subject of considerable disagreement and debate within feminist oriented cultural and film studies.[53] Given this disagreement and debate, it is difficult to formulate a summary definition of what post-feminism *is*. As Sarah Gamble notes:

> 'Postfeminism' is a term that is very much in vogue these days. In the context of popular culture it's the Spice Girls, Madonna and the *Girlie Show*: women dressing like bimbos, yet claiming male privileges and attitudes. Meanwhile, those who wish to maintain an allegiance to more traditional forms of feminism circle around the neologism warily, unable to decide whether it represents a con trick engineered by the media or a valid movement.[54]

As the term arose in the popular media of the 1980s, it was frequently used in articles seeking to review, summarise and historicise second-wave feminism. In October 1982, *The New York Times Magazine* cover featured an article entitled 'Voices from the Post-Feminist Generation', written by Susan Bolotin, which attempted to distinguish between an anachronistic form of feminism and a new generation of young women who were moving away from its 'outdated' beliefs and demands.[55] Similarly, in December 1989, the cover of *Time* magazine declared 'in the 80s they tried to have it all. Now they've just plain had it. Is there a future for feminism?'[56]

A similar strategy is evident in the British media context. Hilary Hinds and Jackie Stacey note that:

> The figure of the feminist has been widely represented in the
> British media for so long as to have become one of the most
> familiar symbols in the contemporary political landscape
> and cultural imagination. Whilst the mainstream press contin-
> ues to circulate the stock-in-trade clichés of bra-burners and
> ruthless career-driven superwomen, these stereotypes
> increasingly operate in tension with a broader media dis-
> course about a potential compatibility between the previously
> polarised categories of feminism and femininity.[57]

The concretising of clichéd images of the second-wave feminist
(bra-burning activist extremists, hard-nosed career women) within
the popular mediascape functioned as an attempt to delineate or
periodise different moments in feminism, suggesting either that
feminism was 'over', or that it had not fulfilled what media commentators constructed as its putatively unified 'project' for a new
generation of women. We can see several key issues here.

Academic discussions of the status of second-wave feminism
have been in dialogue both with popular media discourses and
shifts in the theoretical terrain of the humanities since the early
1980s. The impact of poststructuralist theories of the subject, and
the agendas of postcolonial theory, produced an increasing
emphasis upon notions of difference in feminist cultural theory.[58]
As Deborah Siegel suggests, 'feminist discourses within and outside the academy have taken a self-reflexive turn',[59] leading to an
increasing engagement with what 'being a feminist' *is* in feminist
cultural criticism, and a pronounced distance from the notion of
'woman' as a unified or 'global' category. This is related not so
much to a fracturing of a previously unified feminist consensus,
but, perhaps, an increasing distance from the category of 'woman'
as singular, and a consequent emphasis upon the differences and
contradictions in female experience. In popular articulations of
post-feminism these contradictions have often been expressed as
the difference between generations of feminism in relation to the
ways in which female agency and desires engage with 'feminine'
desires and choices for heterosexuality and family.

This difference is identified by Charlotte Brunsdon in her examination of two film texts that both engage with and simultaneously

'disavow' feminism.[60] Brunsdon's specific focus is on *Working Girl* (Mike Nichols, 1988) and *Pretty Woman*, films that she suggests are both formed by feminism and which, in the narrative presentations of their heroine figures, simultaneously mark their difference and distance from feminism. In concert with the commentators and perspectives that I have cited above, Brunsdon locates post-feminist shifts in configurations of female identity to new modes of consumerism developing in the 1980s: 'something happens in the 1980s in the conjunction (in the West) of the new social movements, with their stress on the claiming and reclaiming of identities, and the expansion of leisure shopping and consumption.'[61] Brunsdon illustrates a clear shift in feminist debates around the status of consumption and its resonance for female identity:

> 1970s feminism, which in both Britain and the USA arose partly out of the New Left and Civil Rights and anti-war movement, and generally involved women with access to higher education... was anti-consumption, often in a quite puritanical manner, across the range of goods (houses, clothes, make-up and high art such as operas). Ideas of identity, which often draw on 'anti-repression' theories, were marked by notions of sincerity, expression, truth-telling. 1990s feminism, in contrast, partly through the 1980s feminist defence of 'women's genres' such as fashion, soap opera and women's magazines, is permissive and even enthusiastic about consumption. Wearing lipstick is no longer wicked, and notions of identity have moved away from a rational/moral axis and are much more profoundly informed by ideas of performance, style and desire.[62]

One of the most visible instances of post-feminist female performativity in the 1980s was Madonna. Her fashioning of her own images, and her engagement with a wide repertoire of different female archetypes, drawn from sources as various as the iconography of classical Hollywood stars, religious iconography and punk subcultural styles, made her a figure of fascination for both the popular media and academic feminism.[63] Madonna-as-commodity-persona was exemplary of a wider post-feminist shift in the relation of women to femininity and its images. Feminist media literacy, combined with a transformation in the status and meaning of consumption, conferred a new 'agency' on the feminine:

> The key point in this popular story is that the post-feminist woman has a different relation to femininity than either the pre-feminist or the feminist woman ... Precisely because this postmodern girl is a figure partly constructed through a relation to consumption, the positionality is more available. She is in this sense much more like the postmodern feminist, for she is neither trapped in femininity (pre-feminist), nor rejecting of it (feminist). She can use it.[64]

The availability of this 'positionality' and the frequency with which post-feminist media representations of women, including mainstream film texts and genres, engage with multiple female roles and female performativity show that the period of the 1980s heralds a moment at which female representation begins to be understood as allied to female agency. If a new generation of young women 'can use' femininity, this agency, and its alliance with consumerism, is understood partly as a range of 'choices' about identity. In turn, these choices are no longer understood as solely generated by a stable ideology of 'patriarchy' as a central generation point of meanings about female identities, desires and roles. They are also generated, as I have noted, by media discourses on shifting female identities, desires and roles very often written by high-profile feminist-identified commentators.[65]

However, the period of the 1980s in which female identity appears to become more fluid, or positionality more 'available', and female sexuality and female sexual literacy part of post-feminist identity 'choices', coincides with vociferous debates about the moral content of American film. As Stephen Prince notes, in the Reagan era debates about portrayals of sex, violence and religion became part of 'a symbolic politics, that is, the waging of political conflicts on cultural terrain'.[66]

> The dominant symbolic motifs of the Reagan period portrayed a society under threat. America and the family were besieged

by resurgent forces of chaos and disorder: communism, gay and women's rights, school busing, abortion. Twentieth-century America had gone astray, had been misled by the hitherto-prevailing liberal culture with its permissive and overly tolerant attitudes … All were threats to the nostalgic vision the [Reagan] administration offered of an America of small government, small business, and local communities organized around family and church. The Reagan "revolution" thus was an attempt to turn back the clock to a more pristine America, to a time when traditional authority was not challenged by oppositional, racial, sexual, political or economic interests.[67]

In this 'highly symbolic era' then, representations of the 'liberated woman', cultural ambivalences to feminism, and post-feminist negotiations about the meanings of femininity and notions of identity-as-performance, take on a particular purchase.

As Yvonne Tasker and Diane Negra suggest: 'existing scholarship on postfeminist media culture tilts heavily toward analysis of romantic comedies and female-centered sitcoms and dramas that have been so strongly associated with female audiences since the 1990s.'[68] Negotiations about the meanings of femininity are configured rather differently in relation to generic varieties of female characterisation and representation. Work on female-addressed sitcoms, such as *Ally McBeal* and *Sex and the City*, reveal ambivalences in these texts. Their protagonists are interestingly positioned as having agency in terms of their career advancements and financial freedoms, but are not so clearly confident in their desires for romance, stable heterosexual union and a family; desires that the broad political project of second-wave feminism sought to reveal as containing or inhibiting female advancement and independence.[69] Yvonne Tasker and Diane Negra pinpoint this ambivalence and the way that it creates a complexity in interpreting post-feminist texts when they note that these texts often function according to a 'double address'[70]. They write:

The achievement of certain important legal rights and enhanced visibility for women (in areas including law, politics, and education) are positioned alongside a persistently articulated dissatisfaction with the rhetoric of second-wave feminism. Thus the continuing contradiction between women's personal and professional lives is more likely to be foregrounded in postfeminist discourse than the failure to eliminate either the pay gap or the burden of care between men and women.[71]

The contradictions between personal and professional are particularly accented in the neo-*noir* crime film and the neo-gothic film. Questions of agency and choice in the neo-*noir* thriller are played out in the figure of the female investigator and legal agent in ways that show that the crime genre, while it bears the traces of postfeminist negotiations, and commodifications of female identity, still advances unresolved questions about women's personal and professional positions. Women's professional and sexual liberation in the crime film frequently clashes with female victimisation, showing that second-wave questions of women's agency are still alive in a 'post' feminist moment, with a particular purchase on the gender reversals of the crime film. Neo-*noir* thrillers in which the neo-*femme fatale* takes centre stage as narrative antagonist, sexual performer and sexual threat reveal cultural ambivalences towards female sexual choice through 'backlash' discourses that arise around the sexually liberated woman. And in the neo-gothic film, examined in Chapter 6, the placement of central female figures within a threatened domestic space also reveals some deep ambivalences about feminist progress, and about post-feminist choices, as I will go on to demonstrate. As Linda Mizejewski argues: '... the messiness of the crime film – its gendered violence, haunted masculinities, and obsession with the body – resists declaring feminism a closed case'.[72]

Women Investigators and the Legal System in Neo-*Noir*

Whereas investigative roles for female characters have an extended history (encompassing both hard and soft-boiled crime, as well as gothic fictions and film), the professionalisation of the female investigator on page and screen gained a distinct momentum in the 1980s and 1990s. A steady growth in commercially successful female crime writers, such as Marcia Muller, Sara Paretsky, Sue Grafton and Patricia Cornwell, brought the professional female investigator a new visibility, as well as a commercial and narrative plausibility. Priscilla Walton and Manina Jones cite *Publishers Weekly* magazine from April 1990: 'the woman as tough professional investigator has been the single most striking development in the detective novel in the last decade.'[73] And in May 1990, *Newsweek* pronounced: 'Call her Samantha Spade or Phillippa Marlowe and she would deck you. A tough new breed of detective is reforming the American mystery novel: smart, self-sufficient, principled, stubborn, funny and female', naming the work of Sara Paretsky and Sue Grafton in particular.[74] In tandem with these new, tough female figures, the long-running success of the female-centred television crime series *Cagney and Lacey* evidenced a 'movement of women in crime fictions from a typical position as *object* of investigation to that of investigator, acquiring the symbolic authority invested in that position'.[75]

As several feminist cultural critics have noted, *Cagney and Lacey*'s production, and its address to a female audience, illustrate some key issues about the cultural representation, and negotiation, of female roles.[76] Addressing the series' mobilisation of the (male) crime genre through and for women, Christine Gledhill argues that:

> Contradictory pressures towards programming that is both recognizably familiar (that conforms to tradition, to formal or generic convention) and also innovative and realistic (offering a twist on, or modernizing, traditional genres) leads to complex technical, formal and ideological negotiations in mainstream media texts ... Conflicting codes of recognition are demanded by the different generic motifs and stereotypes drawn into the series: the cop show, the buddy relationship, the woman's film, the independent heroine ... When female protagonists have to operate in a fictional world organized by male authority and criminality, gender conflict is inevitable.[77]

Negotiation is a particularly productive notion through which to view the complex and diverse meanings that cluster around women in the neo-*noir* crime thriller. For Christine Gledhill, 'negotiation' is central to the ways in which mainstream texts can be meaningful to female viewers, and one capable of 'bridging the gap between the textual and social subject'[78], that is between theorised female spectators positioned by the dominant ideology of the text, and female viewers consuming media texts in ways informed by their social, and subjective, experience:

> As a model of meaning production, negotiation conceives cultural exchange as the intersection of processes of production and reception, in which overlapping but non-matching determinations operate. Meaning is neither imposed, nor passively imbibed, but arises out of a struggle or negotiation between competing frames of reference, motivation and experience.[79]

Contextually positioned as they are within a network of discourses about the meanings of genres, and a nexus of debates about the status of women's roles articulated by feminism, female roles and agency in the crime film are subject to explicit negotiations with cultural resonances. Female agency has a double meaning in the neo-*noir* crime film. Female cops, lawyers and government agents are characters placed within and empowered by their position as representatives of the moral authority of the criminal and judicial systems. They are women who must embody and play out the rules of those systems, and must do so within their codes, procedures and frameworks. Related to this, their position and agency within the crime narrative is frequently marked as exceptional, by their presence in a male space and as central female characters in a male generic system. And it is this negotiation that is frequently dramatised and played out around the female legal agent.

With the exception of William Covey's discussion, there has been a tendency to categorise the female legal agent outside the boundaries of neo-*noir*. Work on gender and neo-*noir* has more frequently focused upon new versions of the *femme fatale* as reworking the 'gender crisis' frequently ascribed to the classic *noir* of the studio era. Interestingly, Covey suggests that neo-*noir* can be 'female-centred',[80] arguing that '[w]omen-centred neo-*noir* films of the 1980s and 1990s showcase tough women cops and detectives operating with action, clarity and decisiveness in a male-centered world'.[81] To his roster of female cops and detectives, I would add the figure of the female lawyer. All of these female figures raise questions of women's professional and personal place in relation to crime, and the criminal and legal systems. The woman-centred neo-*noir* thriller encompasses both the police procedural film and the legal thriller. The films revolve around narrative enigmas that draw their female protagonists into investigative processes in two ways. In playing out the processes and procedures of female investigation, they frequently place the female legal professional across two spheres of action. The first is the intellectual process of the legal system which takes place in offices, law libraries and courtrooms. The second is the more visceral, physical investigative process of the spaces of crime, which include the forensics' morgue, the spaces of suspect's houses and, often, darkened urban locales. Narrative resolution in the woman-centred neo-*noir* thriller is dependent upon female action across these two, often opposing, spheres. Clarity in the legal process is dependent upon the female protagonist who has a professional stake, and permitted position as a woman in the system, both deploying her intellect and facing physical threat in the opposing dark and ambiguous space of crime. But a recurrent and concomitant threat to the female legal professional, given the still exceptional place of women in the criminal and legal spheres, is her position as a professional with all that connotes. The stakes for female protagonists, then, cross personal and professional spheres. Professional women in the neo-*noir* crime thriller must think actively, and act intellectually to survive both personally and professionally.

Key to the narrative trajectories of the neo-*noir* thrillers is the shifting positioning of female characters. Yvonne Tasker writes that:

> Female protagonists and characters can be understood as located across three sites or realms within crime genres: the active, knowledgeable (or at least inquiring) space of the

investigator, that of the criminal/object of investigation, and that of the victim of crime. While it is the first that might be held to have arrived only recently, it is nonetheless the case that female characters and protagonists frequently exist across or move between these three textual realms or positions.[82]

In moving across these realms, female professionals in the neo-*noir* crime thriller frequently confront victimisation, that of another female character, and frequently their own as well. In her analysis of gender and film production in the New Hollywood era of the 1980s and 1990s, Christina Lane notes the emergence of thrillers that 'centralize female protagonists as investigative heroines trying to overcome their own powerlessness through their conviction to stop some kind of male villain from preying on women'.[83] Examining titles such as *Love Crimes*, *Blue Steel*, *Silence of the Lambs*, *Sleeping with the Enemy* and *Copycat*, calling these films 'the woman's psychothriller/"rising heroine" films',[84] Lane notes them as 'one of the few genres that focus on women's subjectivities, especially women's experience as sexual objects'.[85] Lane's notion of the 'rising heroine' is particularly apt to the narrative trajectories of the neo-*noir* crime thriller, the narrative negotiations of the female professional, and the personal and professional stakes that this involves.

Investigation, Identification, Victimisation: Femininity and Professionalism in the Neo-*Noir* Crime Thriller

In *Jagged Edge*, brilliant female lawyer Teddy Barnes (Glenn Close) reluctantly takes on the high-profile defence case of Jack Forrester (Jeff Bridges), accused of brutally murdering his wealthy wife, Page (Maria Mayenzet), in order to acquire her money. In offering a scenario in which a female lawyer wins a seemingly impossible case, but makes fallible personal choices in falling for the client who is ultimately proved to be guilty, the film narrative is double edged. The film's ambivalence about the relationship between personal and professional spheres for legal women makes it a difficult, but interesting, text. It does not straightforwardly present a narrative of feminist 'progression', but Teddy's intersecting personal and professional dilemmas, and the portrayal of her place within the male legal system, illustrate the film's currency within both feminist and post-feminist debates. It was scripted by the blockbusting thriller writer Joe Eszterhas, who also wrote screenplays for *Betrayed*, *Music Box* (Costa-Gavras, 1989), *Basic Instinct*, *Nowhere to Run* (Robert Harmon, 1993), *Sliver* (Philip Noyce, 1993) and *Jade* (William Friedkin, 1995), and who is, as Linda Ruth Williams notes, a figure strongly associated with neo-*noir*.[86]

Jagged Edge opens by showing the murder sequence. It is a stylised sequence that explicitly presents the sex-crime around which Jack Forrester's trial revolves. Set in the Forrester's luxurious, but remote, beach house which is bathed in deep blue light, the sequence deploys visual and aural codes of presentation from the *noir*-horror traditions. Mobile steadycam shots, motivated by the unseen killer's point-of-view, trace his movement up the stairs, with strong 'threat' motifs being signalled in John Barry's accompanying score. His hand reaches into the frame on his entry into Page's bedroom, where the vicious sex-crime is enacted.

The direct and visceral presentation of the murder constructs high stakes for Teddy, both professionally and personally. The eventual revelation of Jack's guilt means he is not the sensitive grieving husband that he appears to be, but an emotionally manipulative monster. *Jagged Edge*'s presentation of its alluring but sadistic male 'hero' intersects with the neo-gothic films examined in the next chapter, particularly in the film's final sequence where Jack threatens to repeat the sex-crime, with Teddy as victim in her own home. This theme, of a woman making a spectacularly 'wrong' romantic choice, bears importantly on perceptions of Teddy's character. However, it is Teddy's place within the legal and investigative criminal process that is intertwined with it that demands discussion alongside other female professionals, and it is that issue I want to explore in placing the film as a neo-*noir* crime thriller. An anxious tension between personal and professional choices for legal and criminal career women also characterise other neo-*noir* thrillers. Scenarios either figure the career woman as 'too' focused on their career to have a personal life – they are 'unfeminine/not really womanly' – or, paradoxically, their presence as women in the sphere of crime sexualises their role – they are 'too feminine/only womanly', making them vulnerable to sexual, and emotional, danger.

In *Suspect*, hard-working public defender Kathleen Riley (Cher) laments that her work pressures deny her the opportunity to date. As she changes from her formal court attire to baggy sweat pants, preparing for yet another long work session preparing her case, she wryly notes to her colleague Morty (Fred Melamed) that she spends most of her time with 'murderers and rapists, and what's really crazy is that I like them'. Morty returns that they are both alike – they stay in public legal work 'for the sake of the one poor bastard who didn't do it'.

In *Black Widow*, Alex Barnes (Debra Winger) turns down an invitation to dinner with her co-worker Michael (D W Moffat) because 'I have work', and later in the film her boss observes that 'in six years you never once came in late on a Monday morning because you had a big weekend. You're not a happy person.' Alex's increasing fixation with tracking the perpetrator of a series of 'black widow' murders, committed by Catherine Petersen (Theresa Russell), gradually dominates her life, to the extent that she resigns her job to go undercover and pursue Catherine to Hawaii. In *Impulse*, undercover vice-cop Lottie (Theresa Russell) is required to undertake therapy sessions, because she shot a 'perp' while on the job. But the sessions involve an exploration of Lottie's sexual history, and her ongoing reluctance towards romantic commitment.[87] *Impulse*'s narrative also plays out one of the commonest ways in which gender reversals of the neo-*noir* thriller deal unequally with male and female protagonists. Where it is common for the tough male police officer, or private eye, to have a string of romantic adventures, sexual or emotional connections for the female legal agent complicate, or compromise, her professional status and make her personally vulnerable. In *Impulse*, Lottie has learned to deal pragmatically with routine sexual harassment from her boss, Joe Morgan (George Dzundza), while also trying to work out an emotional connection with district attorney Stanley (Jeff Fahey). In *Blue Steel*, newly qualified cop Megan Turner (Jamie Lee Curtis) has to deal with the killer Eugene (Ron Silver), who fetishises her status as a gun-toting female cop, and who threatens her sexually and threatens her lover Nick (Clancy Brown). In *Love Crimes*, tough, androgynous district attorney Dana Greenaway (Sean Young) becomes entangled with a man posing as David Hanover, a famous photographer, in order to prey upon, and sexually manipulate, women that he picks up. Seeking to understand why the women that Hanover has seduced are reluctant to press charges, Dana goes undercover, becoming nearly lethally involved with her quarry.

In *Copycat*, criminal psychologist Dr Helen Hudson (Sigourney Weaver), already scarred by a vicious attack on her by grisly 'fan' Darryl Cullum (Harry Connick Jr), endures the attention of copycat serial killer Peter Foley (William McNamara), who is fixated on her. In *Shadow of Doubt*, top-flight defence lawyer Kitt Devereux (Melanie Griffith) takes on a high-profile murder case, defending an up-and-coming rap star Bobby Medina (Wade Dominguez), accused of a brutal sex murder of a young girl from a prominent, and politically connected, White Anglo-Saxon Protestant (WASP) family. As well as dealing with her ex-husband Jack Campioni (Tom Berenger) as her opposing prosecutor, Kitt has to contend with being stalked by a former client, Laird Atkins (Craig Sheffer). She had previously successfully defended Laird against a rape charge, only to discover, when they become sexually involved, that he was guilty all along. *Copycat* and *Shadow of Doubt* are interesting in that the female protagonists are older women, and already highly successful in their criminal fields. Their outstanding performance in their careers has brought them financial gain, but both films imply their success as implicitly costing them personally. They both live alone in expensive homes, fitted with high-tech surveillance systems with which they attempt to keep their stalkers at bay. In *Twisted*, tough, hard-drinking female detective Jessica Shepherd (Ashley Judd) moves up the career ladder after solving a high-pro-file serial killer case. When a string of her former lovers are mur-dered, Jessica herself becomes part of the case that she is investigating: a move that is recurrent in the neo-*noir* crime thriller with a central female investigator. Personal choices, alliances and issues of emotional (and sexual) trust are often reflexive in relation to the female legal agent, forcing a (self) examination of the stakes of her professional position and abilities.

This is also evident in *Taking Lives*, where the brilliant, and workaholic, FBI criminal profiler Illeana (Angelina Jolie) is called in by the French Canadian police to help catch a serial killer who takes on the identities of his victims. Illeana succeeds in mapping the crucial links across a long string of murders, but becomes personally (and so, read professionally) vulnerable when she allows herself to get close to the key witness in the case, Costa (Ethan Hawke). Illeana is herself acutely aware of the dangers of mixing her personal and professional lives, and when she feels herself drawn to Costa she plans to withdraw from the case, telling the lead investigator Leclair (Tchéky Karo) that she has had a 'reaction' to the witness. Leclair is a mentor figure for Illeana, having been one of the people who trained her in profiling for the FBI. Leclair has observed Illeana's rigorous personal discipline. At training school she never once accepted an invitation for a date with one of her colleagues, and he encourages her to be open to Costa, in effect ratifying for her the briefly blissful encounter that ensues. However, as in the other neo-*noir* crime thrillers cited, opening up to emotional and sexual closeness is (potentially) deadly for the female professional. Costa, it turns out, has been cunningly playing Illeana, and the rest of the investigative team. He is not the vulnerable witness, but a psychopath who, in Illeana's profile summation, 'can't stand to be himself'.

The processes and procedures of female investigation in the neo-*noir* thriller interestingly illustrate some key tensions that arise out of the gender reversals of the genre, and the extension of the female legal professional's investigation across both intellectual interpretation and physical action. In the neo-*noir* thrillers with female lawyer protagonists, such as *Jagged Edge*, *Suspect* and *Shadow of Doubt*, the professional standing of the female lawyers permits them to hire (male) investigative help on their cases, while they act, in the initial parts of the investigations, as interpreters and processors of the leads or evidence brought back from the field. In *Shadow of Doubt*, Kitt's status is signalled by her ability to employ a skilled support team: Al Gordon (Huey Lewis), a private investigator with skills in surveillance technologies; and a private assistant, Cheryl (Danielle Nicolet). In *Suspect*, Kathleen hires a private investigator (Lloyd White) to help her build her defence case to exonerate Carl Anderson (Liam Neeson), the homeless deaf-mute Vietnam veteran charged with the murder of legal secretary Elizabeth Quinn. In *Jagged Edge*, Teddy hires private investigator Sam Ransom (Robert Loggia) to help on the Forrester case. Sam is someone Teddy knows and trusts from her early career prosecuting cases in the district attorney's office. The different ways in which Sam and Teddy approach the Forrester case illustrate tensions between differently gendered modes of investigation. Teddy's remit is to marshall evidence and use her knowledge and command of the legal process to prove Jack's innocence. She consults with other experts, a specialist on polygraph tests and a criminal psychologist, to 'test' Jack. These experts do not offer Teddy any significant reasons to doubt her client's innocence, and Teddy's approach is thus both rational and highly professional. It is Sam who sounds caution about Jack's character. Cynical in his world view, hard-boiled in his filthy speech styles, dressed in mac and trilby hat, old-fashioned in his investigative process, 'unprofessional' in his drinking habits, Sam is a generic throwback to the classic detective film. The generic connotations of Sam's character allow the film to quote from the hard-boiled crime tradition, while marking its own distinctive and updated treatment of the legal thriller. Sam is key to focusing the narrative ambivalence that centres upon Jack's character, and he functions to contrast an old, established and 'male' mode of investigation with Teddy's mobilisation of criminological experts. Sam is working from 'the gut'. Despite Jack's exemplary performance on the polygraph and psychological tests, Sam 'has a hunch' that Jack is guilty. Crime aficionados will immediately recognise the rhetorical power of the 'hunch'. It is what drives the hard-boiled investigator to pursue certain leads of investigation, even when those leads are seemingly hopeless. The hunch also connotes male intuition and it is often privileged as part of a male investigator's hunting instinct, and it has a relation to male knowledge of male motivations and the criminal capacity of male behaviour. It is distinct from a more disengaged, intellectual approach to crime solving, or, in Teddy's case, her command of the legal process and argument to mount a brilliant exploitation of the prosecution's weak case. Sam, therefore, has the privilege of a generic authority. He 'just knows' that something does not sit right with Jack, but he is not bound by the necessity of corroborating his hunch, whereas Teddy's professional status and personal safety founder upon her trust of the technologies of investigation, and her own (personal, emotional) 'hunch' that Jack is innocent. In mapping different processes and approaches to investigation for male and female characters, the ambivalence of the film mobilises tensions between personal and professional for its central female protagonist.

In *Suspect*, Kathleen's private investigator is brutally attacked when he goes out to try to corroborate Carl's alibi for where he was on the night of Elizabeth Quinn's murder. Kathleen's case seems increasingly weak, until she herself reluctantly (and 'unprofessionally') collaborates with Eddie Sangar (Dennis Quaid), one of the jurors on her case. Both she and Eddie are threatened as they attempt to gain clarity among Washington's disenfranchised homeless underclass. This underclass figures the dark underside to the powerful and privileged political milieu in which Eddie (a political lobbyist) makes his living. It is by transgressing the rules of the system, through her collaboration with Eddie, and by tracing Elizabeth Quinn's discovery of judicial impropriety, that Kathleen reveals the corruption that leads right back into her own courtroom and its presiding judge Matthew Bishop Helms (John Mahoney).

In *Shadow of Doubt*, Kitt, with the support of Al, traces a network of criminal alliances that have covered up young Jana Calloway's (Sandra Guibord) brutal murder. Jana's party-girl lifestyle and her connections to the celebrity music scene easily implicate the film's prime suspect, Bobby Medina, as guilty. But it is by confronting her nemesis, Laird, and trapping him into a confession, that Kitt uncovers Jana's troubled relationship to the politically ambitious WASP family of the Saxons. Kitt's opponent on the Medina case is her ex-husband Jack, the district attorney who, it emerges, has sacrificed his ethics for his ambition to hitch his wagon to Paul Saxon's (James Morrison) campaign to run for senator. As in *Jagged Edge* and *Suspect*, the female protagonist uncovers corruption that leads right back to the heart of her own case.

A feature of these films' investigative narrative structures is that the key to the criminal enigma is found by the female protagonist herself. In other words, plotting affords the female legal agent investigative and interpretive agency at the revelatory moment of narrative exposition. During the Forrester case in *Jagged Edge*, Sam and Teddy receive messages from a mystery source, which help them defend Jack. The messages are distinctive in that they are typed on an old machine which prints a raised letter 't'. It is Teddy's discovery of a 1942 Remington typewriter in a linen cupboard at Jack's house that definitively reveals his guilt even as she wishfully types 'he is innocen^t'. In *Suspect*, Kathleen's investigative foray to the parking lot where Elizabeth's car is still parked yields a taped confession from Justice Lowell (Thomas Barbour), for whom Elizabeth worked, revealing that he took bribes in a series of cases. Kathleen's research into these cases links them with her own case. In *Shadow of Doubt*, Kitt's search of Jana's apartment yields a distinctive piece of jewellery belonging to her ex-husband Jack, which places him at the murder scene.

It is in bringing these key revelations into the light and expediting the completion of the legal process that the female protagonist confronts her antagonist, and consequently her own victimisation. In *Jagged Edge*, Teddy's realisation that Jack is guilty is succeeded by a sequence that precisely reprises the visual and aural structures of the opening murder sequence. Masked and gloved, Jack breaks into Teddy's house: a roving mobile shot shows him moving upstairs to Teddy's bedroom, holding a jagged hunting knife identical to the one he used to slaughter his wife Page. But though Teddy is positioned as the victim of his intention, she is armed with knowledge and a gun, and when Jack refuses to remove his mask, she shoots him dead. The structural repetition of the murder sequence, and Teddy's identification with the victimisation of another woman, suggests the film's reference to a female gothic structure. Just as scenarios of confrontation in these films gain their charge from the last-minute victories of their endangered heroines, whose suspicions about their husbands/lovers are corroborated by intended male violence, so Teddy's victimisation is concurrent with her position as the moral centre of the film.[88]

In *Suspect*, Kathleen is pursued through the cavernous spaces of the courtroom building's holding cells by an unseen antagonist. She is disturbed by her assailant as she makes a night-time visit to the courtroom to prepare for the next day in the trial. She arms herself with a knife, the murder weapon that was used to kill Elizabeth Quinn, the legal worker and victim, with whom Kathleen is now clearly identified. The sequence of pursuit is highly stylised. Low-key lighting and a restrained colour palette of blues and greys marks the neo-*noir* threat to Kathleen as she struggles to locate her pursuer. The shots alternate between tight framings of Kathleen, revealing her fear as she navigates the space, and a more distanced version of the events through the monitors of the building's closed circuit surveillance system. These monitors present a highly conscious view of the threat to the investigative female protagonist, offering a mise-en-abîme of the ambivalent position of the female legal agent and the demands and dangers of her place in the legal system. Kathleen comes into direct physical confrontation with her antagonist as he grabs and holds her in a stranglehold from behind. She escapes by slashing his arm with the knife. The visceral confrontation is brought into the courtroom the next day when Kathleen brings the legal system to bear upon Judge Helms. Citing the cases in which Helms presided corruptly, Kathleen turns the power of the system against its manipulator, calling Helms to the stand as a suspect in Elizabeth Quinn's murder. The combination of her investigative and intellectual action links the different spheres of the criminal process, unmasking the real murderer and resolving the enigma of the case. Similarly, in *Shadow of a Doubt*, Kitt publicly exposes Jack, and the corruption of the politically ambitious Saxon family, by arriving at a fundraising rally with a phalanx of police officers.

Other neo-*noir* thrillers also show female protagonists confronting their victimisation by male characters. In *Love Crimes*, Dana's ambivalent relationship to photographer Hanover necessitates her dealing with her past, and her father's serial victimisation of women with whom he had affairs. *Blue Steel* concludes with Megan gaining vengeance for Eugene's treatment of her in an extended and bloody shoot-out. The denouement of *Taking Lives* interestingly plays with the notion of woman-as-victim. After the Costa-case, in which criminal profiler Illeana became involved with the killer, unravels and Costa eludes the police, Illeana appears to be exiled from her professional realm and professional identity. She is shown as heavily pregnant, living in a remote, snowbound farmhouse, and living a solitary existence. The new setting appears to domesticate Illeana in a realm and persona contrasted with her previously androgynous and career-focused incarnation. The strong narrative drive of the investigation also seems to have been suspended by this dislocation. But when Costa turns up, personal and professional collide in a bloody and direct physical confrontation. When Illeana resists Costa's ramblings about their future together, he becomes violent, stabbing Illeana's pregnant belly. But at the moment that Illeana seems most helpless, most vulnerable and most 'feminine', she reveals the belly as a prosthetic disguise and dispatches him.

The neo-*noir* crime thrillers examined often present a play of female 'strength' and victimisation, and require negotiations of ambivalent personal and professional identities for their female profession within the legal and crime systems. It is clear, then, that the presence of the female criminal/legal professional within the workplace of the 1980s-present bears a weighty burden of representation. These are female characters that are exceptional, in the sense of being (still) unusual in a male world and male space, and exceptional in the qualities, attributes and skills that permit them to be there. In both these senses, the terms of being an exceptional heroine in these films are still resonant for a feminist critique. As Linda Mizejewski argues: '[while] the heroine single-handedly kills off the villain in the final scene... the real peril in these films is the slippery standing of the exceptional woman, who, as Adrienne Rich warned us a generation ago, "encounters male hostility in the form of psychic rape, often masked as psychic or physical seduction".'[89]

The *Femme Fatale* of Neo-*Noir*: Sexuality and Feminism

The *femme fatale* figure of neo-*noir* also has a highly complex, and often ambivalent, relationship to feminist and post-feminist debates. New versions of the *femme fatale* that arise in this period, and their placement and treatment in neo-*noir* narratives, are interesting in the questions that they ask about the difficult interrelationships between sex and power that circle around a set of representations of contemporary femininities and the commodifications of female identity outlined earlier. This ambivalence is central to questions of the currency and meanings of the *femme fatale* in contemporary cinema.

As I have noted in earlier chapters, feminist film criticism of the 1970s focused a distinctive and transgressive form of female agency onto the *femme fatale* figure of 1940s *film noir*. My examination of a broader range of 1940s *films noirs*, and a variety of neo-*noir* crime and legal thrillers of the 1980s and 1990s, has illustrated that women in the crime film, and the ways in which female agency is represented and explored, are not reducible to this figure.

The 1940s *femme fatale* always contained a central ambivalence for feminist interpretation, partly because of perceptions of *film noir*'s male address and partly because of the figure's agency as sexually motivated.[90] Feminist readings of the *film noir* in the 1970s sought to acknowledge and exploit this ambivalence. Reading the *femme fatale* 'against the grain' suggested that the transgressive potential of the *femme fatale* in 1940s *films noirs* was not, or not simply, her definition as a sexual object, but the woman's access to, and use of, her sexuality as an active force, notwithstanding its containment by narrative closures required by the Production Code. Yvonne Tasker suggests that the appeal that the *femme fatale* figure has had for feminist criticism is located in this ambivalence, in reading the *femme fatale* against the ideological grain of Hollywood's containment of female sexuality: 'it is the sheer *energy* and *vitality* of the *femme fatale* that stands out.'[91]

In an important sense, then, the *femme fatale*'s currency for feminism is precisely in her resistance to stable meanings of femininity. Her presence within crime narratives upsets patriarchal mastery, both in the sense of narrative control and of the containment of female sexuality within the social institutions of the family, to which she is frequently opposed. The *femme fatale* figure also reworks understandings of character stability. Her central ambivalence is founded not only on what she does, but also on the enigma of why she does it. All these elements are behind Mary Ann Doane's concept of the *femme fatale* as 'the figure of a certain discursive unease, a potential epistemological trauma. For her most striking characteristic, perhaps, is the fact that she never really is what she seems to be.'[92]

On the one hand, then, the *femme fatale* figure can never be known; on the other hand, she has become iconic as a productively troubling figure whose presence refuses containment. As one of the key generic representatives of *film noir*'s image, within its critical constructions at least, the redeployment of this figure as a referential icon in neo-*noir*'s 'memorialisation' of its cinematic past condenses some key questions about the interrelationships between gender and genre, as well as their historical and socio-cultural shifts.

Body Heat's focus upon a story of dangerous desire, deception and destruction, is, as Carroll suggests, both 'an old story' and 'a new movie'.[93] It appeals to myths of a ruthless, highly sexualised feminine figure who is both 'as old as Eve and as current as today's movies'.[94] The first encounter between the film's small-town corruptible lawyer Ned Racine (William Hurt) and Matty Walker (Kathleen Turner) at an open-air jazz concert is pervaded by a strong mood of inevitability. As Ned stands watching the band, Matty, shown in a long shot, walks up through the audience to the diegetic strains of 'that old feeling'. Carroll himself argues that the film's focus on fatal desire can only be understood with reference to its antecedents, films such as *Double Indemnity* and *The Postman Always Rings Twice*.[95] But while Matty's sleek and expensive costuming, her white silk shirt dresses and hair styling recall the glamorous studio polish of classic Hollywood stars like Lauren Bacall and Jane Greer, the socio-cultural resonances of her character, and the narrative operations of the neo-*noir* thriller, have been refashioned and speak to the cultural and economic climate of the 1980s.

Todd Erickson argues that the 'yuppie' era in which neo-*noir* arises was 'a time when virtually everything – old standards, morals, sometimes even the truth – was sacrificed in the almighty hunt for the Big Deal'.[96] Erickson also argues that the cultural visibility of women's economic, and sexual, independence became foregrounded in the period. He cites *Body Heat*'s director Lawrence Kasdan as noting the cultural effects of feminism: 'it created an atmosphere during the seventies where there was [the] same type of distrust of women that the guys returning from World War II had when they wondered where their women had been at night while they were away fighting the war'.[97] While Kasdan's focus is male anxiety, advertisers in the 1980s understood both the possibilities for, and pressures upon, women. Leslie Shelton writes: 'the pressure to achieve in a lot of areas within a relatively short period of time, which is new to women, has created unsettling feelings, which are evidenced in guilt and insecurity'.[98]

Both these contradictory connotations coalesce around new versions of the *femme fatale* in neo-*noir*, and explore the meanings of female agency in relation to sexuality and economics. In films such as *Presumed Innocent*, *Disclosure* and *The Last Seduction*, ambitious women are located in the workplace. Their rapid rise to success and competent command of the spheres in which they work is, though, frequently interwoven with their sexuality, collapsing distinctions between brilliant performance at work, and sexual talent. In *Presumed Innocent*, rookie lawyer Carolyn Polhemus (Greta Scacchi) quickly establishes herself at her legal firm, displaying a hunger and aptitude for success as she processes advice from her more senior colleague, Rusty Sabich (Harrison Ford), with whom she has a fatal affair. In *Disclosure*, Meredith Johnson (Demi Moore) gains a high-profile executive appointment at Seattle's Digicom Corporation, over the head of her former lover Tom Sanders (Michael Douglas). *The Last Seduction* opens by showing Bridget Gregory (Linda Fiorentino) commanding the New York office space of her telesales team, whom she bullies if they do not close successfully. When Bridget later flees to small-town Beston, taking with her drugs money that her husband Clay (Bill Pullman) acquired in a deal, she easily lands another sales job. She playfully illustrates her talent for manipulation when she shows her lover Mike (Peter Berg) that she could sell anything, when she makes a cold call selling a veiled offer to kill a woman's husband after she has trawled a database of life insurance.

New incarnations of the *femme fatale* in neo-*noir* combine an increasing centrality of active sexuality with character elements of deception and/or disguise, in ways that both explicitly show an active femininity and leave motivation cloaked in mystery. *Body*

Heat contains repeated scenarios of the coupling of Ned and Matty. *Presumed Innocent* and *Disclosure* stage sex at the office, within the space of work. *Basic Instinct* opens with a notoriously explicit sexual sequence. An unidentified female figure (available to be read as either the film's central female figure Catherine Tramell (Sharon Stone) or her lesbian lover Roxy (Leilani Sarelle)) dominates and kills her male partner at the point of climax. In *Body of Evidence* (Uli Edel, 1993), Rebecca Carlson (Madonna), accused of murdering her millionaire lover, becomes involved in a kinky affair with her lawyer Frank Dulaney (Willem Dafoe).

The explicit, and active, sexual scenarios in which the neo-*femme fatale* is shown in the neo-*noir* thriller mark these films' complex address. The visualisations of the sexually liberated woman, who is unapologetic about the often aggressive pursuit of her desire, coincide with the 'new femininities' that Hilary Radner traces as appearing in the post-feminist period, in which capital is constituted by the female body and sexual expertise 'which she herself exchanges ... as a "free" agent'.[99] The extent of this liberation, though, is precariously dependent upon sexual action, and upon a shifting mediascape in which the meanings of female sexual liberation and commodifications of it anxiously collide.

Kate Stables has argued that 'postmodern film employs the *femme fatale* as a universal archetype, as a marketing ploy, but most significantly as an anxiety pointer, a figure who processes and displays cultural concerns through popular film'.[100] Stables points to the increasing emphasis on the neo-*noir femme fatale* as a sexual performer,[101] noting that the neo-*noir* thriller's utilisation of soft-core pornography is a key element of its contemporary form. *Noir* elements in the erotic thriller are also covered in Linda Ruth Williams' history of the genre, in which she maps the interpenetration of *noir* narrative elements and character types across direct-to-video and mainstream release formats. Williams argues: 'Erotic thrillers are *noir*ish stories of sexual intrigue incorporating some form of criminality or duplicity, often as the flimsy framework for on-screen softcore sex.'[102] Williams suggests that the landscape across which new versions of the femme fatale are located affords a new range of meanings for the figure:

Not only is she sassy, strong and spectacular, epitomising avarice and lust in a way which appeals to an international audience, this focus on money and sex means that she readily lends herself to a cross-fertilisation of *noir* and porn, leading female viewers into new generic territory. She is a handy genre trope which has continued to sell – the covert pleasures women have found in the 1940s punished *femme fatale* have mutated into the overt saleability of the 1990s get-away-with-it version.[103]

The ambiguous endings of films such as *The Last Seduction*, where Bridget eludes the male censure of a detective, her lover and her husband to get away in a limousine with the money, or *Basic Instinct*'s famously unstable final shot, where Catherine's and Nick's (Michael Douglas) tryst is undercut by the shot of an ice pick concealed beneath her bed, are both instances evidencing neo-*noir*'s new treatment of female criminal sexuality. Screenwriter Sharon Cobb suggests that 'new *noir*' offers audiences the subversive delights of narratives free from the ideological demands of character redemption.[104] This is an aspect discussed by both Julianne Pidduck and Deborah Jermyn. Pidduck sees the increased narrative centrality of the 1990s *femme fatale* as of a piece with the figure's irrepressibility.[105] *Basic Instinct*'s Catherine Tramell might be (partly) positioned as the narrative enigma for the film's detective Nick Curran (Michael Douglas), but as an author of blockbusting crime novels she is interestingly positioned as anticipating, authoring and controlling his character moves and motivations, suggesting 'an outright battle over the power of naming, narrative and endings'.[106] Pidduck argues that the appearance of ultra-violent, ultra-sexy 'psycho-femme' figures evident across a range of film titles in the 1990s, such as *The Grifters* (Stephen Frears, 1990), *The Hand That Rocks the Cradle* (Curtis Hanson, 1992), *Final Analysis* (Phil Joanou, 1992), *Poison Ivy* (Katt Shea, 1992), *Basic Instinct*, *Body of Evidence*, *The Crush* (Alan Shapiro, 1993), *The Temp* (Tom Holland, 1993) and *The Last Seduction* offer excessive, even ironic, figures for feminism. She locates their (potential) appeal as figures of power:

Where in our everyday lives as women we are bombarded by
the evidence of our increasing vulnerability, poverty, and lim-
ited social power, the fatal femme's embodied social, sexual,
and physical powers offer an imagined point of contact, if not
simply identification – an imagined momentum or venting of
rage and revenge fantasies – the importance of which cannot
be underestimated.[107]

Deborah Jermyn also argues for a critical 'appropriation' of the
female psychopath as a way of 'recover[ing] moments of resistance
and disruption ... moments which are plentiful in the excess of the
female psychopath'.[108] Whereas the new *femme fatale* figure can
be seen as an appropriable and intriguing feminist revenge fantasy,
this is just one form of escape from the complex narrative negotiations for women in the neo-*noir* crime film. These appropriations
are one productive way in which feminist-oriented criticism can
engage with female villainess figures, which illustrate both
vibrant and politically complex representations of femininity in contemporary cinema. However, Christine Holmlund has noted that
despite the vibrancy and energy of the 'deadly doll' within
Hollywood narratives, the figure marks some of the limits of what
is representable in contemporary cinema. The social conditions
of violence against women are masked by the narrative modes
and codes of representation that dwell upon sensational and
sexual violence committed *by*, rather than endured by, women
on screen.[109]

The emphasis upon female sexual agency, and the move in films
of the 1980s and 1990s to 'package' forms of female agency
as commodities,[110] suggests that the renewals and reworkings of
the *femme fatale* figure in the neo-*noir* thriller is still an area
requiring feminist attention. As Tasker and Negra argue: 'although
a variety of films and genres of the late 1990s and early 2000s
hype empowerment, these texts do not sustain any easy or
straightforward relationship to women's experiences and social
health. Indeed, scholars, popular critics and mass audiences
often report a "hollow quality" at the heart of many postfeminist
media texts.'[111]

Conclusions

The modifications of the neo-*noir* crime thriller and its female characterisations discussed in this chapter show continuities and transformations in *noir*'s gender relations. Neo-*noir* both addresses and commodifies feminism in its female legal agents and new femme fatales. The presence of female characters, and the narrative negotiations to which they are subject, suggest that the terms of being a heroine within the crime genre is a complex position, but one that illustrates some key issues about women's socio-cultural place in the 1980s and 1990s. This socio-cultural place will be examined in the next chapter, which traces revivals, modifications and transformations in the female gothic film in contemporary cinema.

Chapter Six

Reworking the Woman's Film: The Neo-Gothic Heroine in Contemporary Cinema

Introduction

In this chapter, I examine a group of films from the 1990s to the present that revive, revisit and rework elements of the female gothic film of the 1940s. Like neo-*noir*, these films have a distinct and clearly articulated relationship to the past through their use of particular stylistic and narrative strategies. They also bring with them new perspectives on female character placement, and are thus consequently engaged in the ongoing debates about the meanings of public femininities, and women's socio-cultural place that arise in the period. It is the way that they straddle both old and new, in style and content, that distinguishes them as 'neo-gothic', and it is these films' navigation of 'old' and 'new' that is discussed below.

Gothic Continuities, Feminism and Post-feminism

As I have demonstrated in this book's earlier chapters, the gothic mode has been characterised by its promiscuity and fertility across a range of media and cultural forms which encompass architecture, fine art, literature, film and television, and which span sensation fictions of the eighteenth and nineteenth centuries and the mass media of film and television in the twentieth and twenty-first centuries.[1] The gothic mode can be seen to have constantly renewed itself and asserted its currency at distinctly different historical moments. It has repeatedly found new outlets, while its dominant mood is an anxious and fraught relationship to the past. The gothic mode, then, recurrently mobilises tensions between the old and the new.

Discourses in feminism since the late 1980s have also sought to engage with questions of 'old' and 'new', with 'old' standing for second-wave feminism and 'new' standing for its transformations. These discourses, which have gone under the labels of both 'post-feminism' and 'third-wave feminism', are, of course, quite heterogeneous; but they are all characterised by an engagement with second-wave feminism, and uses, or appropriations, of it to rearticulate understandings of what feminism means in the contemporary media landscape.

As I have shown in Chapter 5, the media has been a generative source for the representations of both feminist and post-feminist 'caricature'. Pamela Church Gibson notes the visibility of popular oppositions of these public femininities that she suggests arise in the 1980s: the feminist as a 'grotesque parody ... [of] the dungaree-wearing, bra-burning, man-hating, crop-haired, strident woman',[2] and the 'postfeminist as "empowered" woman with no need for outmoded second wave ideas, first presented to us in the eighties as shoulder-padded, lipstick-wearing and stiletto-borne'.[3] Feminist interpretive and critical work on these public femininities, and the inflections of these meanings within distinct film genres, has been of central importance. Frequently, discussions have addressed 'exceptional' female characters, figures inhabiting male-addressed genres, such as the *femme fatale* figure in crime film of the classical and new Hollywood eras or central female protagonists in female-addressed genres such as the 'domestic melodrama',[4] and latterly, representations of women in romantic comedy and female-addressed television series such as *Ally McBeal, Sex and the City* and *Desperate Housewives*.[5]

The protocols of second-wave feminist film theory, and its attention to politically engaged reading strategies of mainstream texts from the classical studio era have been reworked in the postfeminist context. Critical paradigms of reading 'against the grain' to reveal the ideological charge and contradictions of studio era *film noir* and the domestic melodrama have shifted, as new public femininities emerged in the period of the 1980s and 1990s. Postfeminist approaches have addressed the different positions of central female protagonists on film, noting their location between independence and 'empowerment' (brought through feminism), and an array of female choices and new forms of female desire expressed through consumerist discourses about female identity in the period. As I have noted in Chapter 5, this has been perceived as a negotiation about the meanings of femininity, and a discursive turn in feminist approaches which chimes with the 'double address'[6] of many post-feminist film texts. As Yvonne Tasker and Diane Negra argue, the post-feminist context offers both new choices and new ambivalences for the meanings of feminism.

The group of films examined in this chapter, and the female figures at the centre of them, are located within this post-feminist ambivalence and 'double address'. The neo-gothic films are female-addressed suspense thrillers such as *Sleeping with the Enemy* (Joseph Rubin, USA, 1991), *Deceived* (Damian Harris, USA, 1991) and *What Lies Beneath* (Robert Zemeckis, USA, 2000), which are the central focus of my discussion. But the group extends outwards to encompass titles such as *Jagged Edge* (Richard Marquand, USA, 1985), a neo-*noir*/neo-gothic hybrid, *The Stepfather* (Joseph Ruben, 1987), *Stepfather II* (Jeff Burr, 1989), *Pacific Heights* (John Schlesinger, USA, 1990), *Dead Again* (Kenneth Branagh, USA, 1991), *The Others* (Alejandro Amenabar, 2001) and *Enough* (Michael Apted, 2002). These films feature a central female protagonist, located in a domestic environment and in an unhappy or dysfunctional heterosexual relationship. When he begins to act strangely, or threateningly, the heroine begins to suspect that her husband or lover has a terrible secret relating to a woman in his past, and as she tries to uncover that secret, typically by discovering a secret room, she begins to fear that he is trying to kill her.

The neo-gothic films are simultaneously 'old' and 'new'. They use literary and filmic gothic modes as central reference points, they are organised around what Claire Kahane identifies as the typical literary gothic plot structure. These include the gothic house, 'an imprisoning structure',[7] a female protagonist, and her compulsion to 'seek out the center of a mystery'[8] while she is subjected to threats from a 'powerful male figure',[9] all elements, Kahane argues, that have been continuous threads in the gothic fabric since the late eighteenth century.

These films also have narrative and stylistic similarities to the female gothic cycle of the 1940s, discussed in earlier chapters of this book: films such as *Rebecca* (Alfred Hitchcock, 1940), *Suspicion* (Alfred Hitchcock, 1941), *Shadow of a Doubt* (Alfred Hitchcock, 1943), *Dark Waters* (André de Toth, 1944), *Experiment Perilous* (Jaques Tourneur, 1944), *Jane Eyre* (Robert Stevenson, 1944), *Gaslight* (George Cukor, 1944), *Dragonwyck* (Joseph Mankiewicz, 1946), *The Two Mrs Carrolls* (Peter Godfrey, 1947), *The Spiral Staircase* (Robert Siodmak, 1946), *Secret Beyond the Door* (Fritz Lang, 1948), *Caught* (Max Ophuls, 1949) and *Under Capricorn* (Alfred Hitchcock, 1949). The neo-gothic films' allusions to narrative and stylistic elements common in the 1940s female gothic cycle suggest the continuing currency of the gothic mode as a reference point. Hitchcock's 1940s films have been a particularly recurrent reference point. In his analysis of the 'allusionistic tendency' in Hollywood cinema since the 1970s, Noel Carroll notes that specific Hitchcock films, and 'Hitchcockian' themes and styles, have been a key resource for contemporary filmmakers.[10]

Contemporary reviews of several of the neo-gothic films remark on the ways in which these films cite and mobilise Hitchcockian motifs and styles, as well as exploring how these motifs and styles are reworked within a different era. In *The Stepfather*, a young girl Stephanie (Jill Schoelen) and her mother Susan (Shelley Hack) gradually come to realise that Susan's second husband, Jerry Blake (Terry O'Quinn), is not the 'ideal man' that he seemed to be, but an unpredictable and violent murderer. In her review of the film, Patricia Erens draws comparisons with Hitchcock's *Psycho*, as well as his *Shadow of a Doubt*, noting the way *The Stepfather* explores a dark underside to the assumed normality of American domesticity and family structures.[11] Writing in *The Village Voice*, Georgia Brown suggests continuities between Joseph Ruben's *The Stepfather* and his later film, *Sleeping With the Enemy*, suggesting both films are examples of 'Americana Gothic', in which ideal fathers and husbands become the antagonists against which female characters must do battle.[12]

Kenneth Branagh's 1991 film *Dead Again* explicitly references Hitchcock, as well as cinematic and narrative styles from the classical Hollywood woman's film. The action of its complex plot is divided across two temporal settings; the 'present' of the 1990s, which forms the narrative frame and the past, in which it is 1948. This division is stylistically and self-consciously marked through the use of flashbacks, to period setting, evoked in black and white cinematography, which contrast with the use of colour stocks for the contemporary scenes. *Dead Again* centres upon Grace (Emma Thompson), an amnesiac uncannily possessed by memories of her 1940s double, Margaret Strauss (also played by Thompson), a woman who was brutally murdered. Grace's 'journey' into the past, a subjective trajectory through which she separates herself from her double Margaret and regains her contemporary and forgotten 'self', is aided by the investigation of private detective Mike Church (Kenneth Branagh). The presence of a detective figure allows the film to reference classical 1940s *film noir*, but it is from the female gothic cycle that *Dead Again* draws its narrative trajectory. The enigma of Margaret's murder can only be resolved by uncovering her relationship with her moody and enigmatic husband, the composer Roman Strauss, a figure who doubles Mike and who is also played by Branagh. *Dead Again* was not enthusiastically received by contemporaneous reviewers: it was criticised for its overt stylisation at the expense of its narrative.[13] Despite this, the film's attempt to remobilise motifs from the Hollywood's cinematic past is interesting, particularly as it reveals the currency of those motifs in a group of films that are female-centred. Branagh as director, the film's cinematographer, Matthew Leonetti, and film music composer Patrick Doyle, gained attention for their experiments in style for their work on *Dead Again*.[14] Interviewed about *Dead Again*, Branagh explains that he was attempting to evoke 'the kind of motion pictures I grew up watching on television, especially the

Hitchcock pictures. If you watch *Vertigo* now, or *Notorious*, they're sort of outrageous.'[15] Branagh acknowledges this stylistic excess as bringing together a set of visual and aural elements that bridge cinematographic and musical design; he asked Patrick Doyle 'for the kind of lush score Bernard Herrmann might have written for the likes of Hitchcock'.[16] As *Dead Again* concerns Margaret's relationship with her composer husband, music provides a key symbolic motif. Branagh notes, 'By the end we must have earned the right to use an opera with crazy, mad, demonic voices tying up the movie.'[17] It is by using this combination of visual and aural excess that Branagh intends to position the film outside the realm of the 'generic thriller'.[18]

Stylistic excesses, and Hitchcockian allusions, are similarly traced in reviews and discussions of Robert Zemeckis' *What Lies Beneath*. In pre-publicity for the film, Zemeckis, a director noted for his command of special visual effects, promised that the film offers 'Hitchcock in the age of computer graphics'.[19] In his review of *What Lies Beneath*, Thomas Doherty traces the film's allusions to Hitchcock's *Rear Window* (1954), as well as the 1940s Hitchcock films *Rebecca* and *Suspicion*.[20] The ways in which *What Lies Beneath* reworks female gothic elements is analysed in more detail below, but it is interesting to note that creative personnel working on the film conceived putting new visual technologies to the service of creating a suspense style with a distinct heritage in classical studio era Hitchcock. Robert Legato, the visual effects supervisor on *What Lies Beneath*, relates that he and his crew reviewed and analysed Hitchcock's creation of mood and suspense, particularly his use of mobile framing within tight spaces on the set.[21] Legato describes how he and his crew used a combination of live-action tracking camera shots during the film's principal shooting phase, and computer-generated effects work in post-production, to create a distinctive and threatening mood for the haunted house, which is the main setting for *What Lies Beneath*. He gives examples of shots in which the effect is of moving 'through' walls of the house; in these shots the 'physical' boundaries were generated by computer graphics in post-production, while the camera movements created in live action were retained to give an uncomfortable feeling that the house was an insecure and easily penetrable space. Legato notes that 'none of [these shots were] "Wow look at me" effects shots; but, together they'd create a mood and a distinctive style'.[22]

The recurrence of allusive cinematic styles drawing upon the repertoire of classical Hollywood genres, notably the 1940s female gothic cycle, suggests these films retain a strong resonance for contemporary filmmakers. But the continuities of style are also always in tension with the new meanings that are produced in relation to the contexts in which a reworked genre reappears. As Noel Carroll argues:

> ... [in a] genre reworking... a traditional schema – that of the western, the thriller, the horror film, or the mystery is changed in its rhythms, characters, plot structures and so forth... the reworking evokes a historical genre and its associated myths, commonplaces, and meanings in order to generate expression through the friction between the old and the new.[23]

In the neo-gothic films, this 'friction between the old and the new' is complex and productive, and signals towards some key questions for feminist and post-feminist approaches to film.

Post-Feminist Women's Film: Neo-Gothic Femininity and its Negotiations

The reworking of elements of the female gothic narrative on film, from the 1980s to the present, allows women's sexual and domestic life to be revisited in ways that rearticulate and renegotiate feminist concerns. Their significance is in stylising and exploring the experience of female victimisation and its relationship to women's socio-cultural place in the post-feminist moment.

In earlier chapters, I have examined why the 1940s female gothic cycle has presented difficulties and ambivalences for feminist interpretive approaches. On the one hand, the cycle centres upon female characters; on the other, the films portray female experience of victimisation as a central strand in their narrative trajectories. The female gothic cycle raises issues of identification

179

and textual pleasure for feminist spectatorship theory that 'test[s] the very limits of the filmic representation of female subjectivity for a female spectator'.[24] Through attention to the generic heritage of the female gothic cycle and the specificities of its complex narrative trajectory, which can be understood precisely as a subjective journey for its heroine, I have argued that the female gothic film cycle works through these difficult issues and presents an important, and historically contextualised, negotiation of gendered identities and agency. As Donna Heiland argues, a central feature in the gothic mode's long popularity is its continuing ability to act both as an expression of the anxiety of gender relations and a critique of them:

> ... The stories of gothic novels are always stories of transgression. The transgressive acts at the heart of gothic fiction generally focus on corruption in, or resistance to, the patriarchal structures that shaped the country's political life and its family life, and gender roles within those structures came in for particular scrutiny. Further ... these acts are often violent, and always frightening. For gothic novels are above all about the creation of fear – fear in the characters represented, fear in the reader.[25]

Throughout my earlier discussions of the female gothic formula on film, I have not denied the uncomfortable questions that these films present to a feminist approach. Rather, I have been interested in trying to open up some of the tensions that arise between gothic fears and feminist concerns. There is no doubt that in the neo-gothics' revival of scenarios of horror – female protagonists menaced by powerful and violent male characters – these films can make for difficult viewing. However, staging scenarios where a female figure is in the position of a victim is only half of the female gothic film's story. My examination of the 1940s female gothic cycle has shown that the films possess a powerful charge by dramatising situations in which female heroines confront tyrannical male figures, exorcising their victimisation, and that of women who have preceded them. As I have demonstrated, this trajectory had distinct resonances with the shifting place of women in the socio-cultural context of the 1940s, particularly with the changing meanings of marriage within the period.

The neo-gothic films, and the narrative trajectories of their heroines, have a different socio-cultural resonance than their 1940s counterparts. As I have noted earlier, the post-feminist public femininities that have been most frequently discussed, and consequently have been most visible within feminist critical discourses on film and television, have tended to be sexually and/or financially empowered female protagonists. This array of female figures has, significantly, not included heroines in the neo-gothic film. At the heart of this critical neglect is, I think, a critical preference for certain kinds of heroine figures over others.

In earlier chapters of this book, I explored how a politics of identification informed feminist approaches to the 1940s female gothic cycle, and had produced a critical distancing and an expression of disidentity, from the female gothic cycle's seemingly disempowered protagonists. I noted that Charlotte Brunsdon's work productively defines the concept of disidentity as central to the workings of second-wave feminist critique, and can be discerned in post-feminism too.[26] I want to re-quote her work here, as she so clearly articulates how feminist, and post-feminist, identities are expressed within critical discourses bearing upon the neogothic films:

> Disidentity – not being like that, not being like those other women, not being like those images of women – is constitutive of feminism, and constitutive of feminism in all its generations. For if second-wave feminists were not like the housewives and sex objects they saw in the media, they were in turn othered by the postcolonial critique of the 1980s. As second-wave feminism interrogated itself, those in the next generation of feminists felt compelled to declare their lack of identity with second-wave feminists. Second-wave feminism is remembered, and demonised, as personally censorious, hairy and politically correct. It has also been the key other for younger women keen to celebrate the femininity and feminism of Buffy and Ally.[27]

The celebration of femininity within some strands of post-feminist criticism might be termed 'feminine feminism', as it enacts a negotiation of the complexities of how contemporary femininity sits in dialogue with, and is different from, second-wave feminism. There is also another significant strand of post-feminist criticism that might be termed 'feisty feminine feminism', which has turned its attention to female figures in 'male' genres. Here it is the action heroine and the neo-*femme fatale* figure who have been understood as 'fighting back' in two different ways. Action heroine figures such as Ripley (Sigourney Weaver) in the *Alien* films,[28] Sarah Connor (Linda Hamilton) in *Terminator 2* (James Cameron, 1991), Jordan O'Neil (Demi Moore) in *G.I. Jane* (Ridley Scott, 1997), Trinity (Carrie Ann Moss) in *The Matrix* (Andy and Larry Wachowski, 1999) and Lara Croft (Angelina Jolie) in *Lara Croft: Tomb Raider* (Simon West, 2001) have been noted for their exhibition of feisty or tomboyish characteristics, which transgress gender boundaries in terms of their actions, bodies or performances.[29] Neo-*femme fatales*, such as Matty Walker (Kathleen Turner) in *Body Heat*, Catherine Tramell (Sharon Stone) in *Basic Instinct* and Bridget Gregory in *The Last Seduction*, characters that have all been discussed in Chapter 5, represent sexual and social transgressions through their determination to seize masculine (phallic) power and their determination to 'use' their femininity to seductively do down the men they encounter.[30]

The neo-gothic heroines have been absent from this list of public femininities and critical personae because, I think, of several factors. Both the feminine feminist and feisty feminist figures possess choice, express desire and are financially and sexually empowered. The neo-gothic heroine does not possess the typical characteristics of other public post-feminist personae: she represents fearful, threatened rather than 'feisty' or 'celebrated' femininity, and her brand of femininity is not available to be understood as 'assumed' as a masquerade. She is coded according to a different visual regime than the glamorous *femme fatale* of neo-*noir* or androgynous action heroine. She is married or already in a long-term relationship, and the neo-gothic plots do not centrally examine the heroine's career. Also, while the neo-gothic films are, importantly, located within the context of a late capitalist consumer economy, the neo-gothic heroine is not a consumer figure herself, but is economically disempowered, being dependent on her husband who is a high earner and successful in his career. In being firmly positioned within the realm of the domestic, the central issues that these films seem to explore are located in the private sphere, which is threatened space. The neo-gothic heroine, then, embodies, in a fictional persona, the housewife; a figure who, as Brunsdon has pointed out, is present in academic discussions as the assumed viewer of 'feminine' genres, but who can all too easily become the 'generalised other' to feminism.[31]

This list of the 'negative' characteristics of the neo-gothic heroine, how she is 'not like' other popular post-feminist personae, should not be taken to indicate that these films have no dialogue with feminist concerns. The fact that their heroines cannot be recuperated through the negotiations common to contemporary post-feminist inquiry is a key issue. Given that issues of periodisation or generational difference have been live in debates about what post-feminism *is*, these films are particularly interesting in that though they arise within the 'post-feminist moment', they forcefully raise issues that were more commonly examined by second-wave feminism: domestic politics, violence and sexuality in a male controlled (patriarchal) environment that disempowers women. The fact that these concerns are being re-articulated in the 1980s, 1990s and 2000s presents a powerful picture of the continued currency of such issues in the face of a picture of 'feminist progress', as well as forcing us to recognise that there are key continuities in feminist debate which are as important as generational difference. And that they re-emerge through the gothic mode, so commonly associated with a return of the past, is felicitous.

I want, now, to go on to explore how three neo-gothic films, *Sleeping with the Enemy* (Joseph Ruben, 1991), *Deceived* (Damian Harris, 1991) and *What Lies Beneath* (Robert Zemeckis, 2000) rework key elements of the gothic mode, particularly its address of female fears, and how this involves a dialogue with feminist and post-feminist concerns. I will draw particular attention to the films' re-configuration of gothic domestic space, and the (dis)placements of the neo-gothic heroine woman within it. And

I will examine how the gothic trope of mirroring or doubling female figures is redeployed.

In their examination of the psychology of the literary gothic mode, Norman Holland and Leona Sherman write that the condensed commercial image of the literary gothic tradition is a woman and a brooding castle or mansion: 'the image of woman-plus-habitation and the plot of dynastic mysteries within the habitation has changed little since the eighteenth century'.[32] Like the 'imprisoning [gothic] structure' identified by Kahane, this enduring image is present in the neo-gothic films, while also being shaped to a contemporary context.

Sleeping with the Enemy uses two contrasting domestic spaces. An ultra-modern Cape Cod beach house in an isolated location, where housewife Laura Burney (Julia Roberts) is imprisoned in an abusive marriage to Martin (Patrick Bergin), a high-powered investment counsellor, stands against an old-fashioned frame house in a small town in Iowa, to which Laura escapes as Sara Waters after faking her death by drowning. The film establishes the 'sleek architect-designed castle'[33] as an alienating space for Laura. Its aspirant, minimalist décor mixes fine-art objects with angular modern furnishings in a restrained palette of blacks, whites and greys, and the lighting design evokes a chilly mood, draining scenes of colour. The restrained colour palette rhymes with the dark formal suits worn by Bergin for most of the film. The mise-en-scène expresses Martin's power, the clinical minimalism and lack of bric-a-brac is suggestive of a masculine, yuppie bachelor pad, and speaks to his position as a 'career player'. He exerts a suffocating and minute control over the domestic realm: objects like hand towels must line up, and groceries in the kitchen cupboards must be arranged to his specification by Laura, or he will brutally 'remind' her of the rules. Although Laura is the keeper of the house, this space has none of the softening 'feminine' touches of idealised domesticity, and her performance of domestic tasks is infused with self-conscious anxiety. She is imprisoned in a cage of hard reflective surfaces of silver, black and glass, surfaces through which Martin can patrol her actions and onto which she falls under the violence of his anger and, in their sexual encounters, his lust.

The figuring of this space as Martin's, and its gendered, masculine style, means that the idealised continuity of woman-home-domesticity, common in mainstream cinema, is broken. It is not simply that Martin belongs to the public sphere of business, career and wealth and that Laura belongs to the private sphere of home and family; rather that Laura belongs to neither public nor private spheres, she belongs *to* Martin's house rather than the home belonging to *her*. By dramatising Martin's control of their domestic space and, by extension, of Laura's feminine role (his supervision of her domestic tasks and choice of clothes), the film locates their relationship within a power dynamic that has been rendered anachronistic by feminist politics. Laura's absolute subjection by Martin and her lack of access to social power in the first part of the film evokes the generic position of the female gothic heroine. In literary and filmic gothic narratives the heroine is frequently a displaced figure; younger, and/or from a lower social class than the (often aristocratic) gothic anti-hero, she suffers in a gendered power differential. This is explored through her difficult search to find a place in the ancestral home of her husband/lover. The literary gothic locations of Udolpho (*The Mysteries of Udolpho*) and Thornfield (*Jane Eyre*), through to the filmic gothic settings of Manderley (*Rebecca*), Dragonwyck (*Dragonwyck*), Thornton Square (*Gaslight*) and Levender Falls (*Secret Beyond the Door*), are all spaces that powerfully and affectively portray a crisis in women's relation to the home and her agency within it. Holland and Sherman's 'dynastic mysteries' represent a patriarchal control of domestic space that is re-negotiated by the heroine through her experience of its imprisonment and her subsequent escape.

That this male dynastic structure re-emerges in the 1990s in films like *Sleeping with the Enemy* suggests that second-wave feminist questions, about the politics of domestic labour, about domestic violence and sexual abuse, can still have significant purchase.[34] The male dynasty in *Sleeping with the Enemy* is signalled through Martin's earning power, and his power extends to his ability to track Laura down in her new and idealised re-located home in Iowa. The contrasting domestic locations in the film offer two distinct takes on the relation of woman to home through feminism, and post-feminism. The antiquated gender relations, evident in the beach house scenes, beg for a sustained and radical feminist critique of domestic imprisonment, while Laura/Sara's new home in Iowa is much more in tune with female-addressed forms of cinema and television which celebrate the 'pleasures' of domesticity and femininity.[35] Sara/Laura's new home is the parallel, idealised and feminine space to the alienated, masculine, domestic space of Cape Cod. Presented in a warm, softly lit montage in which she cleans old furniture, paints kitchen cupboards and arranges house-plants on her window-sill, the mise-en-scène expresses the house as structuring Sara/Laura's new self-determination. Where Cape Cod had displaced Laura from friends and family, the Iowa house re-places Sara/Laura into a small town community, and intertwines the recovery of her femininity with the possibility of romance with 'the boy next door', a drama teacher Ben (Kevin Anderson).

Sara/Laura's re-discovery of her femininity is offered as both a 'progressive' step and a 'return' to an authentic self. Previously, Martin selected her designer wardrobe, loomed in the background of her mirror, and at one point, even dressed her up – in a red silk nightgown which was a 'peace offering' after a bout of violence. All of these aspects suggest the constriction of a male-defined femininity, and Martin's unhealthily obsessive fixation on fitting Laura to an abstract ideal of 'wife' and 'lover'. Martin's fixation is clear in their sexual encounters, initiated by his demands, and structured by his fantasies, to the diegetic strains of Berlioz's *Symphonie Fantastique*. Berlioz's music – in which a musician is obsessed with a vision of a lover who spurns him – serves as a telling nineteenth-century intertext of obsession and death. While on the surface Martin seems controlled, what lies beneath is his investment in a chaotic narrative of sadistic passion and male fury. The *Symphonie Fantastique* is an apt expression for the anxious interchangeability of sex and violence which frequently characterises gothic gender relations, and which is vividly played out in *Sleeping with the Enemy*. That Martin's pathology is partly signalled through music, and through excessive stylistic uses of it, echoes the strategies that 1940s female gothic film uses to signal unstable masculine subjectivity, which I have discussed in Chapter 4.

The film interestingly lays out different modes of femininity through Laura's experience. We see her discomfort as Martin forces her into a male-defined (and outdated) feminine role. Then, we witness her 'regaining' her 'own' femininity in Iowa. For her transitional journey between Cape Cod and Iowa, Laura dons a black wig, but we understand this as a necessary disguise rather than a playful masquerade with femininity. In Iowa, Laura/Sara assumes an informal style of dress (jeans, long flowing skirts, unstructured cardigans, pastel shades) as her 'own', and with her hair curlier and 'naturally' styled, Laura does interestingly indulge in the playfulness of 'dressing up' at the instigation of her new boyfriend, Ben. One evening he takes her to the school where he works, and putting her on the stage he shines the spotlight on her and switches on a starlit sky behind her. Then, in a backstage montage sequence, Laura tries on a whole array of costumes and hats, and Ben teaches her to jive. This sequence's self-conscious staging of romance evokes a key moment in *Singin' in the Rain* (Stanley Donen and Gene Kelly, 1952) and, more widely, the reflexivity of the musical. It's intertextual reference to the shopping-and-dressing-up sequence in *Pretty Woman*[36] works around Julia Roberts' star image. By explicitly putting Sara/Laura in the spotlight, the film intertwines star and character personae as Laura expresses the carefree aspect of her character for the first time in the film through Roberts' famous smile. Thus, an authenticity or naturalness that, as Brunsdon and Read note,[37] is central to Roberts' image is produced through the playfulness of dressing up. We are to understand that Laura *can* enter into, and enjoy, this masquerade because it is safely staged *as* role playing, and not threatening to her identity, as the play with Berlioz and the red silk nightgown is. The way that Ben looks encouragingly on at Laura trying on costumes is in marked contrast to Martin's exacting gaze.

As I have noted in earlier chapters, costume has a privileged place in the woman's film, and those in the gothic mode are no exception.[38] I suggested that the displacements of the heroine are often signalled through a self-consciousness about her image, and its suitability to the role of wife and keeper of the ancestral home. This self-consciousness is commonly expressed in the 1940s gothic films, illustrated by Joan Fontaine (in *Rebecca*) wishing she 'were a woman of thirty-six, dressed in black satin with a string of pearls'. Many of the 1940s gothic heroines are made to feel gauche (*Rebecca*), bookish (*Undercurrent*) and socially awkward (*Gaslight*), compared with the sophistication of their husbands. This is how the 1940s gothic films express the unfitness of the gothic husband for the heroine, as well as a (proto)-feminist concern about the shaping of a feminine image for the approval of men. In the post-feminist moment of the neo-gothic illustrated by *Sleeping with the Enemy*, femininity is no longer exclusively generated for the approval of a powerful male figure, but 'belongs' to women. This is not unproblematic, dangerously close as it is to essentialism, but the coding of femininity-for-women contains a correspondence between the old and neo-gothic films, and their heroines. The 'naturalness' generated through Roberts' star image, and the relaxed 'normalness' of the Sara Waters persona, fit the tradition that the female gothic heroine manifests an unspectacular femininity. This sets the gothic heroine apart from the exceptional popular femininities, like the femme fatale, and shows she offers something different. Writing about the 1940s female gothic films, Andrea Walsh suggests that the gothic heroine (in films like *Suspicion* and *Gaslight*) 'symboli[ses] Everywoman',[39] and was, therefore, an identificatory figure for 1940s female audiences. This 'everywoman' persona also has relevance to the female protagonists of the neo-gothics: the coding of Sara Waters persona is shared by Adrienne Saunders (Goldie Hawn) in *Deceived* and by Claire Spencer (Michelle Pfeiffer) in *What Lies Beneath*.

As indicated in earlier chapters, questions of identification have become key in feminist approaches to the woman's film, and are particularly focused on the gothic and neo-gothic heroines as victim figures and their relationship to the film's female spectators. However, the gothic mode dramatises questions of identification (and disidentification), through the generic gothic trope of female mirroring or doubling, and through the affective operation of the gothic as an experiential mode. Examining how identification, and disidentification, are repeatedly foregrounded and dealt with in the neo-gothic group will reveal that the films' victimisation of female figures is part of the process of narrativity, and one of a series of different positionalities the heroine occupies, rather than an essentially gendered, and static, position of the genre.

Deceived shows what happens when the picture perfect marriage of Adrienne to Jack is exposed as a sham when Jack's past begins to intrude upon the present. The opening of the film with the couple's 'whirlwind' romance makes them seem a perfect fit. She restores antique artefacts, he is a museum curator. On their first date they talk animatedly all night, uncovering common family holiday locations and musical tastes, and a montage condenses the early years of their marriage and the birth of their daughter, Mary (Ashley Peldon), all located in a luxurious New York loft. Jack appears to be an ideal husband, listening and attentive to Adrienne, and a devoted father, tucking Mary into bed after telling her the stories from a family photo album. Adrienne's suspicions are prompted when Jack begins to act more unpredictably, and the transparent communication between them breaks down – she suspects him of having an affair. Leaving their apartment abruptly, Jack appears to die in a car crash.

Inconsolable with grief, Adrienne gradually uncovers a past life of Jack's, of which she was totally unaware during their courtship and marriage, and she learns that Jack is as fake as the replica objects that he uses as switches to steal priceless antique artefacts from the museum – like the Egyptian necklace that is hidden in their apartment. His real name is Frank Sullivan, and Jack Saunders was a close friend of his from high school who died in a plane crash, upon which Frank assumed his identity. When Adrienne traces family of the real Jack Saunders, Evelyn Wade (Amy Wright), reminisces about the closeness between the two men, saying 'Jack was Frank's only friend, they were inseparable, like one person'. She fills in Frank's deprived family background, and recalls a time when Frank listened to her all night, encouraging her dreams and future plans, in a tone that clearly signals a young romance, as well as having an eerie correspondence with Adrienne's first date with Jack/Frank. From Evelyn, Adrienne traces Frank's mother, Rosalie (Kate Reid), to her dingy, rundown apartment. Assuming Frank was dead, Rosalie is bitter to find he has been living in the same city all the time.

Scenes concurrent with Adrienne's investigation portray the loft apartment that she shared with Jack as an increasingly uneasy and threatened space. She and Mary are woken in the night by strange sounds and the distinct presence of an unidentified 'someone'. In these night-time shots the apartment appears cavernous, with shadowy boundaries, and a distinctive colour palette of deep reds and greens is used in the lighting design and mise-en-scène to create a sense of threat. Adrienne and her au pair Ellen (Anais Granofsky) repeatedly find windows ajar, and slow, menacing mobile shots, apparently unmotivated by an embodied character, give a strong suggestion of a haunting presence. After waking one night, Adrienne sits in the kitchen poring over an old high-school file of Jack's, and after she goes to bed the frame slowly tracks forwards to reveal a shadowy figure watching her from a deserted apartment opposite, which is in the process of renovation. The threats become manifest when Adrienne returns from visiting Rosalie to find the loft ransacked, and Ellen attacked. In the aftermath, Adrienne ruefully observes to Harvey (Tom Irwin), a friend and colleague of Jack's, 'I didn't know anything about him. Everything I believed was a lie.' The theme of 'marrying a stranger', common in the 1940s gothic films, is the shadowy underside to the whirlwind romance. It had considerable purchase in the wartime and post-war period, dramatising female concerns about hasty wartime marriages, and post-war readjustments to returning husbands and lovers.[40] It is exploited in films such as *The Stranger* (Orson Welles, 1946) and *Secret Beyond The Door* (Fritz Lang, 1948), and it continues to have a purchase in the neo-gothic *Deceived* through the hastiness with which Adrienne and Jack get together. In the neo-gothics, though, the unhappy marriage carries with it a much more explicit and direct threat of physical violence.

Of course, the shadowy intruder is Jack/Frank, who has shifted from his position as husband and father within the home, to a figure who has excluded himself from it, and looks on from outside. Adrienne encounters her husband, estranged from her by his faked death, when he arranges a meeting between them at his mother's apartment. Frank tells of how he took on Jack's identity, saying that 'he was everything I wanted to be', and recalling that the night that Jack died 'was a dream, a nightmare'. The story of Jack's 'becoming' is simultaneously the story of Adrienne Saunder's dissolution, in that her patronymic place as wife and mother is erased as Jack's fake identity is exposed. Jack/Frank justifies his dissembling by saying he is being blackmailed by Daniel Sherman, who is forcing him to deal in faked artefacts by threatening to reveal his past. Jack/Frank tells Adrienne that Sherman is demanding a priceless Egyptian necklace hidden in their apartment. But Adrienne's search uncovers a further layer to Frank/Jack's dissembling, when she finds an identity card bearing the name Daniel Sherman but with Jack's photograph on it. Sherman is simply another alias for Frank/Jack to use. Going to Sherman's address, a spacious house in the suburbs, Adrienne finds a heavily pregnant Cathy Sherman (Mary Kane) unpacking boxes from a recent move. The house is dotted with 'family' photographs, including a wedding photograph of Frank/Jack/Daniel with Cathy, and a picture of Mary, who Cathy maintains is Daniel's mother. The Sherman household is an uncanny 'mirror' family to the Saunders one. Jack/Frank has fabricated his own identity by rearranging the names and identities of his family in the past. The Sherman house is an idealised domestic space under construction, while the Saunders apartment, through Jack's ransacking of it, is in dissolution.

Encountering this parallel space elicits a vertiginous loss of identity for Adrienne, because the household, and Jack, have been so constitutive of her position as wife, mother and lover. The figures of Cathy Sherman, and of Evelyn Wade earlier, are a specific focus as women who act as 'double' figures for Adrienne. Evelyn's memories of the development of a closeness between herself and Frank, and then Frank's abrupt disappearance, present a kind of parallel past to Adrienne, and Cathy Sherman is presenting a parallel future. Adrienne understands her own situation as threatened by discovering, and interpreting, the stories of these two other women, and the way that they locate the neo-gothic male antagonist figure: Frank/Jack/Daniel.

As I have shown in earlier chapters, female double figures recurrently haunt the gothic mode. This haunting is stylistically expressed in 'double' imagery, such as the portraits discussed in Chapter 3, or through an insistent and uncanny 'voice' from the past, discussed in Chapter 4. The recurrent double figure represents the position and identity from which the heroine must distinguish and individuate herself. Sherman writes that 'the primary motivating fear in the gothic is of nothingness or nonseparation',[41] and that the gothic allows women to confront this fear and to confirm a feminine identity.[42] Kahane explores the 'ambivalent' pleasures of the Gothic experience: the exploration of gothic space allows the female protagonist to be an adventurer figure, but, Kahane writes, what the heroine and reader must 'ultimately ... confront are the mysteries of identity'.[43] These perspectives explore issues of feminine boundaries and identities that are still stake in the neo-gothic films, but female doubles are configured slightly differently in these films.

The neo-gothic films show their heroines engaged in an intra-textual, and shifting, process of identification with and disidentification from with these female doubles and mirror figures, foregrounding both questions of identification and of identity. Evelyn's story about Frank puts Adrienne in a double process of listening to the past and simultaneously recasting her *own* position in relation to it. Similarly, in her meeting with Cathy Sherman, Adrienne realises her displacement from the position of 'wife'. These realisations come through uncovering and interpreting another woman's story; they also confirm suspicions about the gothic husband's past which bear upon his relation to the heroine in the present. These moments yoke together conflicting emotions, combining sympathy and dread, and in the oscillation between these emotional poles, the heroine must register both her closeness *to*, and distance herself *from*, the double or mirror figure in a series of shifting positions; she is 'simultaneously persecuted victim and courageous heroine'.[44] This is also the moment that 'disidentity' is asserted. The neo-gothic heroine must recognise likeness to her mirror figure and escape by 'not being like those other women',[45] a strategy that is, as Brunsdon suggests, 'constitutive of feminism'.[46]

It is this double move that is at the heart of the neo-gothic's ambivalent relationship to feminism. On the one hand, the films solicit sympathy for the story of a suffering woman, inviting the idea of an understanding between women which connotes essential femininity, 'what all women know about bad men'. On the other, the survival of the heroine depends upon her not being like the woman in the story, and upon determining a different narrative outcome for herself. Although they are ambivalent, the films do not jettison feminism. In *What Lies Beneath*, we encounter a narrative that, I will argue, retains a feminist cast in the ways in which relations between women become central to the drama.

Claire (Michelle Pfeiffer) and Norman Spencer (Harrison Ford) live in a luxurious, remote, old lakeside house in New England, inherited from Norman's father. Norman is a 'brilliant' and career-driven research scientist in genetics, Claire a sensitive and emotional figure retired from a glittering career as a concert cellist. The film explores the gradual breakdown of the couple's relationship when Claire's daughter, Caitlin (Katharine Towne), leaves for college. Claire discovers Norman's past affair with a postgraduate student, Madison Frank (Amber Valetta), who has disappeared, and later uncovers evidence that Norman has murdered her.

Claire's emotional and psychological perspective is the focalising frame of events, but they are also intertwined with a supernatural theme. Alone, and increasingly isolated in the remote house, Claire 'experiences a series of bizarre and uncanny incidents, open to ambiguous interpretation'.[47] In 1940s female gothic films such as *Suspicion*, *Gaslight*, *Experiment Perilous* and *Undercurrent*, there is the potential for what Diane Waldman refers to as 'the invalidation of feminine experience',[48] though all of these films eventually corroborate their heroine's perceptions. *What Lies Beneath* references this possibility by putting Claire's interpretations under pressure, particularly through the trope of the double or mirror figure.

The first double figure is Claire's neighbour, Mary Feur (Miranda Otto). After overhearing violent arguments, hearing Mary weeping and seeing Warren Feur (James Remar) loading his car on a stormy night, Claire is convinced Mary has been murdered. Her spying on the couple is made highly referential to *Rear Window* (Alfred Hitchcock, 1954) in both its theme and style. There is even a moment that Warren Feur looks back at Claire, which is framed and edited to closely, and playfully, cite the famous moment in Hitchcock's film when L B Jefferies (James Stewart) is 'caught' in the act of looking by Lars Thorwald (Raymond Burr). Claire's suspicions increase as she believes that noises and presences in her house are 'clues' to Mary's murder. Egged on by her old friend

Jody (Diana Scarwid), she uses a ouija board, which spells out the initials 'M' and 'F'. Claire's investigation and her intuition make her so positive about Mary's murder that she publicly confronts Warren (an academic, like Norman) in front of a group of his colleagues, only to find that Mary is alive and well.

Despite this public exposure, Claire's suspicions are both wrong and right. She correctly identifies Mary's marital unhappiness because it mirrors her own, and when they do meet, Mary confesses to being 'overwhelmed' in her marriage. Claire's mistake is that she has imaginatively extended the unhappiness and distress to its expression in violence and murder. A murder has taken place, of Madison, who is the film's second double figure to Claire. Claire's belief that the uncanny events signify something are validated as she uncovers Madison's death and Norman's involvement. Combining deduction, intuition and her developing interest in the supernatural, her investigation is a specifically 'feminine one'.

Claire witnesses Madison's presence in the bathroom of the house, where the bath fills with water on its own, and Madison's reflection eerily appears in the water and bathroom mirrors. She bears an uncanny resemblance to a younger version of Claire, and in keeping with the processes of doubling, identification and disidentification that are features of the neo-gothic. The staging of these doublings in the bathroom is interesting. It is at once a space of feminine transformation and fabrication through toilette, and the space of female nakedness and vulnerability. There is also a privileged cinematic heritage of bathrooms as spaces of horror, or threat, which can be traced from films such as *The Seventh Victim* (Mark Robson, 1943), through *Psycho* (Alfred Hitchcock, 1960), to *Fatal Attraction* (Adrian Lyne, 1987). These connotations are exploited in the confrontation between Norman and Claire. The film's watery theme also exploits associative links between water and femininity; water is both Madison's grave and the element through which she returns to exert her power.

Madison's supernatural return foregrounds the theme of female doubling, and it occurs twice in the final part of the film, which is an extended, suspenseful and bloody struggle between Norman and Claire. Having drugged her with a paralysing nerve agent, Norman puts Claire in the bath, intending to drown his wife and staging her death as suicide. Watching over her prone body, he notices her necklace, a love token he bought for Madison, and which Claire has recovered from the lake. As he examines it, Madison supernaturally appears in and through Claire, shocking him into knocking himself out. This buys Claire a temporary escape, and she tries to get away from the house in their pick-up truck. But Norman has managed to clamber into the back, and tries to strangle Claire as she veers off into the lake. This disturbs Madison's grave and releases her body, and she returns a second time, now re-embodied in her own (now decaying) flesh to hold Norman down under water, freeing Claire to swim to the surface and safety.

This moment of collaboration, and that earlier in the bathroom, replays the neo-gothic strategy of colliding then distancing feminine identities. Madison's reappearance through Claire's paralysed body offers both the terror of identity loss, the 'non-separateness' which erases individuality, *and* the way that Claire's sympathy with Madison and investigation into her death allows her story to be told, and exposes Norman's guilt, validating Claire's fears. The final shots of the film suggest the closeness of this interchange by showing Claire laying a red rose on Madison's grave.

The relationship between Claire and Madison, and Madison's watery reappearance, show *What Lies Beneath* both drawing upon, and reworking, the filmic female gothic mode. As indicated, the film allies itself with suspense and horror sequences in Hitchcock films, but it is to *Rebecca*, both novel and film, that *What Lies Beneath* owes its greatest debt. *Rebecca* is also the story of a marriage powerfully haunted by another woman. The murder and disposal of Madison's body echoes *Rebecca*, where Maxim purposefully (the novel) or accidentally (the film version, bound by the Production Code) kills his wife, and then scuppers her boat to make her death appear as suicide. When a ship runs aground in fog, Rebecca's boat – significantly named *'Je Reviens'* – is found. Rebecca has returned, and Maxim and his second wife have to endure an inquest. However, *What Lies Beneath* reworks the returning woman in Claire's attachment to Madison. Claire is older and more experienced than the heroine of *Rebecca*, and the crisis in her relationship comes into focus when her daughter – of

Madison's age – flies the nest. There are hints that Norman intends to prey upon Caitlin, as he has on Madison, and so the uncanny and supernatural interchange between Claire and Madison suggests an older and younger woman acting in and for each other's interests, even as it stages the generational differences between two women in relation to the same powerful male figure.

A narratively significant collaboration between female figures also occurs in *The Stepfather*. Jerry Blake, the overtly controlling male figure in this film, decides to eliminate his new family, as he has done in the past, after he argues with his stepdaughter Stephanie over her goodnight kiss with her boyfriend. In the film's climactic and bloody conclusion, Jerry attacks Stephanie's mother, Susan, and pursues Stephanie through the house, trapping her in the bathroom. Grasping a shard from the mirror that has been shattered by Jerry's attempts to break in, Stephanie fights back, and in concert with her mother, who recovers to arm herself with Jerry's pistol, Jerry is finally overcome. In her discussion of the film, Erens argues that the film 'serves to valorise women's maternal role and the strong female bonding which exists between mothers and daughters. Such valorisation is an exception in mainstream cinema, both past and present.'[49]

Conclusions: Bringing It All Back Home

To conclude, I now want to return to the contemporary resonances of the neo-gothic films, and to point again to their cinematic and cultural contexts. Reviewing the generic and narrative characteristics of the top 20 grossing films at the American box office since 1977, Peter Krämer argues that 'family-adventure movies are the most successful production trend in American cinema since the late 1970s'.[50] Krämer suggests that 'the cultural work that films' narratives perform to reconcile family members with each other on the screen translates into a kind of social work performed by the films on the familial units in the auditorium'.[51] While none of the neo-gothic films discussed reached the blockbusting levels of family films that Krämer discusses, several of these films had a significant, or respectable, box office presence.[52] These films are interesting in the ways that they exploit the shadows or undercurrents of the family film. As Robin Wood has argued, in the period since the release of *Psycho*, 'the horror film has become both American and familial and the monster has taken on a new guise'.[53] The threatening domestic spaces of the neo-gothic films have strong parallels with Wood's 'terrible house', which he sees as a feature of family horror. The neo-gothic films recast the continuum between woman–home–family–domesticity by exploring the potentially sinister side of this picture for women. As I have illustrated, issues of financial entrapment, emotional distress, physical violence and a crisis of trust in gender relations are played out from a female perspective. In his review of *What Lies Beneath*, Doherty argues that the film is:

> ... emphatically female-centered and overtly feminist: it reads like a large scale, big star version of the kind of woman-fights-back melodramas that supply the Lifetime network with the bulk of its original programming. A courageous journey to self-actualization by a spunky female is set against the self-absorption of a male who at once neglects her needs and smothers her life force.[54]

These films suggest that the power differentials between men and women are still a live and vibrant issue through the 1990s and into the early twenty-first century, despite the social and cultural advances made by women through feminism, and however complicated the balance between femininity and heterosexual desire might be in the post-feminist moment. Susan Faludi forcefully argues that American women's most pressing concerns are not with 'missing out' on the ideals of home and hearth, but with equality in the division of labour, at home and in the workplace:

> In public opinion surveys, women consistently rank their own inequality, at work and at home, among their most urgent concerns. Over and over, women complain to pollsters about a lack of economic, not marital, opportunities; they protest that working men, not working women, fail to spend time in the nursery and the kitchen... it is justice for their gender, not

wedding rings and cradles, that women believe to be in desperately short supply.[55]

It is through these films' use of the gothic mode that these questions, 'old' or established in feminist discourses, come back to haunt the contemporary moment and force us to experience a rearticulation or recasting of female fears by bringing questions of female agency back home.

Conclusions

The Currency of
Hollywood Heroines

The preceding chapters of this book have demonstrated that Hollywood heroines are complex and highly engaging figures. They are often the starting point for the viewing of Hollywood cinema by film fans, historians, critics and theorists alike. Hollywood heroines are generated out of particular moments in Hollywood production, and are conditioned by the structures of genre and of narrative. They are also, though, generative of questions and debates about female identities, desires and roles. The forms in which they emerge are conditioned by textual processes of narrativity, and by a web of socio-cultural discourses existent in the contexts of these texts, a web that encompasses discourses in the popular and the critical spheres. Hollywood heroines, then, are generative figures.

In my discussions of heroines in *film noir*, and the female gothic film, their generic constitution and their generic transformations, I hope I have captured some of these complexities. In my chapters examining *film noir* and neo-*noir*, I have traced female characters and stories that are telling of women's identities across private and public spheres, and which explore the specificities of women's working lives and their professional identities as offering a way of thinking of women as narratively and socially active in ways that exceed their sexuality. In my chapters on female modifications of *film noir* in the 1940s, and on female-addressed neo-*noir* of the 1980s and 1990s, I have tried to look across a range of female characters that extends far beyond a 'vice–virtue' polarity of *femme fatale* versus female redeemer. In my chapters examining the female gothic film, and its contemporary neo-gothic revival, I have tried to address the gendered dynamics of the woman's film and the ways in which the gothic mode is deployed on film. I have examined the ways in which the complex processes of its narrativity offers ways of thinking about questions of women's relation to the domestic sphere, heterosexual relations and their transformations from the 1940s to the present.

The impulse to write this book began with my desire to examine a wider array of public femininities in *film noir* and the female gothic film; to revisit and to tell, or retell, the stories of an array of female figures in two particular genres that had been, in some senses, at the margins of feminist attention. I have tried to argue for the meanings, the currency, of these figures, to bring them out of the shadows and to realise these meanings through my discussion. A wide, vibrant and fascinating array of Hollywood heroines, of course, extends far beyond the orbit of this book. There have been many female figures that I encountered in my research that I could not cover within the framework of my discussion. But I hope that others will also engage with this array and enjoy the process of tracing these women, and bringing their stories into the light.

Notes

Notes to Introduction

1 Barry Keith Grant, *Film Genre Reader* (Austin: University of Texas Press, 1986), p. ix; cited in Steve Neale, *Genre and Hollywood* (London and New York: Routledge, 1999), p. 9.

2 Braudy, Leo, 'Genre: The Conventions of Connection', from *The World in a Frame: What We See in Films* (New York: Anchor Press, 1976); reprinted in Gerald Mast, Marshall Cohen and Leo Braudy (eds) *Film Theory and Criticism: Introductory Readings Fourth Edition* (New York and Oxford: Oxford University Press, 1992), pp. 435–452.

3 Steve Neale, *Genre* (London: BFI, 1980).

4 Steve Neale, 'Questions of Genre', *Screen*, 31 (1) (1990), 45–66.

5 Neale, cites G Lukow and S Ricci, 'The "Audience" Goes "Public": Inter-Textuality, Genre and the Responsibilities of Film Literacy', *On Film*, 12 (1984), 29–36, in Neale: *Genre and Hollywood*, p. 39.

6 Christine Gledhill, 'Rethinking genre', in Christine Gledhill and Linda Williams (eds) *Reinventing Film Studies* (London: Arnold, 2000), p. 221.

7 See, for example, E Ann Kaplan (ed) *Women in Film Noir* (London: BFI, 1978), and Kaplan (ed) *Women in Film Noir: New Edition* (London: BFI, 1998); Michael Renov, *Hollywood's Wartime Women: Representation and Ideology* (London: UMI Research 1988); Mary Ann Doane *Femmes Fatales: Feminism, Film Theory, Psychoanalysis* (New York and London: Routledge, 1991).

8 See, for example, the collected contributions in Christine Gledhill (ed) *Home is Where the Heart Is: Essays on Melodrama and the Woman's Film*; Mary Ann Doane, *The Desire to Desire: The Woman's Film of the 1940s* (Bloomington: Indiana University Press, 1987); Jeanine Basinger, *A Woman's View: How Hollywood Spoke to Women 1930–1960* (New York: Knopf, 1993).

9 Doane: *The Desire to Desire*, pp. 123–175.

10 H Porter Abbot, *The Cambridge Introduction to Narrative* (Cambridge: Cambridge University Press, 2002), p. 188. See also David Bordwell, *Narration in the Fiction Film* (London: Methuen, 1985).

11 Abbott: *The Cambridge Introduction to Narrative*, p. 187.

12 Teresa de Lauretis, *Alice Doesn't: Feminism, Semiotics, Cinema* (Bloomington: Indiana University Press, 1984), pp. 105–106.
13 Hilary Radner, 'Pretty Is as Pretty Does: Free Enterprise and the Marriage Plot' in Jim Collins, Hilary Radner and Ava Preacher Collins (eds) *Film Theory Goes to the Movies* (New York and London: Routledge, 1993), p. 58.

Notes to Chapter 1

1 John Houseman, 'Today's Hero: A Review', *Hollywood Quarterly* Vol. 2, No. 2 (Jan 1947), pp. 161–163, p. 163.
2 Raymond Borde and Étienne Chaumeton, 'Towards a Definition of *Film Noir*', from *Panorama du Film Noir Americain* (Paris: Les Éditions de Minuit, 1955); reprinted in Alain Silver and James Ursini (eds) *Film Noir Reader* (New York: Limelight Editions, 1996), pp. 17–25, p. 25. The first use of the term *'film noir'* is attributed to Nino Frank, 'Un Nouveau Genre 'Policier': l'Aventure Criminelle', *L'Écran Français* (August, 1946), reprinted in Alain Silver and James Ursini (eds) *Film Noir Reader: 2* (New York: Limelight Editions, 1999), p. 18. Jean-Pierre Chartier also uses the term in his essay 'Les Américains aussi font des films "noirs"', *La Révue de Cinéma* (November, 1946), trans. by Alain Silver and reprinted in *Film Noir Reader: 2*. Both these essays differentiated *film noir* from existing Hollywood genres. Frank saw the 'new' films as breaking with a previous Hollywood style, both visually and in terms of character representation. Chartier compares the American films to French *films noirs* of the 1930s, arguing that the American *films noirs* present a darker perspective on human relationships. On French *films noirs* as preceding the American ones, see Ginette Vincendeau, 'Noir is also a French Word, the French Antecedents of Film Noir', in Ian Cameron (ed) *The Movie Book of Film Noir* (London: Studio Vista, 1992). The first critical work that attempted a larger scale delineation of *film noir* as a group of films is usually taken as being Raymond Borde and Étienne Chaumeton's *Panorama du Film Noir Américain*.
3 Borde and Chaumeton: 'Towards a Definition of *Film Noir*', p. 25, emphases in original.
4 Steve Neale, *Genre and Hollywood* (London: Routledge, 2000), p. 161.
5 Neale: *Genre and Hollywood*, p. 160.
6 Christine Gledhill, '*Klute* 1: A Contemporary *Film Noir* and Feminist Criticism', in E Ann Kaplan (ed) *Women in Film Noir: New Edition* (1978; London: BFI, 1998).
7 Janey Place, 'Women in *Film Noir*', in E Ann Kaplan (ed.) *Women in Film Noir: New Edition* (1978; London: BFI, 1998).
8 Gledhill: '*Klute* 1', p. 27.
9 Gledhill: '*Klute* 1', p. 28.
10 Gledhill: '*Klute* 1', p. 28.
11 Place: 'Women in *Film Noir*', p. 47.

12   Place: 'Women in *Film Noir*', p. 47.

13   Place: 'Women in Film Noir', p. 47.

14   Neale: *Genre and Hollywood*, p. 160.

15   Lester Asheim, 'Film and the Zeitgeist', *Hollywood Quarterly*, Vol. 2, No. 4 (July 1947), pp. 414–416, p. 415.

16   Asheim: 'Film and the Zeitgeist', p. 415. Asheim lists *Variety*'s top ten money-makers as follows: *Bells of St Mary's* (Leo McCarey, 1945), *Leave Her to Heaven* (John Stahl, 1945), *Blue Skies* (Stuart Heisler, 1946), *Road to Utopia* (Hal Walker, 1946), *Spellbound* (Alfred Hitchcock, 1945), *The Green Years* (Victor Saville, 1946), *Adventure* (Victor Fleming, 1945), *Easy to Wed* (Edward Buzzell, 1946), *Notorious* (Alfred Hitchcock, 1946), and *Two Years Before the Mast* (John Farrow, 1946). Asheim cites a 1946 Gallup poll of movie-goers' favourite movies as follows: *Bells of St Mary's*, *State Fair* (Walter Lang, 1945), *The Green Years*, *Mildred Pierce* (Michael Curtiz, 1945), *Leave Her to Heaven*, *Anna and the King of Siam* (John Cromwell, 1945), *Spellbound*, *Rhapsody in Blue* (Irving Rapper, 1945), and *Love Letters* (William Dieterle, 1945).

17   See also Mike Chopra Gant, *Hollywood Genres and Postwar America: Masculinity, Family and Nation in Popular Movies and Film Noir* (London: I.B.Tauris, 2005).

18   Examples cited in *Picturegoer*, 'Will the Goody-Goody Heroine Survive?', October 1946, include: (*Kitty* (Mitchell Leisen, 1945), *Diary of a Chambermaid* (Jean Renoir, 1946) and *Pink String and Sealing Wax* (Robert Hamer, 1946)), the epic in Technicolor (*Caesar and Cleopatra* (Gabriel Pascal, 1946)), the western (*Duel in the Sun* (King Vidor, 1946)), the 'woman's picture' drama (*A Stolen Life* (Curtis Bernhardt, 1946)), the cycle of British Gainsborough costume dramas are cited alongside 'the ruthless woman' in the crime film such as *Scarlet Street* (Fritz Lang, 1945), *The Postman Always Rings Twice* (Tay Garnett, 1946), *Gilda* (Charles Vidor, 1946) and *The Big Sleep* (Howard Hawks, 1946).

19   Neale: *Genre and Hollywood*, p. 163.

20   See Herb Lightman, 'The Subjective Camera', *American Cinematographer*, February 1946, p. 46 and p. 66, Herb Lightman, 'The Fluid Camera', *American Cinematographer*, March 1946, p. 82 and pp. 102–103, and Herb Lightman, 'Mood in the Motion Picture', *American Cinematographer*, February 1947, pp. 48–49 and p. 69.

21   Elizbeth Cowie, '*Film Noir* and Women', in Joan Copjec (ed) *Shades of Noir* (London: Verso, 1993), p. 130.

22   Frank Krutnik, *In a Lonely Street: Film Noir, Genre, Masculinity* (London and New York: Routledge, 1991), p. 86, in Cowie: '*Film Noir* and Women', p. 125.

23   Cowie: '*Film Noir* and Women' cites James Damico, 'Film Noir: A Modest Proposal', *Film Reader*, No. 3 (1978), Foster Hirsch, *Film Noir: The Dark Side of the Screen* (New York: A S Barnes, 1981), and Marc Vernet, 'The Filmic Transaction: On the Openings of *Films Noirs*', *Velvet Light Trap*, No. 20 (Summer 1983), in Cowie, pp. 122–123.

24 Cowie: '*Film Noir* and Women', p. 126.

25 Cowie: '*Film Noir* and Women', p. 135.

26 Cowie: '*Film Noir* and Women', pp. 132–137.

27 Cowie: '*Film Noir* and Women', p. 137.

28 Cowie: '*Film Noir* and Women', p. 137.

29 Richard Maltby, 'The Politics of the Maladjusted Text', in Ian Cameron (ed) *The Movie Book of Film Noir* (London: Studio Vista, 1992).

30 Angela Martin, "Gilda Didn't Do Any of Those Things You've Been Losing Sleep Over!': The Central Women of 40s *Films Noirs*', in E Ann Kaplan (ed) *Women in Film Noir: New Edition* (London: BFI, 1998).

31 Martin: 'The Central Women of 40s *Films Noirs*', p. 205.

32 For example, Vera Caspary wrote the source novel for *Laura* with Betty Reinhardt collaborating with male writers on the screenplay, Virginia Van Upp wrote the screenplay for *Gilda* and produced the film, Joan Harrison collaborated on screenplays for *Suspicion* (Alfred Hitchcock, 1941) and *Saboteur* (Alfred Hitchcock, 1942), and produced *Phantom Lady* (Robert Siodmak, 1944), *Dark Waters* (André de Toth, 1944), *The Strange Affair of Uncle Harry* (Robert Siodmak, 1945), *Nocturne* (Edwin L Marin, 1946) and *They Won't Believe Me* (Irving Pichel, 1947); Ida Lupino directed *Outrage* (1950) and *The Hitch-hiker* (1953).

33 Martin: 'The Central Women of 40s *Films Noirs*', p. 209.

34 Kathryn Kalinak, 'The Fallen Woman and the Virtuous Wife: Musical Stereotypes in *The Informer*, *Gone with the Wind*, and *Laura*', *Film Reader*, 5 (1982), 76–82, and Richard Dyer, 'Postscript: Queers and Women in Film Noir', in E Ann Kaplan (ed) *Women in Film Noir: New Edition* (London: BFI, 1998).

35 Joyce Nelson, '*Mildred Pierce* Reconsidered', *Film Reader*, No. 2 (1977); Pam Cook, 'Duplicity in *Mildred Pierce*', in E Ann Kaplan (ed) *Women in Film Noir* (London: BFI, 1978); Linda Williams, 'Feminist Film Theory: *Mildred Pierce* and the Second World War', in E Deirdre Pribram (ed) *Female Spectators: Looking at Film and Television* (London: Verso, 1988); and Mary Beth Haralovich, 'Selling *Mildred Pierce*: A Case Study in Movie Promotion', in Thomas Schatz, *Boom and Bust: The American Cinema in the 1940s* (New York: Charles Scribner's Sons, 1997), pp. 196–202.

36 Richard Dyer, 'Resistance Through Charisma: Rita Hayworth and *Gilda*', in E Ann Kaplan (ed) *Women in Film Noir* (London: BFI, 1978).

37 Elizabeth Ward, 'The Unintended *Femme Fatale*: *The File on Thelma Jordan* and *Pushover*', in Alain Silver and James Ursini (eds) *Film Noir Reader 2* (New York: Limelight Editions, 1999).

38 See also Julie Grossman, 'Film Noir's "*Femme Fatales*": Hard-Boiled Women and Moving Beyond Gender Fantasies', *Quarterly Review of Film and Video*, Vol. 24, No. 1 (Jan 2007), forthcoming.

39 Thomas Schatz *Boom and Bust: American Cinema During the 1940s* (Berkeley: University of California Press, 1999), p. 71.

40 Schatz: *Boom and Bust*, pp. 69–71; D'Ann Campbell, *Women at War with America: Private Lives in a Patriotic Era* (Cambridge, Mass and London: Harvard University Press, 1984), p. 11.

41 Schatz: *Boom and Bust*, p. 70.

42 Schatz: *Boom and Bust*, p. 70.

43 *Motion Picture Herald*, 'Romantic Drama Customer Choice', 8 June 1946.

44 Schatz: *Boom and Bust*, p. 76.

45 Lizzie Francke, *Script Girls: Women Screenwriters in Hollywood* (London: BFI, 1994), p. 45.

46 Catherine Turney, quoted in Francke: *Script Girls*, p. 47.

47 For a longer discussion of Van Upp's role, see Francke: *Script Girls*, pp. 60–65; Sheri Chinen Biesen, 'Joan Harrison, Virginia Van Upp and Women Behind-the-Scenes in Wartime Film Noir', *Quarterly Review of Film and Video*, 20 (2) (2003), 125–144.

48 See Francke: *Script Girls*, pp. 80–85; Naomi Wise, 'The Hawksian Woman', *Take One*, Vol. 3, No. 3, January–February 1971, and Leigh Brackett, 'A Comment on "The Hawksian Woman"', *Take One*, Vol. 3, No. 8, July–August 1971, both reprinted in Jim Hillier and Peter Wollen (eds) *Howard Hawks: American Artist* (London: BFI, 1996).

49 Francke: *Script Girls*, pp. 55–56.

50 Barbara Berch, 'A Hitchcock Alumna: Introducing Joan Harrison, Hollywood's Only Full-Fledged Woman Producer', *New York Times*, 27 June 1943.

51 Fred Stanley, 'Hollywood Bows to the Ladies', *New York Times*, 7 January 1945, p.1 and p. 3, p. 1, also cited in Chinen Biesen, p. 127.

52 Stanley's discussion includes stars in producing roles: Constance Bennett's production of *Paris Underground* (Gregory Ratoff, 1945), Bette Davis' production of *A Stolen Life* (Curtis Bernhardt, 1946), and Ginger Rogers' plans to star-produce at RKO later in 1945, Stanley: 'Hollywood Bows to the Ladies', p. 1.

53 William Chafe, *The American Woman: Her Changing Social, Economic and Political Roles, 1920–1970* (London: Oxford University Press, 1974), Betty Friedan, *The Feminine Mystique* (1963; London and New York: Penguin, 1992), Rosen: *Popcorn Venus*, pp. 215–218.

54 Marjorie Rosen, *Popcorn Venus: Women, Movies and the American Dream* (New York: Avon Books, 1973), p. 201.

55 Chinen Biesen: 'Women Behind-the-Scenes in Wartime Film Noir', p. 125.

56 Maureen Honey, *Creating Rosie the Riveter: Class, Gender, and Propoganda During World War II* (Amherst: University of Massachusetts Press, 1984).

57 http://www.rosietheriveter.org/ Accessed 23 February 2006, 10.43.

58 Michael Renov, *Hollywood's Wartime Woman: Representation and Ideology* (Ann Arbor/London: UMI Research Press, 1988), p. 46, Honey: *Creating Rosie the Riveter*, p. 97, and D'Ann Campbell, *Women at War With America: Private Lives in a Patriotic Era* (Cambridge, Mass and London: Harvard University Press, 1984), p. 72.

59 Campbell: *Women at War With America*, p. 72.

60 Campbell: *Women at War With America*, p. 72.

61 Campbell: *Women at War With America*, p. 72.

62 Campbell: *Women at War With America*, p. 72.

63 Campbell: *Women at War With America*, p. 5.
64 Source: Women's Bureau, *Women as Workers: A Statistical Guide* (Washington D.C. 1953), cited in Campbell: *Women at War With America*, p. 239.
65 Campbell: *Women at War With America*, p. 108.
66 Leah Price and Pamela Thurschwell, 'Introduction: Invisible Hands', in Price and Thurschwell (eds) *Literary Secretaries/Secretarial Culture* (London: Ashgate, 2005), pp. 3–4.
67 Price and Thurschwell: 'Introduction: Invisible Hands', p. 7, and Carolyn Christensen Nelson, *A New Woman Reader* (London: Broadview Press, 2001).
68 Honey: *Creating Rosie the Riveter*, pp. 201–202.
69 Campbell: *Women at War With America*, p. 108.
70 Honey: *Creating Rosie the Riveter*, pp. 120–122.
71 'When it becomes a souvenir', Smith-Corona, *Saturday Evening Post*, 4 November 1944, cited in Honey: *Creating Rosie the Riveter*, p. 121.
72 Raymond Chandler, 'The Simple Art of Murder', *Atlantic Monthly*, December 1944, reprinted in *Pearls Are a Nuisance* (1950; London: Penguin, 1976), p. 198.
73 Chandler: 'The Simple Art of Murder', p. 198.
74 Krutnik: *In a Lonely Street*, p. 86.
75 Maltby: 'The Politics of the Maladjusted Text', p. 39.
76 *Variety*, Review of *Phantom Lady*, 26 January 1944.
77 *Variety*, Review of *Phantom Lady*, 26 January 1944.
78 See Laura Mulvey, 'Visual Pleasure and Narrative Cinema', *Screen*, 16 (3) (1975), 6–18; reprinted in *The Sexual Subject: A Screen Reader in Sexuality* (London: Routledge, 1992).
79 Krutnik: *In a Lonely Street*, p. 194.
80 Krutnik: *In a Lonely Street*, p. 194.
81 Krutnik: *In a Lonely Street*, p. 194.
82 Krutnik: *In a Lonely Street*, p. 194.
83 Krutnik: *In a Lonely Street*, p. 194.
84 On Nancy Drew see Sally Parry, 'The Secret of the Feminist Heroine: The Search for Values in Nancy Drew and Judy Bolton', and Deborah L Siegel, 'Nancy Drew as New Girl Wonder: Solving It All for the 1930s', in Sherrie Inness (ed) *Nancy Drew and Company: Culture, Gender and the Girls' Series* (Bowling Green State University Press, 1997); and Melanie Rehak, *Girl Sleuth: Nancy Drew and the Women Who Created Her* (London: Harvest Books, 2006).
85 On the history of the female investigator figure in literary fiction, see Jane Pennell, 'The Female Detective: Pre and Post Women's Lib', *Clues: A Journal of Detection*, Vol. 6, No. 2 (1985), pp. 85–98.
86 Neale: *Genre and Hollywood*, p. 72.
87 Cowie: 'Film Noir and Women', p. 132.
88 Cowie: 'Film Noir and Women', p. 133.
89 Cowie: 'Film Noir and Women', p. 133.

90 David Bordwell, *Narration in the Fiction Film* (London: Methuen, 1985), p. 65, cited in Neale: *Genre and Hollywood*, p. 75.
91 Neale: *Genre and Hollywood*, p. 75.
92 Bordwell: *Narration in the Fiction Film*, p. 65, in Neale: *Genre and Hollywood*, p. 75.
93 *Variety*, Review of *Phantom Lady*, 26 January 1944.
94 Krutnik: *In a Lonely Street*, p. 95.
95 Virginia Wright Wexman, *Creating the Couple: Love, Marriage and Hollywood Performance* (Princeton, Princeton University Press, 1993), p. 25.
96 Wexman: *Creating the Couple*, p. 31.
97 Molly Haskell, 'Man's Favourite Sport? (Revisited)', pp. 107–109, in Jim Hillier and Peter Wollen (eds) *Howard Hawks: American Artist* (London: BFI, 1996), p. 109.
98 Haskell: 'Man's Favourite Sport? (Revisited)', p. 109.
99 Wise: 'The Hawksian Woman', p. 112.
100 Brackett: 'A Comment on "The Hawksian Woman"', p. 120.
101 Todd McCarthy, *Howard Hawks: The Grey Fox of Hollywood* (New York: Grove Press, 1997), pp. 347–348.
102 Twentieth Century-Fox, Pressbook for *Hot Spot*, 1941.
103 Universal, Pressbook for *Phantom Lady*, 1944.
104 Universal, Pressbook for *Phantom Lady*, 1944.
105 Twentieth Century-Fox, Pressbook for *The Dark Corner*, 1946.

Notes to Chapter 2

1 Fred Botting, *Gothic* (London and New York: Routledge, 1996), pp. 1–2.
2 Botting: *Gothic*, p. 2.
3 Botting: *Gothic*, p. 3.
4 Botting: *Gothic*, p. 3.
5 Ellen Moers, *Literary Women* (London: The Women's Press, 1963).
6 Moers: *Literary Women*, p. 121.
7 Moers: *Literary Women*, p. 121.
8 Moers: *Literary Women*, p. 122.
9 Moers: *Literary Women*, p. 122.
10 Moers: *Literary Women*, p. 122.
11 Moers: *Literary Women*, p. 123.
12 Moers: *Literary Women*, p. 126.
13 Moers: *Literary Women*, p. 126.
14 Moers: *Literary Women*, p. 126.
15 Moers: *Literary Women*, p. 126.
16 Moers: *Literary Women*, p. 91.
17 Moers: *Literary Women*, p. 126.
18 Norman Matson, 'Gooseflesh Special', *New York Times*, 28 May 1944, p. 7 and p. 23, p. 7.

19 Donald Barr, 'Don't Look Behind You', *New York Times*, 10 November 1946, p. 167.

20 Howard Mumford Jones, 'Publishing Time, Literary Time', *New York Times*, 29 June 1947, p. 1 and p. 24, p. 24.

21 Howard Mumford Jones, 'Publishing Time, Literary Time', *New York Times*, 29 June 1947, p. 1 and p. 24, p. 24.

22 Fred Stanley, 'Hollywood Shivers', *New York Times*, 28 May 1944, p. 3.

23 *Variety* Review for *Shadow of a Doubt*, 13 January 1943.

24 *Variety* Review for *The Spiral Staircase*, 9 January 1946.

25 *Variety* Review for *Undercurrent*, 2 October 1946.

26 *Variety* Reviews for *The Two Mrs Carrolls*, 2 April 1947, and *Sleep My Love*, 14 January 1948.

27 Lightman, Herb, '"Sleep My Love": Cinematic Psycho-thriller', *American Cinematographer*, February 1948, pp. 46–47 and p. 55.

28 Thomas Elsaesser, 'Tales of Sound and Fury: Observations on the Family Melodrama', *Monogram* 4 (1972), 2–15; reprinted in Christine Gledhill (ed) *Home is Where the Heart is: Studies in Melodrama and the Woman's Film* (London: BFI, 1987), p. 59.

29 Elsaesser: 'Tales of Sound and Fury', p. 58.

30 Elsaesser: 'Tales of Sound and Fury', p. 58.

31 Waldman, Diane, '"At last I can tell it to someone!": Feminine Point of View and Subjectivity in the Gothic Romance Film of the 1940s', *Cinema Journal* 23 (2) (1983), 29–40, 29.

32 Tania Modleski, *Loving with a Vengeance: Mass Produced Fantasies for Women* (New York and London: Methuen, 1984), p. 21.

33 Guy Barefoot, *Gaslight Melodrama: From Victorian London to 1940s Hollywood* (New York and London: Continuum, 2001).

34 Mary Ann Doane, *The Desire to Desire: The Woman's Film of the 1940s* (London: Macmillan, 1987), p. 123.

35 Andrew Britton, *Movie* 31/32.

36 Neale: *Genre and Hollywood*, p. 43.

37 Tzvetan Todorov, *Genres in Discourse*, trans. C. Porter (Cambridge: Cambridge University Press, 1990), p. 17, cited in Neale: *Genre and Hollywood*, p. 42.

38 Neale: *Genre and Hollywood*, p. 43.

39 Murray Smith, '*Film Noir*: The Female Gothic and *Deception*', *Wide Angle* 10, 1, pp. 62–75, p. 63.

40 Smith: '*Film Noir*: The Female Gothic and *Deception*', p. 64.

41 Smith: '*Film Noir*: The Female Gothic and *Deception*', p. 64.

42 Robert L Carringer, *The Making of Citizen Kane* (London: John Murray, 1985), p. 20; James Naremore, *The Magic World of Orson Welles* (New York: Oxford University Press, 1978), p. 112; and James Naremore, *More Than Night: Film Noir in its Contexts* (Berkeley: University of California Press, 1998), p. 4.

43 Neale: *Genre and Hollywood*, p. 164.

44 Norman Holland and Leona Sherman, 'Gothic Possibilities', *New Literary History*, Vol. 8, No. 2 (Winter, 1977), pp. 279–294; Claire Kahane, 'Gothic Mirrors and Feminine Identity', *Centennial Review*, 24 (1980), pp. 43–64.

45 Christopher Robinson, 'Daphne Du Maurier's *Rebecca*', Theatre Programme for Frank McGuinness Production of *Rebecca*, Theatre Royal, Plymouth, 7–12 February 2005.

46 Patsy Stoneman, *Brönte Transformations: The Cultural Dissemination of Jane Eyre and Wuthering Heights* (London: Prentice Hall/Harvester Wheatsheaf, 1996).

47 Thomas Schatz, *The Genius of the System: Hollywood Film-making in the Studio Era* (London: Faber and Faber, 1988), p. 327.

48 Schatz: *The Genius of the System*, p. 328.

49 Schatz: *The Genius of the System*, pp. 327–328.

50 Schatz: *The Genius of the System*, p. 327.

51 Schatz: *The Genius of the System*, p. 328.

52 Schatz: *The Genius of the System*, p. 329, and Jeffrey Sconce, 'Narrative Authority and Social Narrativity: The Cinematic Reconstitution of Brontë's *Jane Eyre*', in Janet Staiger (ed) *The Studio System* (New York: Rutgers University Press, 1995).

53 Schatz: *The Genius of the System*, p. 329.

54 Barefoot: *Gaslight Melodrama*, p. 4.

55 Barefoot: *Gaslight Melodrama*, p. 4.

56 Karen Anderson, *Wartime Women: Sex Roles, Family Relations and the Status of Women During World War II* (Westport, Connecticut: Greenwood Press, 1981), p. 84.

57 Campbell: *Women at War With America*, p. 5; Andrea Walsh, *Women's Film and Female Experience 1940–1950* (New York: Praeger, 1984), pp. 67–69.

58 Walsh: *Women's Film and Female Experience 1940–1950*, p. 67.

59 Modleski: *Loving With a Vengeance*, pp. 21–22; and Waldman 'At last I can tell it to someone!', pp. 38–40.

60 Modleski: *Loving With a Vengeance*, pp. 21–22.

61 Christine Gledhill (ed) *Home is Where the Heart Is: Essays on Melodrama and the Woman's Film* (London: BFI, 1987); Mary Ann Doane, *The Desire to Desire: The Woman's Film of the 1940s* (Bloomington: Indiana University Press, 1987); E Deidre Pribram (ed) *Female Spectators: Looking at Film and Television* (London: Verso, 1988); Jeanine Basinger, *A Woman's View: How Hollywood Spoke to Women 1930–1960* (New York: Knopf, 1993); Judith Mayne, *Cinema and Spectatorship* (London and New York: Routledge, 1993); and Jackie Stacey, *Star Gazing: Hollywood Cinema and Female Spectatorship* (London: Routledge, 1994).

62 Waldman, 'At last I can tell it to someone!', p. 31.

63 Waldman, 'At last I can tell it to someone!', p. 31, my emphasis.

64 Doane: *The Desire to Desire*, p. 123.

65 Doane: *The Desire to Desire*, p. 126.

66 Doane: *The Desire to Desire*, p. 179.

67   Doane: *The Desire to Desire*, p. 177.

68   Doane: *The Desire to Desire*, p. 126.

69   Mulvey, 'Visual Pleasure and Narrative Cinema' (1975), reprinted in *Screen* (ed) *The Sexual Subject: A Screen Reader in Sexuality* (London: Routledge, 1992), p. 28.

70   Mary Ann Doane, 'Film and the Masquerade: Theorizing the Female Spectator' *Screen*, Vol. 23, Nos 3–4 (1982), pp. 74–87; reprinted in *Screen* (ed) *The Sexual Subject: A Screen Reader in Sexuality*, pp. 233–234.

71   John Ellis, *Visible Fictions: Cinema, Television, Video, Revised Edition* (1982; London and New York: Routledge, 1995), p. 43.

72   Ian Green, 'Malefunction: A Contribution to the Debate on Masculinity in the Cinema', *Screen*, Vol. 25, Nos 4–5 (July–Oct 1984), pp. 36–48, p. 38.

73   Green, 'Malefunction', p. 38.

74   Green, 'Malefunction', p. 39.

75   Green, 'Malefunction', pp. 39–40.

76   Green, 'Malefunction', p. 40.

77   Botting: *Gothic*, p. 3.

78   Botting: *Gothic*, p. 3.

79   Moers: *Literary Women*, p. 90.

80   Coral Ann Howells, *Love, Mystery and Misery: Feeling in Gothic Fiction* (London: Athlone Press, 1978), p. 1. Howells takes her title from Anthony Frederick Holstein's novel, *Love, Mystery and Misery* (London: Minerva Press, 1810).

81   Heiland: *Gothic and Gender*, p. 5.

82   Heiland: *Gothic and Gender*, p. 5.

83   Charlene Bunnell, 'The Gothic: A Literary Genre's Transition to Film', in B Grant (ed) *Planks of Reason: Essays on the Horror Film* (London: Scarecrow Press, 1984), p. 81.

84   Elizabeth Cowie, *Representing the Woman: Cinema and Psychoanalysis* (Basingstoke: Macmillan, 1997), p. 42.

85   Cowie: *Representing the Woman*, p. 41.

86   Bordwell: *Narration in the Fiction Film*, p. 52, cited in Cowie: *Representing the Woman*, p. 44.

87   Cowie: *Representing the Woman*, p. 44.

88   Cowie: *Representing the Woman*, p. 42.

89   Cowie: *Representing the Woman*, p. 43.

90   Cowie: *Representing the Woman*, p. 45.

91   Cowie: *Representing the Woman*, p. 45.

92   This is Roland Barthes' 'hermeneutic code', Roland Barthes, *S/Z* (1970), trans. Richard Miller (London: Johnathan Cape, 1974), p. 79, cited in Cowie: *Representing the Woman*, p. 49.

93   Cowie: *Representing the Woman*, p. 49.

94   Waldman, 'At last I can tell it to someone!', pp. 29–30.

95   Bordwell: *Narration in the Fiction Film*, p. 65, in Neale: *Genre and Hollywood*, p. 75.

96   Alfred Hitchcock interviewed by Francois Truffaut, *Hitchcock* (New York: Simon and Schuster, 1967), p. 80, cited in Cowie: *Representing the Woman*, p. 51.
97   Cowie: *Representing the Woman*, pp. 52–53.
98   Moers: *Literary Women*, p. 91.
99   Pam Cook, 'No fixed address: the women's picture from *Outrage* to *Blue Steel*', in Steve Neale and Murray Smith (eds) *Contemporary Hollywood Cinema* (London and New York: Routledge, 1998), p. 235.
100 Botting: *Gothic*, p. 3.
101 Elsaesser: 'Tales of Sound and Fury', p. 51.
102 Elsaesser: 'Tales of Sound and Fury', p. 47.
103 Charlotte Brunsdon, 'Feminism, Postfeminism, Martha, Martha and Nigella', *Cinema Journal* 44, No. 2 (2005), pp. 110–116, p. 112. Brunsdon's discussion, focused on stylistic shifts in mainstream British and American lifestyle television programming, includes a key conceptualisation of how shifts in feminism can be traced through feminist assertions of identity and 'disidentity'. Her conceptualisation is highly relevant to feminist identity in film criticism on the female gothic film.
104 Moers: *Literary Women*, p. 126.

Notes to Chapter 3

1   Jeanine Basinger, *A Woman's View: How Hollywood Spoke to Women 1930–1960* (Hanover, New England: Wesleyan University Press, 1993), p. 319.
2   Waldman, 'At last I can tell it to someone!', p. 30.
3   Walker, '*Secret Beyond the Door*', p. 19.
4   David Bordwell, Janet Staiger and Kristin Thompson, *The Classical Hollywood Cinema: Film Style and Mode of Production to 1960* (London: Routledge, 1985), p. 16.
5   Bordwell, Staiger and Thompson: *The Classical Hollywood Cinema*, p. 16.
6   Lynne Pearce and Jackie Stacey, 'Introduction', in Pearce and Stacey (eds) *Romance Revisited* (London: Lawrence and Wishart, 1995), p. 15.
7   Pearce and Stacey: *Romance Revisited*, p. 16.
8   See, for example, Janice Radway, *Reading the Romance: Women, Patriarchy and Popular Literature* (1984; Chapel Hill and London: University of North Carolina Press, 1991); Modleski: *Loving with a Vengeance*; Helen Taylor, 'Romantic Readers', in Helen Carr (ed) *From My Guy to Sci Fi: Genre and Women's Writing in the Postmodern World* (London: Pandora Press, 1989), and Lynne Pearce and Gina Wisker (eds) *Fatal Attractions: Rescripting Romance in Contemporary Literature and Film* (London: Pluto Press, 1998).
9   Pearce and Stacey: *Romance Revisited*, p. 14.
10   Lynne Pearce and Gina Wisker, 'Rescripting Romance: An Introduction', in Pearce and Wisker (eds) *Rescripting Romance*, p. 1.
11   Pearce and Stacey: *Romance Revisited*, p. 15.

12 Maria LaPlace, 'Producing and Consuming the Woman's Film: Discursive Struggle in *Now Voyager*', in Gledhill: *Home is Where the Heart Is*, p. 139.

13 Marina Warner, 'The Uses of Enchantment', in Duncan Petrie (ed) *Cinema and the Realms of Enchantment: Lectures, Seminars and Essays by Marina Warner and Others, BFI Working Papers* (London: BFI, 1993), p. 29.

14 Marina Warner, 'The Uses of Enchantment', in Duncan Petrie (ed) *Cinema and the Realms of Enchantment: Lectures, Seminars and Essays by Marina Warner and Others, BFI Working Papers* (London: BFI, 1993), p. 29.

15 Marina Warner, 'The Uses of Enchantment', p. 29.

16 Warner, 'The Uses of Enchantment', p. 30.

17 François Truffaut, *Hitchcock*, Revised Edition with the collaboration of Helen G Scott (New York: Touchstone, Simon and Schuster, 1983), p. 132.

18 Truffaut, *Hitchcock*, p. 132, original emphasis.

19 Warner: 'The Uses of Enchantment', p. 30.

20 Warner: 'The Uses of Enchantment', p. 30.

21 Warner: 'The Uses of Enchantment', p. 30.

22 Cowie: 'Film Noir and Women', pp. 156–157.

23 For discussions of class in *Rebecca*, see Alison Light, 'Returning to Manderley': Romance Fiction, Female Sexuality and Class, *Feminist Review*, No. 16, Summer 1984, pp. 7–25, and Gina Wisker, 'Dangerous Borders: Daphne du Maurier's *Rebecca*: shaking the foundations of the romance of privilege, partying and place', *Journal of Gender Studies*, Vol. 12, No. 2, 2003, pp. 83–97.

24 Botting: *Gothic*, p. 11.

25 Botting: *Gothic*, p. 11.

26 Botting: *Gothic*, p. 11.

27 Annette Kuhn, with Frances Borzello, Jill Pack and Cassandra Wedd, 'Living dolls and "real women"', in Annette Kuhn, *The Power of the Image: Essays on Representation and Sexuality* (London: Routledge, 1985), p. 13.

28 Modleski: *The Women Who Knew Too Much*, p. 52.

29 Modleski: *The Women Who Knew Too Much*, p. 52.

30 Modleski: *The Women Who Knew Too Much*, p. 53.

31 Jane Gaines, 'Costume and Narrative: How Dress Tells the Woman's Story', in Jane Gaines and Charlotte Herzog (eds) *Fabrications: Costume and the Female Body* (New York and London: Routledge, 1990), p. 181.

32 Ruth Roland, 'Personality in Dress', *Photoplay* 8, No. 1 (June 1915), p. 134, cited in Gaines: 'How Dress Tells the Woman's Story', p. 187.

33 Gaines: 'How Dress Tells the Woman's Story', p. 203.

34 Pressbook for *Rebecca*, Selznick International Pictures, 1940.

35 Pressbook for *Rebecca*, Selznick International Pictures, 1940.

36 Doane: *The Desire to Desire*, p. 163.

37 Modleski: *The Women Who Knew Too Much*, p. 45.

38 Modleski: *The Women Who Knew Too Much*, p. 50.

39 Modleski: *The Women Who Knew Too Much*, p. 46.

40 Modleski: *The Women Who Knew Too Much*, p. 50.

41   Modleski: *The Women Who Knew Too Much*, p. 50, original emphases.

42   Modleski: *The Women Who Knew Too Much*, p. 50, original emphases.

43   Radway: *Reading the Romance*, p. 134.

44   Modleski: *The Women Who Knew Too Much*, p. 45.

45   Botting: *Gothic*, p. 11.

46   Bonitzer: 'Partial Vision: Film and the Labyrinth', p. 58, cited in Modleski, *The Women Who Knew Too Much*, p. 53.

47   Woodall: 'Introduction: facing the subject', p. 3.

48   Woodall: 'Introduction: facing the subject', p. 2.

49   Woodall: 'Introduction: facing the subject', p. 3.

50   Elisabeth Bronfen, *Over Her Dead Body: Death, femininity and the aesthetic* (Manchester: Manchester University Press, 1992), p. x.

51   Woodall: 'Introduction: facing the subject', p. 1.

52   Woodall: 'Introduction: facing the subject', p. 8. Woodall cites Aristotles's *Poetics*, iv 3; iv 8; xv 8.

53   Woodall: 'Introduction: facing the subject', p. 8.

54   David Piper: *Personality and the Portrait* (London: BBC Publications, 1973), p. 11.

55   Piper: *Personality and the Portrait*, p. 11. André Bazin also discusses the role of images of the dead in ancient cultures in 'The Ontology of the Photographic Image', in *What Is Cinema?: Volume I*, pp. 9–10.

56   Piper: *Personality and the Portrait*, p. 11.

57   Otto Rank, *The Double: A Psychoanalytic Study*, ed. and trans. by Harry Tucker, JR (London: Maresfield Library, 1989).

58   Sigmund Freud, 'The Uncanny' (1919), reprinted in *Penguin Freud Library Volume 14: Art and Literature*, ed. by Albert Dickson (1985; London: Penguin, 1990), p. 356.

59   Freud: 'The Uncanny', p. 357.

60   Freud: 'The Uncanny', p. 357.

61   Bronfen: *Over Her Dead Body*, p. xii.

62   Bronfen: *Over Her Dead Body*, p. xii.

63   Bronfen: *Over Her Dead Body*, p. xii.

64   Bronfen: *Over Her Dead Body*, p. xii.

65   Bronfen: *Over Her Dead Body*, p. x.

66   Edgar Allan Poe, 'The Oval Portrait', in *Tales of Mystery and Imagination* (Hertfordshire: Wordsworth Editions, 1993).

67   Bronfen: *Over Her Dead Body*, p. 112.

68   Bronfen: *Over Her Dead Body*, p. x.

Notes to Chapter 4

1   Thomas Elsaesser, 'Tales of Sound and Fury: Observations on the Family Melodrama', *Monogram* No. 4, p. 972, pp. 2–15; reprinted in Christine Gledhill (ed) *Home is Where the Heart Is: Studies in Melodrama and the Woman's Film* (London: BFI, 1987), pp. 43–69, p. 50.

2   Elsaesser: 'Tales of Sound and Fury', p. 51.

3   Modleski: *The Women Who Knew Too Much*, p. 53.

4   Modleski: *The Women Who Knew Too Much*, p. 53.

5   Michel Chion, *The Voice in Cinema*, ed. and trans. Claudia Gorbman (1982; New York: Columbia University Press, 1999), p. 49.

6   Chion: *The Voice in Cinema*, p. 49.

7   Rick Altman, 'Moving Lips: Cinema as Ventriloquism', *Yale French Studies*, 60 (1980), 67–79, 73–74.

8   Altman: 'Moving Lips', p. 74.

9   Altman: 'Moving Lips', p. 74.

10 Chion: *The Voice in Cinema*, p. 18, original emphasis.

11 Chion: *Audio-Vision*, p. 72.

12 Chion: *The Voice in Cinema*, p. 21, original emphasis.

13 Chion: *The Voice in Cinema*, p. 6, original emphases.

14 Chion: *The Voice in Cinema*, p. 5.

15 Chion: *The Voice in Cinema*, p. 5.

16 Roland Barthes, 'The Grain of the Voice', in *Image/Music/Text* (London: Fontana, 1977), Essays selected and translated by Stephen Heath, p. 188.

17 Barthes: 'The Grain of the Voice', pp. 181–182.

18 Chion: *The Voice in Cinema*, p. 126.

19 Chion: *The Voice in Cinema*, p. 125.

20 Gill Branston, '... Viewer, I Listened to Him ..., Voices, Masculinity, *In the Line of Fire*', in *Me Jane: Masculinity, Movies and Women*, ed. by Pat Kirkham and Janet Thumim (London: Lawrence and Wishart, 1995), pp. 38–39.

21 Chion: *The Voice in Cinema*, p. 21.

22 Pascal Bonitzer, 'Partial Vision: Film and the Labyrinth', p. 58, cited in Modleski, *The Women Who Knew Too Much*, p. 53.

23 Chion: *The Voice in Cinema*, p. 23.

24 Chion: *The Voice in Cinema*, pp. 23–24.

25 Mary Ann Doane, '*Caught* and *Rebecca*: The Inscription of Femininity as Absence', *Enclitic*, 5–6 (1981–1982), 75–89, 88–89.

26 Chion: *The Voice in Cinema*, p. 140.

27 Chion: *The Voice in Cinema*, p. 140.

28 Alan Williams, 'Historical and Theoretical Issues in the Coming of Recorded Sound to the Cinema', in Rick Altman (ed) *Sound Theory and Sound Practice* (London: Routledge, 1992), pp. 134–135, cited in Branston, 'Viewer, I Listened to Him', p. 42.

29 On voice and speech styles in the action movie, see Yvonne Tasker, 'Tough Guys and Wise Guys', in her *Spectacular Bodies: Gender, Genre and the Action Cinema* (New York and London: Routledge, 1993), pp. 73–90.

30 Branston: 'Viewer, I Listened to Him', p. 44.

31 Jane Tompkins, *West of Everything: The Inner Life of Westerns* (Oxford: Oxford Unversity Press, 1992), cited in Branston: 'Viewer, I Listened to Him', p. 44.

32 Branston: 'Viewer, I Listened to Him', p. 44.

33 Branston: 'Viewer, I Listened to Him', p. 46.

34 The effect of Rebecca's laughter on the men in the film is discussed by Modleski: *The Women Who Knew Too Much*, p. 54. For a fascinating discussion of the laugh of Bertha Mason, the woman in the past in *Jane Eyre*, see Cora Kaplan, *Seachanges: Culture and Feminism* (London: Verso, 1986), pp. 171–174.

35 Branston: 'Viewer, I Listened to Him', p. 45.

36 Freud: 'The Uncanny', p. 356.

37 Chion: *Audio-Vision*, p. 80.

38 Claudia Gorbman, *Unheard Melodies: Narrative Film Music* (London: BFI, 1987), pp. 2–3.

39 Gorbman: *Unheard Melodies*, p. 3, original emphases.

40 Gorbman: *Unheard Melodies*, p. 3.

41 Gorbman: *Unheard Melodies*, p. 3.

42 Steve Neale has examined the sound of bells as forming part of a pattern of meaningful sounds in *Letter From an Unknown Woman* (Max Ophuls, 1948) in his 'Narration, Point of View and Patterns in the Soundtrack of *Letter of an Unknown Woman*', in John Gibbs and Douglas Pye (eds) *Style and Meaning: Studies in the Detailed Analysis of Film* (Manchester: Manchester University Press, 2005), pp. 98–107.

43 Gorbman: *Unheard Melodies*, pp. 22–23.

44 Gorbman: *Unheard Melodies*, p. 23.

45 Elsaesser: 'Tales of Sound and Fury', p. 51.

46 Bronfen: *Over Her Dead Body*, p. x.

47 Gorbman, citing Roger Manvell and John Huntley, *The Technique of Film Music* (New York: Hastings House, 1975), pp. 20–21, in her *Unheard Melodies*, p. 39.

48 Gorbman: *Unheard Melodies*, p. 40.

49 Gorbman: *Unheard Melodies*, p. 39.

50 Gorbman: *Unheard Melodies*, p. 6.

51 Gorbman cites Didier Anzieu, "L'enveloppe sonore du soi", *Nouvelle Revue de Psychanalyse*, 13 (1976), 161–179, 175, in her *Unheard Melodies*, p. 6.

52 Francis Hofstein, 'Drogue et musique', *Musique en jeu* 9 (November 1972), 111–115, cited in Gorbman, *Unheard Melodies*, p. 63.

53 Guy Rosolato, 'La Voix: Entre corps et langage', *Revue francaise de psychanalyse* 38, 1 (Jan. 1974), 75–94, cited in Gorbman, p. 63.

54 Gorbman, citing Roger Manvell and John Huntley, *The Technique of Film Music* (New York: Hastings House, 1975), pp. 20–21, in her *Unheard Melodies*, p. 39.

55 Patrick McGilligan discusses the production history of *Gaslight* in his biography of George Cukor. He suggests that the scriptwriters, Walter Reisch and John Van Druten, were concerned about the casting of Ingrid Bergman in the part of Paula. McGilligan relates that Reisch could not see how 'a powerful woman with enormous shoulders, strong and healthy' could play the fragile character. Cukor, however, considered the transformation to be a challenge: 'What's the difference? What if we do have a powerful woman? It will be twice

as interesting to see whether she will be able to fight back, whether he will be able to really ruin her, or break her.' McGilligan also states: 'According to Reisch, Cukor gave the ending particular emphasis: where Gregory Anton is strapped to a chair and Paula Alquist becomes for a passing moment, "a goddess of vengeance" (Reisch's words).' (Patrick McGilligan, *George Cukor: A Double Life* (London: Faber and Faber, 1992), pp. 176–177.)

56 Doane: *The Desire to Desire*, p. 135.
57 Waldman: 'At last I can tell it to someone!', p. 36.
58 Sandra Gilbert and Susan Gubar, *The Madwoman in the Attic: The Woman Writer and the Nineteenth Century Literary Imagination* (New Haven and London: Yale University Press, 1979).
59 Cook: 'No fixed address', p. 235.
60 Botting: *Gothic*, p. 98.
61 Botting: *Gothic*, p. 99.
62 Florett Robinson, 'Hiss-s-s-s-s Through the Years: Styles in movie villains change, but whether Western desperadoes, city slickers or Japs, they're all bad men', *New York Times*, 15 August 1943, p. 16.
63 Barbara Deming, *Running Away From Myself: A Dream Portrait of America Drawn from the Films of the Forties* (New York: Grossman Publishers, 1969), p. 96. Deming's book was written in 1950, but was not published until 1969.
64 Deming: *Running Away From Myself*, p. 99.
65 Kaja Silverman, *Male Subjectivity at the Margins* (New York and London: Routledge, 1992), p. 53.
66 Silverman: *Male Subjectivity at the Margins*, p. 52.
67 Andrea Walsh, *Women's Film and Female Experience 1940–1950* (New York: Praeger, 1984), p. 182.
68 Marina Warner, 'The Uses of Enchantment', p. 29.
69 Through her research on women readers of romance fiction, Janice Radway asserts that the hero of the ideal romance is characterised by the nurturing and caring role that he takes on in relation to the heroine. See Janice Radway, *Reading the Romance: Women, Patriarchy and Popular Literature* (1984; Carolina: University of North Carolina Press, 1991), pp. 134–147.
70 See Diane Waldman, 'At last I can tell it to someone!', p. 33, and Alfred Hitchcock's interview with Francois Truffaut in *Hitchcock* (New York: Secker and Warburg, 1967), pp. 101–103.
71 Waldman: 'At last I can tell it to someone!', p. 38.
72 Radway: *Reading the Romance*, p. 134.
73 Basinger: *A Woman's View*, p. 319.

Notes to Chapter 5

1 Noel Carroll, 'The Future of Allusion: Hollywood in the Seventies (and Beyond)', *October*, No. 2 (Spring 1982), pp. 51–81; reprinted in Carroll, *Interpreting the Moving Image* (Cambridge: Cambridge University Press,

1998), p. 253. On the development of a critically engaged 'fan base' for noir, see also: Marc Vernet, '*Film Noir* on the Edge of Doom', in Joan Copjec: *Shades of Noir* (London: Verso, 1993), p. 26; and Peter Stanfield, ' "Film Noir Like You've Never Seen": Jim Thompson Adaptations and Cycles of Neo-Noir', in Steve Neale (ed) *Genre and Contemporary Hollywood* (London: BFI, 2002), pp. 254–256.

2   Geoffrey O'Brien, 'The Return of Film Noir!', *New York Review of Books*, 14 August 1991; also cited in Naremore: *More Than Night*, p. 168.

3   Carroll: 'The Future of Allusion', p. 240.

4   Carroll: 'The Future of Allusion', p. 241.

5   Carroll: 'The Future of Allusion', p. 241.

6   Thomas Schatz, 'The New Hollywood', in Jim Collins, Hilary Radner and Ava Preacher Collins (eds) *Film Theory Goes to the Movies* (New York and London: Routledge, 1993), p. 8.

7   Schatz: 'The New Hollywood', p. 11; Peter Krämer, 'Post-Classical Hollywood', in John Hill and Pamela Church Gibson (eds) *The Oxford Guide to Film Studies* (Oxford: Oxford University Press, 1998), pp. 289–307.

8   Schatz: 'The New Hollywood', p. 11.

9   Schatz: 'The New Hollywood', p. 12.

10   Naremore: *More Than Night*, p. 258.

11   Naremore: *More Than Night*, p. 258.

12   Naremore: *More Than Night*, p. 259.

13   Naremore: *More Than Night*, p. 259.

14   Naremore: *More Than Night*, p. 259.

15   Naremore: *More Than Night*, p. 259.

16   Naremore: *More Than Night*, p. 259.

17   Naremore: *More Than Night*, p. 259. On *The Fugitive* and *Miami Vice*, see James Ursini, 'Angst at Sixty Fields Per Second', and Jeremy Butler, '*Miami Vice*: The Legacy of *Film Noir*', in Alain Silver and James Ursini (eds) *Film Noir Reader* (New York: Limelight Editions, 1996).

18   Schatz: 'The New Hollywood', p. 13.

19   Schatz: 'The New Hollywood', p. 13.

20   See Thomas Doherty, *Teenagers and Teenpics: The Juvenilization of American Movies in the 1950s* (Boston and London: Unwin Hyman, 1988).

21   Linda Ruth Williams and Michael Hammond, 'Introduction: The 1960s', in Linda Ruth Williams and Michael Hammond (eds) *Contemporary American Cinema* (New York: Open University Press/McGraw Hill, 2006), p. 5.

22   Williams and Hammond: 'Introduction: The 1960s', in *Contemporary American Cinema*, p. 6.

23   Williams and Hammond: 'Introduction: The 1960s', in *Contemporary American Cinema*, p. 6.

24   Williams and Hammond: 'Introduction: The 1960s', in *Contemporary American Cinema*, p. 6.

25   Schatz: 'The New Hollywood', p. 17.

26   Schatz: 'The New Hollywood', pp. 19–20.

27   Schatz: 'The New Hollywood', p. 20.

28   Schatz: 'The New Hollywood', p. 25.

29   Schatz: 'The New Hollywood', p. 25.

30   Schatz: 'The New Hollywood', p. 25.

31   Schatz: 'The New Hollywood', p. 33; see also Justin Wyatt, *High Concept: Movies and Marketing in Hollywood* (Austin: University of Texas Press, 1994).

32   Mark Crispin Miller, 'Hollywood: The Ad', *Atlantic Monthly*, April 1990, pp. 49–52, and Richard Schickel, 'The Crisis in Movie Narrative', *Gannett Centre Journal*, 3, Summer 1989, cited in Schatz: 'The New Hollywood', pp. 32–33.

33   Schatz: 'The New Hollywood', p. 34.

34   Schatz: 'The New Hollywood', p. 34.

35   Schatz: 'The New Hollywood', p. 35.

36   Schatz: 'The New Hollywood', p. 35.

37   Linda Ruth Williams, *The Erotic Thriller in Contemporary Cinema* (Edinburgh: Edinburgh University Press, 2005), pp. 253–276.

38   Carroll: 'The Future of Allusion', p. 244.

39   Todd Erickson, 'Kill Me Again: Movement Becomes Genre', in Silver and Ursini (eds) *Film Noir Reader*.

40   Erickson: 'Movement Becomes Genre', in Silver and Ursini (eds) *Film Noir Reader*.

41   Rosalind Coward, '"Sexual Liberation" and the family', *m/f*, No. 1 (1978), pp. 7–24, p. 7.

42   Coward: '"Sexual Liberation" and the family', p. 7; on feminist activism against the Miss America beauty pageant; see also Suzanna Danuta Walters, *Material Girls: Making Sense of Feminist Cultural Theory* (Berkeley and London: University of California Press, 1995), pp. 30–31.

43   Coward: '"Sexual Liberation" and the family', pp. 7–8.

44   Coward: '"Sexual Liberation" and the family', pp. 14–15.

45   Coward: '"Sexual Liberation" and the family', p. 15.

46   Maria LaPlace, 'Producing and Consuming the Woman's Film: Discursive Struggle in *Now Voyager*', in Gledhill: *Home is Where the Heart Is*, p. 139.

47   Hilary Radner, 'Pretty Is as Pretty Does: Free Enterprise and the Marriage Plot', in Jim Collins, Hilary Radner and Ava Preacher Collins (eds) *Film Theory Goes to the Movies* (New York and London: Routledge, 1993), p. 58.

48   Radner: 'Free Enterprise and the Marriage Plot', p. 59.

49   Radner: 'Free Enterprise and the Marriage Plot', p. 58.

50   Radner: 'Free Enterprise and the Marriage Plot', p. 57.

51   Charlotte Brunsdon, *Screen Tastes: Soap Opera to Satellite Dishes* (London and New York: Routledge, 1997), p. 48.

52   Brunsdon: *Screen Tastes*, p. 48.

53   See, for example, Tania Modleski, *Feminism Without Women: Culture and Criticism in a 'Postfeminist' Age* (New York and London: Routledge, 1991); Susan Faludi, *Backlash: The Undeclared War Against Women* (London: Chatto and Windus, 1991); Michèle Barratt and Anne Phillips, 'Introduction' to Barratt and Phillips (eds) *Destabilizing Theory: Contemporary Feminist Debates*

(London: Polity Press, 1992); Imelda Whelehan, *Modern Feminist Thought: From Second Wave to 'Post-feminism'* (Edinburgh: Edinburgh University Press, 1995); Deborah L Siegel, 'Reading Between the Waves: Feminist Historiography in a "Postfeminist" Moment', in Leslie Heywood and Jennifer Drake (eds) *Third Wave Agenda: Being Feminist, Doing Feminism* (Minneapolis: University of Minnesota Press, 1997); Sarah Gamble, 'Postfeminism', in Gamble (ed) *The Routledge Companion to Feminism and Postfeminism* (London and New York: Routledge, 2001); and Yvonne Tasker and Diane Negra (eds) 'In Focus: Postfeminism and Media Studies', *Cinema Journal*, Vol. 44, No. 2 (2005), pp. 107–133.

54   Gamble: 'Postfeminism', p. 43.

55   Susan Bolotin, 'Voices from the Post-Feminist Generation', *New York Times Magazine*, 17 October 1982, p. 31, cited in Walters: *Material Girls*, p. 118.

56   Claudia Wallis, 'Onward Women!', *Time*, 4 December 1989, p. 81, cited in Walters: *Material Girls*, p. 118.

57   Hilary Hinds and Jackie Stacey, 'Imaging Feminism, Imaging Femininity: The Bra-Burner, Diana, and the Woman Who Kills', *Feminist Media Studies*, Vol. 1, No. 2 (2001), pp. 153–177, p. 153.

58   See Michèle Barratt and Anne Phillips, 'Introduction', in Barratt and Phillips (eds) *Destabilizing Theory: Contemporary Feminist Debates*, pp. 1–10; Sylvia Walby, 'Post-Post Modernism? Theorizing Social Complexity', in Barratt and Phillips (eds) *Destabilizing Theory: Contemporary Feminist Debates*, pp. 31–52; and Chandra Talpade Mohanty, 'Feminist Encounters: Locating the Politics of Experience', in Barratt and Phillips (eds) *Destabilizing Theory: Contemporary Feminist Debates*, pp. 74–92.

59   Siegel: 'Reading Between the Waves', p. 59.

60   Brunsdon: 'Post-feminism and Shopping Films', in *Screen Tastes*, p. 83.

61   Brunsdon: 'Post-feminism and Shopping Films', in *Screen Tastes*, pp. 83–84.

62   Brunsdon: 'Post-feminism and Shopping Films', in *Screen Tastes*, pp. 84–85.

63   See bell hooks, *Black Looks* (Boston: Southend Press, 1992); Cathy Schwitchenberg (ed) *The Madonna Connection* (Boulder: Westview Press, 1993); and Walters: *Material Girls*, pp. 1–3 and pp. 43–44.

64   Brunsdon, 'Post-feminism and Shopping Films', in *Screen Tastes*, pp. 85–86.

65   On the impact of 'celebrity' feminists, such as Camille Paglia, Kate Roiphe and Naomi Wolf on popular understandings of feminism, see Jennifer Wicke, 'Celebrity material: materialist feminism and the culture of celebrity', *The South Atlantic Quarterly*, Vol. 93, No. 4 (1995), pp. 751–778; Siegel: 'Reading Between the Waves', pp. 74–75; and Gamble: 'Postfeminism', p. 45.

66   Stephen Prince, *A New Pot of Gold: Hollywood Under the Electric Rainbow 1980–1989* (Berkeley and London: University of California Press, 2000), p. 341.

67   Prince: *Hollywood under the Electric Rainbow 1980–1989*, p. 342.

68   Yvonne Tasker and Diane Negra, 'Introduction' to Tasker and Negra (eds) 'In Focus: Postfeminism and Contemporary Media Studies', *Cinema Journal*, Vol. 44, No. 2 (2005), pp. 107–133, p. 107.

69 Rachel Moseley and Jacinda Read, 'Having it Ally: Popular Television (Post) Feminism', *Feminist Media Studies* 2, No. 2 (July 2002), pp. 231–249; Kristyn Gorton '(Un)fashionable Feminists: The Media and *Ally McBeal*', in Gillis, Howie and Munford (eds) *Third Wave Feminism*; Joanna Di Mattia, '"What's the harm in believing?" Mr Big, Mr Perfect and the romantic quest for *Sex and the City*'s Mr Right', in Kim Akass and Janet McCabe, *Reading Sex and the City* (London: I.B.Tauris, 2004).

70 Yvonne Tasker and Diane Negra, 'In Focus: Postfeminism and Contemporary Media Studies', *Cinema Journal* 44, No. 2 (Winter 2005), pp. 107–110, p. 108.

71 Tasker and Negra: 'In Focus: Postfeminism and Contemporary Media Studies', p. 108.

72 Linda Mizejewski, 'Dressed to Kill: Postfeminist Noir', in Tasker and Negra (eds) 'In Focus: Postfeminism and Contemporary Media Studies', pp. 121–127, p. 126.

73 Carolyn Anthony, 'Mystery Books: Crime Marches On', *Publishers Weekly*, 13 April 1990, pp. 24–29, p. 28, cited in Priscilla L Walton and Manina Jones, *Detective Agency: Women Rewriting the Hard-Boiled Tradition* (Berkeley and London: University of California Press, 1999), p. 10. See also Yvonne Tasker, *Working Girls: Gender and Sexuality in Popular Cinema* (London and New York: Routledge, 1998), p. 91.

74 *Newsweek*, cited in Walton and Jones: *Detective Agency*, p. 10.

75 Tasker: *Working Girls*, p. 91.

76 Christine D'Acci, 'The Case of *Cagney and Lacey*', in Helen Baehr and Gillian Dyer (eds) *Boxed In: Women and Television* (London: Pandora Press, 1987).

77 Christine Gledhill, 'Pleasurable Negotiations', in E Deirdre Pribram (ed) *Female Spectators: Looking at Film and Television* (London and New York: Verso, 1988), pp. 69–70.

78 Gledhill: 'Pleasurable Negotiations', p. 67.

79 Gledhill: 'Pleasurable Negotiations', pp. 67–68.

80 William Covey, 'Girl Power: Female-Centered Neo-*Noir*', in Alain Silver and James Ursini (eds) *Film Noir Reader 2* (New York: Limelight Editions, 1999), pp. 311–328.

81 Covey: 'Female-Centered Neo-*Noir*', p. 311.

82 Tasker: *Working Girls*, p. 92.

83 Christina Lane, *Feminist Hollywood: From Born in Flames to Point Break* (Detroit: Wayne State University Press, 2000) p. 137.

84 Lane: *Feminist Hollywood*, p. 137.

85 Lane: *Feminist Hollywood*, p. 138.

86 Williams: *The Erotic Thriller in Contemporary Cinema*, pp. 149–163.

87 See Tasker: *Working Girls*, pp. 100–102.

88 See Christine Gledhill's discussion of *Jagged Edge* and its construction of distinct moral opposites through its characters in her essay 'Women Reading Men', in Pat Kirkham and Janet Thumim (eds) *Me Jane: Masculinity, Movies and Women* (London: Lawrence and Wishart, 1995).

89 Adrienne Rich, 'The Anti-Feminist Woman', in *On Lies, Secrets and Silence: Selected Prose 1966–1978* (New York: Norton, 1979), p. 82, cited in Mizejewski: 'Dressed to Kill: Postfeminist Noir', p. 125.

90 See Janey Place, 'Women in *Film Noir*' p. 47.

91 Tasker: *Working Girls*, p. 120, emphases in original.

92 Mary Ann Doane, *Femmes Fatales: Feminism, Film Theory, Psychoanalysis* (New York and London, Routledge, 1991), p. 1.

93 Carroll: 'The Future of Allusion', p. 240.

94 Janey Place: 'Women in *Film Noir*', p. 47.

95 Carroll: 'The Future of Allusion', p. 240.

96 Bryan Burrough, 'Top Deal Maker Leaves a Trail of Deception in Wall Street Rise', *Wall Street Journal*, 22 January 1990, p. 1, cited in Erickson: 'Movement Becomes Genre', p. 312.

97 Erickson, interview with Lawrence Kasdan 10 November 1989, cited in 'Movement Becomes Genre', p. 313.

98 Leslie Shelton, in Ron Gales, 'As the '80s Wane, a New View of the Good Life Emerges', *Adweek*, 13 February 1989, p. 34, cited in Erickson, 'Movement Becomes Genre', pp. 313–314.

99 Radner: 'Free Enterprise and the Marriage Plot', p. 59.

100 Kate Stables, 'The Postmodern Always Rings Twice: Constructing the *Femme Fatale* in 90s Cinema', in E Ann Kaplan (ed) *Women in Film Noir: New Edition* (London: BFI, 1998), p. 171.

101 Stables: 'Constucting the *Femme Fatale* in 90s Cinema', pp. 172–173.

102 Williams: *The Erotic Thriller in Contemporary Cinema*, p. 1.

103 Williams: *The Erotic Thriller in Contemporary Cinema*, p. 122.

104 Sharon Cobb, 'Writing the New *Noir* Film', in Silver and Ursini (eds) *Film Noir Reader 2*, p. 211.

105 Julianne Pidduck, 'The 1990s Hollywood *Femme Fatale*: (Dis)figuring Feminism, Family, Irony, Violence', *CineAction*, No. 38, September 1995, pp. 65–72, p. 69.

106 Pidduck: 'The 1990s Hollywood *Femme Fatale*', p. 69. See also Williams: *The Erotic Thriller in Contemporary Cinema*, p. 188, and Robert E Wood, 'Somebody Has To Die: *Basic Instinct* as White *Noir*', *Post Script*, Vol. 12, No. 3, Summer 1993, pp. 44–51.

107 Pidduck: 'The 1990s Hollywood *Femme Fatale*', p. 72.

108 Deborah Jermyn, 'Rereading the bitches from hell: a feminist appropriation of the female psychopath', *Screen*, Vol. 37, No. 3, Autumn 1996, pp. 251–267, p. 266.

109 Christine Holmlund, 'A Decade of Deadly Dolls: Hollywood and the Woman Killer', in Helen Birch (ed) *Moving Targets: Women, Murder, Representation* (London: Virago, 1993), pp. 127–151.

110 Tasker and Negra: 'In Focus: Postfeminism and Contemporary Media Studies', p. 107.

111 Tasker and Negra: 'In Focus: Postfeminism and Contemporary Media Studies', p. 107.

Notes to Chapter 6

1   For a discussion of the televisual gothic, see Helen Wheatley, *Gothic Television* (Manchester: Manchester University Press, 2006).

2   Pamela Church Gibson, 'Introduction: Popular Culture', in Stacy Gillis, Gillian Howie and Rebecca Munford (eds) *Third Wave Feminism: A Critical Exploration* (London: Palgrave Macmillan, 2004), p. 138.

3   Church Gibson, 'Introduction: Popular Culture', p. 139.

4   Laura Mulvey, 'Visual Pleasure and Narrative Cinema', *Screen*, Autumn 1975, Vol. 16, No. 3, pp. 6–18; E Ann Kapan (ed) *Women in Film Noir* (London: BFI, 1978); Christine Gledhill, 'Klute 1: a contemporary film noir and feminist criticism', in Kaplan (ed) *Women in Film Noir*; and Christine Gledhill (ed) *Home is Where the Heart Is: Studies in Melodrama and the Woman's Film* (London: BFI, 1987).

5   See Moseley and Read: 'Having it Ally', Gorton, 'The Media and *Ally McBeal*', Joanna Di Mattia, 'The romantic quest for *Sex and the City*'s Mr Right', Akass and McCabe (eds) *Reading 'Desperate Housewives'*.

6   Yvonne Tasker and Diane Negra, 'In Focus: Postfeminism and Contemporary Media Studies', *Cinema Journal* 44, No. 2 (Winter 2005), pp. 107–110, p. 108.

7   Claire Kahane, 'Gothic Mirrors and Feminine Identity', *Centennial Review*, 24 (1980), 43–64, 45.

8   Kahane: 'Gothic Mirrors and Feminine Identity', p. 45.

9   Kahane: 'Gothic Mirrors and Feminine Identity', p. 45.

10 Carroll: 'The Future of Allusion', pp. 244–245.

11 Patricia Erens, 'Review: *The Stepfather*', *Film Quarterly*, Vol. 41, No. 2 (Winter 1987–1988), pp. 48–54.

12 Georgia Brown, 'Americana Gothic', *The Village Voice*, 12 February 1991, p. 55.

13 Charles Leayman, 'A passionless fusion of neo-film *noir* and Hollywood romance', *Cinefantastique*, Vol. 22, No. 4, February 1992, pp. 59–60.

14 On Leonetti's work for *Dead Again*, see David Heuring, 'Déjà Vu Fuels Dread in *Dead Again*', *American Cinematographer*, Vol. 72, No. 9, September 1991, pp. 50–54, 56 and 58.

15 Dann Gire, 'Director Kenneth Branagh on *Dead Again*, sending up Sir Alfred Hitchcock', *Cinefantastique*, Vol. 22, No. 4, February 1992, p. 58.

16 Gire: 'Director Kenneth Branagh on *Dead Again*', p. 58.

17 Gire: 'Director Kenneth Branagh on *Dead Again*', p. 58.

18 Gire: 'Director Kenneth Branagh on *Dead Again*', p. 58.

19 Cited by Thomas Doherty, 'Review of *What Lies Beneath*', *Cinefantastique*, Vol. 32, No. 2, August 2000, pp. 4–5, p. 4.

20 Doherty: 'Review of *What Lies Beneath*', p. 4.

21 Jody Duncan, 'Hitchcock Homage', *Cinefex*, No. 83, October 2000, pp. 57–60, 65–66 and 154; p. 58.

22 Legato, cited in Duncan: 'Hitchcock Homage', p. 58.

23 Carroll: 'The Future of Allusion', p. 245.

24 Doane: *The Desire to Desire*, p. 125.

25 Donna Heiland, *Gothic and Gender: An Introduction* (Oxford: Blackwell, 2004), p. 5.

26 Charlotte Brunsdon, 'Feminism, Postfeminism, Martha, Martha and Nigella', *Cinema Journal*, 44, No. 2, Winter 2005, pp. 110–116. On *Buffy The Vampire Slayer*, see Patricia Pender, 'Kicking Ass is Comfort Food: Buffy as Third Wave Feminist Icon', in Gillis, Howie and Munford (eds) *Third Wave Feminism*.

27 Brunsdon, 'Feminism, Postfeminism, Martha, Martha and Nigella', p. 112.

28 *Alien* (Ridley Scott, 1979), *Aliens* (James Cameron, 1986), *Alien*³ (David Fincher, 1992) and *Alien: Resurrection* (Jean-Pierre Jeunet, 1997).

29 Yvonne Tasker, *Spectacular Bodies: Gender, Genre and the Action Cinema* (London: Routledge, 1993); Sherrie Inness, *Tough Girls: Women Warriors and Wonder Women in Popular Culture* (Philadelphia: University of Pennsylvania Press, 1999); Sherrie Inness (ed) *Action Chicks: New Images of Tough Women in Popular Culture* (New York: Palgrave Macmillan, 2004); Yvonne Tasker (ed) *The Action and Adventure Cinema* (Oxon: Routledge, 2004).

30 Julianne Pidduck, 'The 1990s Hollywood Femme Fatale (Disfiguring Feminism, Family, Irony, Violence'), *Cineaction*, September 1995; Kate Stables, 'The Postmodern Always Rings Twice: Constructing the *Femme Fatale* in 90s Cinema', in E Ann Kaplan (ed) *Women in Film Noir: New Edition* (London: BFI, 1998).

31 Charlotte Brunsdon, *Screen Tastes: Soap Opera to Satellite Dishes* (London: Routledge, 1997), p. 180.

32 Norman N Holland and Leona F Sherman, 'Gothic Possibilities', *New Literary History*, Vol. 8, No. 2 (Winter 1977), pp. 279–294, p. 279.

33 Georgia Brown, 'Americana Gothic', *The Village Voice*, 12 February 1991, p. 55.

34 See Ann Oakley, *Housewife* (London: Pelican, 1976) and *The Sociology of Housework* (Oxford: Blackwell, 1985).

35 See Rachel Moseley, 'Makeover Takeover on British Television', *Screen* 41, No. 3 (Autumn 2000), pp. 299–314; Charlotte Brunsdon, Catherine Johnson, Rachel Moseley and Helen Wheatley, 'Factual Entertainment on British Television', *European Journal of Cultural Studies*, 4, No. 1 (February 2001), pp. 29–62, and Brunsdon: 'Feminism, Postfeminism, Martha, Martha and Nigella'.

36 Jane Caputi, '*Sleeping with the Enemy* as *Pretty Woman Part II*? Or What Happened After the Princess Woke Up', *Journal of Popular Film and Television*, Vol. 19, No. 1, Spring 1991, pp. 2–8, p. 4; Brunsdon: *Screen Tastes*, p. 202; Tasker: *Working Girls*, note 4, p. 207; Jacinda Read, *The New Avengers: Feminism, Femininity and the Rape Revenge Cycle* (Manchester: Manchester University Press, 2000), p. 58.

37 Brunsdon: *Screen Tastes*, p. 94 and p. 99; Read: *The New Avengers*, p. 64. The 'down-home' persona of Sara Waters is of a piece with the Roberts' star image, with its connotations of ordinariness and accessibility, one that has been cemented in later films such as *Notting Hill* (Roger Michell, 1999), *Erin Brockovich* (Steven Soderburgh, 2000) and *America's Sweethearts* (Joe Roth, 2001).

38   See Jane Gaines, 'Costume and Narrative: How Dress Tells the Woman's Story', in Jane Gaines and Charlotte Herzog (eds) *Fabrications: Costume and the Female Body* (New York and London: Routledge, 1990).

39   Andrea Walsh, *Women's Film and Female Experience: 1940–1950* (New York: Praeger, 1984), p. 184.

40   Walsh: *Women's Film and Female Experience*, p. 184.

41   Leona Sherman in Holland and Sherman, 'Gothic Possibilities', p. 283.

42   Leona Sherman in Holland and Sherman, 'Gothic Possibilities', p. 283.

43   Kahane: 'Gothic Mirrors', p. 52.

44   Moers: *Literary Women*, p. 91.

45   Brunsdon: 'Feminism, Postfeminism, Martha, Martha and Nigella', p. 112.

46   Brunsdon: 'Feminism, Postfeminism, Martha, Martha and Nigella', p. 112.

47   Waldman: 'Gothic Romance Film of the 1940s', pp. 29–30.

48   Waldman: 'Gothic Romance Film of the 1940s', p. 31.

49   Erens: 'Review: *The Stepfather*', p. 49.

50   Peter Krämer, 'Would you take your child to see this film: the cultural and social work of the family-adventure movie', in Steve Neale and Murray Smith (eds) *Contemporary Hollywood Cinema* (London: Routledge, 1998), p. 295.

51   Krämer: 'the family adventure movie', p. 295.

52   *Sleeping With the Enemy*, released February 1991, accrued box office rentals of $46,300,000, No. 8 for the year; *Deceived*, released September 1991, accrued rentals of $12,000,000, No. 54 for the year. (Source: *Variety*, 6 January 1992, p. 82.) From 1993, *Variety* tracked the top box-office performers in the calendar year in terms of their domestic and international grosses. *What Lies Beneath* earned a domestic gross of $155.4m, and an international gross of $120m, giving a total global gross of $275.4m, and at No. 9 for the year. (Source: *Variety*, 15–21 Jan. 2001, p. 24.)

53   Robin Wood, 'An Introduction to the American Horror Film,' in Richard Lippe and Robin Wood (eds) *American Nightmare: Essays on the Horror Film* (Toronto: Festival of Festivals, 1979), pp. 7–28, cited in Erens: 'Review: *The Stepfather*', p. 49.

54   Doherty: 'Review of *What Lies Beneath*', p. 5.

55   Susan Faludi, *Backlash: The Undeclared War Against Women* (London: Chatto and Windus, 1991), p. 9. Faludi cites the Annual Study of Womens' Attitudes (1988, Mark Clements Research); *New York Times* poll, 1989, and The Roper Organisation, Bickley Townsend and Kathleen O'Neill, 'American Women Get Mad,' *American Demographics*, Aug. 1990, p. 26.

Appendix

The Female Gothic Cycle of the 1940s

Listed Chronologically

* Indicates the involvement of women in the writing of a film's screenplay or source material.

Rebecca (dir. Alfred Hitchcock, 1940)*
Screenplay by Joan Harrison and Robert E Sherwood, from the novel by Daphne du Maurier, adaptation by Philip MacDonald and Michael Hogan.

The Man I Married aka *I Married a Nazi* (dir. Irving Pichel, 1940)
Screenplay by Oliver Garret, from the novel *Swastika* by Oscar Shisgau.

Suspicion (dir. Alfred Hitchcock, 1941)*
Screenplay by Joan Harrison, Samson Raphaelson and Alma Reville, from the novel *Before the Fact*, by Francis Iles.

I Walked with a Zombie (dir. Jacques Tourneur, 1943)*
Screenplay by Curt Siodmak and Ardel Wray, from the story by Inez Wallace.

Shadow of a Doubt (dir. Alfred Hitchcock, 1943)*
Screenplay by Sally Benson, Alma Reville and Thornton Wilder, based on an original story by Gordon McDonell.

When Strangers Marry aka *Betrayed* (dir. William Castle, 1944)
Screenplay by Philip Yordan and Dennis J Cooper, from a story by George Moscov.

Dark Waters (dir. Andre de Toth, 1944)*
Screenplay by Marian Cockrell and Joan Harrison, from a story by Frank and Marian Cockrell.

Experiment Perilous (dir. Jacques Tourneur, 1944)*
Screenplay by Warren Duff, from a novel by Margaret Carpenter.

Gaslight (dir. George Cukor, 1944)
Screenplay by John Van Druten, John L Balderston and Walter Reisch, based on the play by Patrick Hamilton.

Jane Eyre (dir. Robert Stevenson, 1944)*
Screenplay by Aldous Huxley, John Houseman and Robert Stevenson, based on the novel by Charlotte Bronte.

The Uninvited (dir. Lewis Allen, 1944)*
Screenplay by Dodie Smith, based on the novel by Dorothy McCardle.

My Name is Julia Ross (dir. Joseph H Lewis, 1945)*
Screenplay by Muriel Bolton, based on the novel *The Woman in Red* by Anthony Gilbert.

Spellbound (dir. Alfred Hitchcock, 1945)
Screenplay by Ben Hect, adaptation by Angus McPhail from the novel *The House of Dr Edwardes* by Francis Beeding.

Notorious (dir. Alfred Hitchcock, 1946)
Screenplay by Ben Hecht.

Shock (dir. Afred Werk, 1946)
Screenplay by Eugene Ling.

Dragonwyck (dir. Joseph L Mankiewicz, 1946)*
Screenplay by Joseph L Mankiewicz, from the novel by Anya Seton.

The Spiral Staircase (dir. Robert Siodmak, 1946)*
Screenplay by Mel Dinelli, from the novel *Some Must Watch* by Ethel Lina White.

The Stranger (dir. Orson Welles, 1946)
Screenplay by Anthony Veiller, adapted by Decla Dunning and Victor Trivas from an original idea by Victor Trivas.

Undercurrent (dir. Vincente Minelli, 1946)*
Screenplay by Edward Chodorow, with contributions from Marguerite Roberts (and uncredited George Oppenheimer), from the novel *You Were There* by Thelma Strabel.

Bury Me Dead (Bernard Vorhaus, 1947)*
Screenplay by Karen DeWolf and Dwight V Babcock, from the radio play by Irene Winston.

Secret Beyond the Door (dir. Fritz Lang, 1947)*
Screenplay by Silvia Richards.

The Two Mrs Carrolls (dir. Peter Godfrey, 1947)
Screenplay by Thomas Job, from the play by Martin Vale.

Sleep My Love (dir. Douglas Sirk, 1948)
Screenplay by St Clair McKelway and Leo Rosten, with contributions by Decla Dunning and Cyril Enfield, from the novel by Leo Rosten.

Sorry Wrong Number (dir. Anatole Litvak, 1948)*
Screenplay by Lucille Fletcher, from her radio play.

Caught (dir. Max Ophuls, 1949)*
Screenplay by Arthur Laurents, from the novel *Wild Calendar* by Libbie Block.

Under Capricorn (dir. Alfred Hitchcock, 1949)*
Screenplay by James Bridie, John Cotton and Margaret Linden, based on the novel by Helen Simpson, adaptation by Hume Cronyn.

Whirlpool (dir. Otto Preminger, 1949)
Screenplay by Lester Barlow (=Ben Hecht) and Andrew Solt, from the novel by Guy Endore.

Box Office Figures and Academy Awards and Nominations

Rebecca (1940) was the third-top earning film of 1940, making $3 million. It won Academy Awards for Best Cinematography (Black and White): George Barnes, and Best Picture: David O Selznick, and it was nominated for a further ten Academy Awards, including Best Actor (Olivier), Best Actress (Fontaine), Best Score (Drama) (Waxman), Best Special Effects (Jack Cosgrove) and Best Sound Effects (Arthur Johns). [Sources: Thomas Schatz, *Boom and Bust: The American Cinema in the 1940s* (Charles Scribner's Sons: New York, 1997), pp. 466–478, and George Turner, 'Du Maurier + Selznick + Hitchcock + *Rebecca*', in *American Cinematographer*, 78, 7 (1997), pp. 84–88.]

Suspicion (1941) was nominated for Best Picture: Harry E Edington (RKO) and for Best Score (Drama): Franz Waxman, and Joan Fontaine won the Academy Award for Best Actress. [Source: *Halliwell's Film and Video Guide 1999*, ed. by John Walker (London: Harper Collins, 1999).]

Shadow of a Doubt (1943) was nominated for Best Original Story (Gordon McDonell). [Source: Walker (ed) *Halliwell's Film and Video Guide 1999*.]

Experiment Perilous (1944) was nominated for Best Art Direction (Black and White): Albert S D'Agostino. [Source: Walker (ed) *Halliwell's Film and Video Guide 1999*.]

Gaslight (1944) earned $3 million, and was the 14-top earning film of 1944. Ingrid Bergman won Best Actress, and Cedric Gibbons and William Ferrari won Best Art Direction (Black and White). It was nominated for a further five awards: Best Picture: Arthur Hornblow Jnr (MGM), Best Screenplay: John Van Druten, John L Balderston and Walter Reisch, Best Cinematography (Black and White): Joseph Ruttenberg, Best Actor: Charles Boyer, and Best Supporting Actress: Angela Lansbury. [Sources: Schatz, *Boom and Bust*, p. 467; Walker (ed), *Halliwell's Film and Video Guide 1999*.]

The Uninvited (1944) was nominated for Best Cinematography (Black and White): Charles Lang.

The 1944 Academy Award for Best Cinematography (Black and White) was given to Joseph La Shelle for *Laura*. [Sources: Schatz, *Boom and Bust*, p. 467; Walker (ed), *Halliwell's Film and Video Guide 1999*.]

Spellbound (1945) was the third-top earning film for 1945, making $4.97 million. It won Academy Awards for Best Score (Drama): Miklos Rozsa, and it was nominated for a further four; Best Picture: David O Selznick, Best Director: Alfred Hitchcock, Best Cinematography (Black and White): George Barnes, Best Supporting Actor: Michael Chekhov. [Sources: Schatz, *Boom and Bust*, p. 467; Walker (ed), *Halliwell's Film and Video Guide 1999*.]

Notorious (1946) was the eighth-top earning film for 1946, making $4.8 million. It was nominated for Academy Awards for Best Screenplay: Ben Hecht and Best Supporting Actor: Claude Rains. [Sources: Schatz, *Boom and Bust*, p. 467; Walker (ed) *Halliwell's Film and Video Guide 1999*.]

The Spiral Staircase (1946) was nominated for an Academy Award for Best Supporting Actress: Ethel Barrymore. [Source: Walker (ed), *Halliwell's Film and Video Guide 1999*.]

The Stranger (1946) was nominated for an Academy Award for Best Original Story: Victor Trivas.

Barbara Stanwyck was nominated for the Academy Award for Best Actress for *Sorry Wrong Number* (1948). [Source: Walker (ed) *Halliwell's Film and Video Guide 1999*.]

Bibliography

Abbot, H Porter, *The Cambridge Introduction to Narrative* (Cambridge: Cambridge University Press, 2002).

D'Acci, Christine, 'The Case of *Cagney and Lacey*', in Helen Baehr and Gillian Dyer (eds) *Boxed In: Women and Television* (London: Pandora Press, 1987).

Akass, Kim, and McCabe, Janet, *Reading 'Desperate Housewives': Beyond the White Picket Fence* (London: I.B.Tauris, 2006).

Altman, Rick, 'Moving Lips: Cinema as Ventriloquism', *Yale French Studies*, 60 (1980), pp. 67–79.

Anderson, Karen, *Wartime Women: Sex Roles, Family Relations and the Status of Women During World War II* (Westport, Connecticut: Greenwood Press, 1981).

Asheim, Lester, 'Film and the Zeitgeist', *Hollywood Quarterly* 2 (4) (Jul. 1947), pp. 414–416.

Barefoot, Guy, *Gaslight Melodrama: From Victorian London to 1940s Hollywood* (New York and London: Continuum, 2001).

Barr, Donald, 'Don't Look Behind You', *New York Times*, 10 November 1946, p. 167.

Barratt, Michèle, and Phillips, Anne (eds) *Destabilizing Theory: Contemporary Feminist Debates* (London: Polity Press, 1992).

Barthes, Roland, 'The Grain of the Voice', in *Image/Music/Text* (London: Fontana, 1977).

Basinger, Jeanine, *A Woman's View: How Hollywood Spoke to Women 1930–1960* (New York: Knopf, 1993).

Berch, Barbara, 'A Hitchcock Alumna: Introducing Joan Harrison, Hollywood's Only Full-Fledged Woman Producer', *New York Times*, 27 June 1943.

Borde, Raymond, and Chaumeton, Étienne, 'Towards a Definition of *Film Noir*', from *Panorama du Film Noir Americain* (Paris: Les Éditions de Minuit, 1955), reprinted in Alain Silver and James Ursini (eds) *Film Noir Reader* (New York: Limelight Editions, 1996).

Bordwell, David, *Narration in the Fiction Film* (London: Methuen, 1985).

Bordwell, David, Staiger, Janet, and Thompson, Kristin, *The Classical Hollywood Cinema: Film Style and Mode of Production to 1960* (London: Routledge, 1985).

Botting, Fred, *Gothic* (London and New York: Routledge, 1996).

Brackett, Leigh, 'A Comment on "The Hawksian Woman"', *Take One* 3 (8) (Jul–Aug 1971), reprinted in Jim Hillier and Peter Wollen (eds) *Howard Hawks: American Artist* (London: BFI, 1996).

Branston, Gill, '... Viewer, I Listened to Him ...', Voices, Masculinity, *In the Line of Fire*, in *Me Jane: Masculinity, Movies and Women*, ed. by Pat Kirkham and Janet Thumim (London: Lawrence and Wishart, 1995).

Braudy, Leo, 'Genre: The Conventions of Connection' from *The World in a Frame: What We See in Films* (New York: Anchor Press, 1976), reprinted in Gerald Mast, Marshall Cohen and Leo Braudy, (eds) *Film Theory and Criticism: Introductory Readings Fourth Edition* (New York and Oxford: Oxford University Press, 1992).

Bronfen, Elisabeth, *Over Her Dead Body: Death, Femininity and the Aesthetic* (Manchester: Manchester University Press, 1992).

Brown, Georgia, 'Americana Gothic', *The Village Voice*, 12 February 1991, p. 15.

Brunsdon, Charlotte, *Screen Tastes: Soap Opera to Satellite Dishes* (London and New York: Routledge, 1997).

Brunsdon, Charlotte, 'Feminism, Postfeminism, Martha, Martha and Nigella', *Cinema Journal* 44 (2) (2005), pp. 110–116.

Brunsdon, Charlotte, Johnson, Catherine, Moseley, Rachel, and Wheatley, Helen, 'Factual Entertainment on British Television', *European Journal of Cultural Studies* 4 (1) (February 2001), pp. 29–62.

Bunnell, Charlene, 'The Gothic: A Literary Genre's Transition to Film', in B. Grant (ed) *Planks of Reason: Essays on the Horror Film* (London: Scarecrow Press, 1984).

Butler, Jeremy, *'Miami Vice*: The Legacy of *Film Noir'*, in Alain Silver and James Ursini (eds) *Film Noir Reader* (New York: Limelight Editions, 1996).

Campbell, D'Ann, *Women at War with America: Private Lives in a Patriotic Era* (Cambridge, Mass and London: Harvard University Press, 1984).

Caputi, Jane, *'Sleeping with the Enemy* as *Pretty Woman Part II?* Or What Happened After the Princess Woke Up', *Journal of Popular Film and Television* 19 (1) (Spring 1991), pp. 2–8.

Carringer, Robert L, *The Making of Citizen Kane* (London: John Murray, 1985).

Carroll, Noel, 'The Future of Allusion: Hollywood in the Seventies (and Beyond)', *October* 2 (Spring 1982), pp. 51–81, reprinted in Carroll, *Interpreting the Moving Image* (Cambridge: Cambridge University Press, 1998).

Chafe, William, *The American Woman: Her Changing Social, Economic and Political Roles, 1920–1970* (London: Oxford University Press, 1974).

Chandler, Raymond, 'The Simple Art of Murder', *Atlantic Monthly*, December 1944, reprinted in *Pearls Are a Nuisance* (1950; London: Penguin, 1976).

Chinen Biesen, Sheri, 'Joan Harrison, Virginia Van Upp and Women Behind-the-Scenes in Wartime *Film Noir'*, *Quarterly Review of Film and Video*, 20, 2 (2003), pp. 125–144.

Chinen Biesen, Sheri, *Blackout: World War II and the Origins of Film Noir* (Baltimore: John Hopkins University Press, 2005).

Chion, Michel, *Audio-Vision: Sound On Screen* edited and translated by Claudia Gorbman (1980; New York: Columbia University Press, 1994).

Chion, Michel, *The Voice in Cinema*, edited and translated by Claudia Gorbman (1982; New York: Columbia University Press, 1999).

Chopra Gant, Mike, *Hollywood Genres and Postwar America: Masculinity, Family and Nation in Popular Movies and Film Noir* (London: I.B.Tauris, 2005).

Church Gibson, Pamela, 'Introduction: Popular Culture', in Stacy Gillis, Gillian Howie and Rebecca Munford (eds) *Third Wave Feminism: A Critical Exploration* (London: Palgrave Macmillan, 2004).

Cobb, Sharon, 'Writing the New *Noir* Film', in Alain Silver and James Ursini (eds) *Film Noir Reader 2* (New York: Limelight Editions, 1999).

Cook, Pam, 'No fixed address: the women's picture from *Outrage* to *Blue Steel*', in *Contemporary Hollywood Cinema*, ed. by Steve Neale and Murray Smith (London and New York: Routledge, 1998).

Cook, Pam, 'Duplicity in *Mildred Pierce*', in E Ann Kaplan (ed) *Women in Film Noir: New Edition* (1978; London: BFI, 1998).

Covey, William, 'Girl Power: Female-Centered Neo-*Noir*', in Alain Silver and James Ursini (eds) *Film Noir Reader 2* (New York: Limelight Editions, 1999).

Coward, Rosalind, '"Sexual Liberation" and the family', *m/f* 1 (1978), pp. 7–24.

Cowie, Elizabeth, '*Film Noir* and Women', in Joan Copjec (ed) *Shades of Noir* (London: Verso, 1993).

Cowie, Elizabeth, *Representing the Woman: Cinema and Psychoanalysis* (Basingstoke: Macmillan, 1997).

Doane, Mary Ann, '*Caught* and *Rebecca*: The Inscription of Femininity as Absence', *Enclitic* 5–6 (1981–1982), pp. 75–89.

Doane, Mary Ann, *The Desire to Desire: The Woman's Film of the 1940s* (Bloomington: Indiana University Press, 1987).

Doane, Mary Ann, *Femmes Fatales: Feminism, Film Theory, Psychoanalysis* (New York and London: Routledge, 1991).

Doane, Mary Ann, 'Film and the Masquerade: Theorizing the Female Spectator', *Screen* 23, (3–4) (1982), pp. 74–87, reprinted in *Screen* (ed) *The Sexual Subject: A Screen Reader in Sexuality* (London: Routledge, 1992).

Doherty, Thomas, *Teenagers and Teenpics: The Juvenilization of American Movies in the 1950s* (Boston and London: Unwin Hyman, 1988).

Doherty, Thomas, 'Review of *What Lies Beneath*', *Cinefantastique* 32 (2) (August 2000), pp. 4–5.

Deming, Barbara, *Running Away From Myself: A Dream Portrait of America Drawn from the Films of the Forties* (New York: Grossman Publishers, 1969).

Duncan, Jody, 'Hitchcock Homage', *Cinefex* 83 (October 2000), pp. 57–60, 65–66 and 154.

Dyer, Richard, 'Resistance Through Charisma: Rita Hayworth and *Gilda*', in E Ann Kaplan (ed) *Women in Film Noir: New Edition* (1978; London: BFI, 1978).

Dyer, Richard, 'Postscript: Queers and Women in *Film Noir*', in E Ann Kaplan (ed) *Women in* Film Noir: *New Edition* (London: BFI, 1998).

Ellis, John, *Visible Fictions: Cinema, Television, Video, Revised Edition* (1982; London and New York: Routledge, 1995).

Elsaesser, Thomas, 'Tales of Sound and Fury: Observations on the Family Melodrama', *Monogram* 4 (1972), pp. 2–15, reprinted in Christine Gledhill (ed) *Home is Where the Heart is: Studies in Melodrama and the Woman's Film* (London: BFI, 1987).

Erens, Patricia, 'Review: *The Stepfather*', *Film Quarterly*, 41 (2) (Winter 1987–1988), pp. 48–54.

Erickson, Todd, 'Kill Me Again: Movement Becomes Genre', in Alain Silver and James Ursini (eds) *Film Noir Reader* (New York: Limelight Editions, 1996).

Faludi, Susan, *Backlash: The Undeclared War Against Women* (London: Chatto and Windus, 1991).

Francke, Lizzie, *Script Girls: Women Screenwriters in Hollywood* (London: BFI, 1994).

Freud, Sigmund, 'The Uncanny' (1919), reprinted in *Penguin Freud Library Volume 14: Art and Literature*, ed. by Albert Dickson (1985; London: Penguin, 1990).

Friedan, Betty, *The Feminine Mystique* (1963; London and New York: Penguin, 1992).

Gaines, Jane, 'Costume and Narrative: How Dress Tells the Woman's Story', in Jane Gaines and Charlotte Herzog (eds) *Fabrications: Costume and the Female Body* (New York and London: Routledge, 1990).

Gamble, Sarah (ed) *The Routledge Companion to Feminism and Postfeminism* (London and New York: Routledge, 2001).

Gilbert, Sandra, and Gubar, Susan, *The Madwoman in the Attic: The Woman Writer and the Nineteenth Century Literary Imagination* (New Haven and London: Yale University Press, 1979).

Gire, Dann, 'Director Kenneth Branagh on *Dead Again*, sending up Sir Alfred Hitchcock', *Cinefantastique*, 22 (4) (February 1992), p. 58.

Gledhill, Christine (ed) *Home is Where the Heart Is: Essays on Melodrama and the Woman's Film* (London: BFI, 1987).

Gledhill, Christine, 'Pleasurable Negotiations', in E Deirdre Pribram (ed) *Female Spectators: Looking at Film and Television* (London and New York: Verso, 1988).

Gledhill, Christine, 'Women Reading Men', in Pat Kirkham and Janet Thumim (eds) *Me Jane: Masculinity, Movies and Women* (London: Lawrence and Wishart, 1995).

Gledhill, Christine, '*Klute* 1: A Contemporary *Film Noir* and Feminist Criticism', in E Ann Kaplan (ed) *Women in Film Noir: New Edition* (1978; London: BFI, 1998).

Gledhill, Christine, 'Rethinking genre', in Christine Gledhill and Linda Williams (eds) *Reinventing Film Studies* (London: Arnold, 2000).

Gorbman, Claudia, *Unheard Melodies: Narrative Film Music* (London: BFI, 1987).

Gorton, Kristyn, '(Un)fashionable Feminists: The Media and *Ally McBeal*', in Gillian Howie, Stacy Gillis, and Rebecca Munford (eds) *Third Wave Feminism: A Critical Exploration* (Basingstoke: Palgrave Macmillan, 2004).

Grant, Barry Keith, *Film Genre Reader* (Austin: University of Texas Press, 1986).

Green, Ian, 'Malefunction: A Contribution to the Debate on Masculinity in the Cinema', *Screen* 25 (4–5) (1984), pp. 36–48.

Grossman, Julie, '*Film Noir*'s "*Femme Fatales*": Hard-Boiled Women and Moving Beyond Gender Fantasies', *Quarterly Review of Film and Video*, 24 (1) (Jan 2007).

Haralovich, Mary Beth, 'Selling *Mildred Pierce*: A Case Study in Movie Promotion', in Thomas Schatz, *Boom and Bust: The American Cinema in the 1940s* (New York: Charles Scribner's Sons, 1997).

Haskell, Molly, '*Man's Favourite Sport?* (Revisited)', in Jim Hillier and Peter Wollen (eds) *Howard Hawks: American Artist* (London: BFI, 1996).

Heiland, Donna, *Gothic and Gender: An Introduction* (Oxford: Blackwell, 2004).

Heuring, David, 'Déjà Vu Fuels Dread in *Dead Again*', *American Cinematographer* 72 (9) (September 1991), pp. 50–54, p. 56 and p. 58.

Hinds, Hilary, and Stacey, Jackie, 'Imaging Feminism, Imaging Femininity: The Bra-Burner, Diana, and the Woman Who Kills', *Feminist Media Studies* 1 (2) (2001), pp. 153–177.

Hirsch, Foster, *Film Noir: The Dark Side of the Screen* (New York: A S Barnes, 1981).

Holland, Norman, and Sherman, Leona, 'Gothic Possibilities', *New Literary History*, 8 (2) (winter, 1977), pp. 279–294.

Holmlund, Christine, 'A Decade of Deadly Dolls: Hollywood and the Woman Killer', in Helen Birch (ed) *Moving Targets: Women, Murder, Representation* (London: Virago, 1993).

Honey, Maureen, *Creating Rosie the Riveter: Class, Gender, and Propoganda During World War II* (Amherst: University of Massachusetts Press, 1984).

Hooks, Bell, *Black Looks* (Boston: Southend Press, 1992).

Houseman, John, 'Today's Hero: A Review', *Hollywood Quarterly* (2) (Jan. 1947), pp. 161–163.

Howells, Coral Ann, *Love, Mystery and Misery: Feeling in Gothic Fiction* (London: Athlone Press, 1978).

Inness, Sherrie, *Tough Girls: Women Warriors and Wonder Women in Popular Culture* (Philadelphia: University of Pennsylvania Press, 1999).

Inness, Sherrie (ed) *Action Chicks: New Images of Tough Women in Popular Culture* (New York: Palgrave Macmillan, 2004).

Jermyn, Deborah, 'Rereading the bitches from hell: a feminist appropriation of the female psychopath', *Screen* 37 (3) (1996), pp. 251–267.

Jones, Howard Mumford, 'Publishing Time, Literary Time', *New York Times*, 29 June 1947, p. 1 and p. 24.

Kahane, Claire, 'Gothic Mirrors and Feminine Identity', *Centennial Review*, 24 (1980), pp. 43–64.

Kalinak, Kathryn, 'The Fallen Woman and the Virtuous Wife: Musical Stereotypes in *The Informer*, *Gone with the Wind*, and *Laura*', *Film Reader*, 5 (1982), pp. 76–82.

Kaplan, E Ann (ed) *Women in Film Noir* (London: BFI, 1978).

Kaplan, E Ann (ed) *Women in Film Noir: New Edition* (London: BFI, 1998).

Krämer, Peter, 'Post-Classical Hollywood', in John Hill and Pamela Church Gibson (eds) *The Oxford Guide to Film Studies* (Oxford: Oxford University Press, 1998).

Krämer, Peter, 'Would you take your child to see this film: The cultural and social work of the family-adventure movie', in Steve Neale and Murray Smith (eds) *Contemporary Hollywood Cinema* (London: Routledge, 1998).

Krutnik, Frank, *In a Lonely Street: Film Noir, Genre, Masculinity* (London and New York: Routledge, 1991).

Kuhn, Annette, *The Power of the Image: Essays on Representation and Sexuality* (London: Routledge, 1985).

Lane, Christina, *Feminist Hollywood: From* Born in Flames *to* Point Break (Detroit: Wayne State University Press, 2000).

LaPlace, Maria, 'Producing and Consuming the Woman's Film: Discursive Struggle in *Now Voyager*', in Christine Gledhill (ed) *Home is Where the Heart Is: Essays on Melodrama and the Woman's Film* (London: BFI 1987).

Lauretis, Teresa de, *Alice Doesn't: Feminism, Semiotics, Cinema* (Bloomington: Indiana University Press, 1984).

Leayman, Charles, 'A passionless fusion of neo-film *noir* and Hollywood romance', *Cinefantastique* 22 (4) (February 1992), pp. 59–60.

Light, Alison, 'Returning to Manderley': Romance Fiction, Female Sexuality and Class, *Feminist Review* 6 (summer, 1984), pp. 7–25.

Lightman, Herb, 'The Subjective Camera', *American Cinematographer*, February 1946, p. 46 and p. 66.

Lightman, Herb, 'The Fluid Camera', *American Cinematographer*, March 1946, p. 82 and pp. 102–103.

Lightman, Herb, 'Mood in the Motion Picture', *American Cinematographer*, February 1947, pp. 48–49 and p. 69.

Lightman, Herb, '"Sleep My Love": Cinematic Psycho-thriller', *American Cinematographer*, February 1948, pp. 46–47 and p. 55.

Lippe, Richard, and Wood, Robin (eds) *American Nightmare: Essays on the Horror Film* (Toronto: Festival of Festivals, 1979).

McCarthy, Todd, *Howard Hawks: The Grey Fox of Hollywood* (New York: Grove Press, 1997).

McGilligan, Patrick, *George Cukor: A Double Life* (London: Faber and Faber, 1992).

Maltby, Richard, 'The Politics of the Maladjusted Text', in Ian Cameron (ed) *The Movie Book of* Film Noir (London: Studio Vista, 1992).

Martin, Angela, '"Gilda Didn't Do Any of Those Things You've Been Losing Sleep Over!": The Central Women of 40s *Films Noirs*', in E Ann Kaplan (ed) *Women in Film Noir: New Edition* (London: BFI, 1998).

Matson, Norman, 'Gooseflesh Special', *New York Times*, May 28, 1944, p. 7 and p. 23.

Mattia, Joanna Di, '"What's the harm in believing?" Mr Big, Mr Perfect and the romantic quest for *Sex and the City*'s Mr Right', in Kim Akass and Janet McCabe (eds) *Reading Sex and the City* (London: I.B.Tauris, 2004).

Mayne, Judith, *Cinema and Spectatorship* (London and New York: Routledge, 1993).

Mizejewski, Linda, 'Dressed to Kill: Postfeminist Noir', *Cinema Journal* 44 (2) (2005), pp. 121–127.

Modleski, Tania, *Loving with a Vengeance: Mass Produced Fantasies for Women* (New York and London: Methuen, 1984).

Modleski, Tania, *The Women Who Knew Too Much: Hitchcock and Feminist Theory* (New York and London: Routledge, 1988).

Modleski, Tania, *Feminism Without Women: Culture and Criticism in a 'Postfeminist' Age* (New York and London: Routledge, 1991).

Moers, Ellen, *Literary Women* (London: The Women's Press, 1963).

Mohanty, Chandra Talpade, 'Feminist Encounters: Locating the Politics of Experience', in Michèle Barratt and Anne Phillips (eds) *Destabilizing Theory: Contemporary Feminist Debates* (London: Polity Press, 1992).

Moseley, Rachel, 'Makeover Takeover on British Television', *Screen* 41 (3) (2000), pp. 299–314.

Moseley, Rachel, and Read, Jacinda, 'Having it Ally: Popular Television (Post) Feminism', *Feminist Media Studies* 2 (2) (July 2002), pp. 231–249.

Motion Picture Herald, 'Romantic Drama Customer Choice', 8 June 1946.

Mulvey, Laura, 'Visual Pleasure and Narrative Cinema', *Screen* 16 (3) (1975), pp. 6–18, reprinted in *Screen* (ed) *The Sexual Subject: A Screen Reader in Sexuality* (London: Routledge, 1992).

Naremore, James, *The Magic World of Orson Welles* (New York: Oxford University Press, 1978).

Naremore, James, *More Than Night:* Film Noir *in its Contexts* (Berkeley: University of California Press, 1998).

Neale, Steve, *Genre* (London: BFI, 1980).

Neale, Steve, 'Questions of Genre', *Screen* 31 (1) (1990), pp. 45–66.Neale, Steve, *Genre and Hollywood* (London and New York: Routledge, 1999).

Nelson, Carolyn Christensen (ed) *A New Woman Reader* (London: Broadview Press, 2001).

Nelson, Joyce, '*Mildred Pierce* Reconsidered', *Film Reader* 2 (1977).

Oakley, Ann, *Housewife* (London: Pelican, 1976).

Oakley, Ann, *The Sociology of Housework* (Oxford: Blackwell, 1985).

O'Brien, Geoffrey, 'The Return of Film Noir!', *New York Review of Books*, 14 August 1991.

Parry, Sally, 'The Secret of the Feminist Heroine: The Search for Values in Nancy Drew and Judy Bolton', in Sherrie Inness (ed) *Nancy Drew and Company: Culture, Gender and the Girls' Series* (Bowling Green State University Press, 1997).

Pearce, Lynne, and Stacey, Jackie (eds) *Romance Revisited* (London: Lawrence and Wishart, 1995).

Pearce, Lynne, and Wisker, Gina (eds) *Fatal Attractions: Rescripting Romance in Contemporary Literature and Film* (London: Pluto Press, 1998).

Pender, Patricia, '"Kicking Ass is Comfort Food": Buffy as Third Wave Feminist Icon' in Gillian Howie, Stacy Gillis and Rebecca Munford (eds) *Third Wave Feminism: A Critical Exploration* (Basingstoke: Palgrave Macmillan, 2004).

Pennell, Jane, 'The Female Detective: Pre and Post Women's Lib', *Clues: A Journal of Detection* 6 (2) (1985), pp. 85–98.

Pidduck, Julianne, 'The 1990s Hollywood Femme Fatale: (Dis)figuring Feminism, Family, Irony, Violence', *CineAction*, 38 (Sept 1995), pp. 65–72.

Piper, David, *Personality and the Portrait* (London: BBC Publications, 1973).

Place, Janey, 'Women in *Film Noir*', in E Ann Kaplan (ed) *Women in Film Noir: New Edition* (1978; London: BFI, 1998).

Poe, Edgar Allan, 'The Oval Portrait', in *Tales of Mystery and Imagination* (Hertfordshire: Wordsworth Editions, 1993).

Pribram, E Deidre (ed) *Female Spectators: Looking at Film and Television* (London: Verso, 1988).

Price, Leah, and Thurschwell, Pamela (eds) *Literary Secretaries/ Secretarial Culture* (London: Ashgate, 2005).

Prince, Stephen, *A New Pot of Gold: Hollywood Under the Electric Rainbow 1980–1989* (Berkeley and London: University of California Press, 2000).

Radner, Hilary, 'Pretty Is as Pretty Does: Free Enterprise and the Marriage Plot', in Jim Collins, Hilary Radner and Ava Preacher Collins (eds) *Film Theory Goes to the Movies* (New York and London: Routledge, 1993).

Radway, Janice, *Reading the Romance: Women, Patriarchy and Popular Literature* (1984; Chapel Hill and London: University of North Carolina Press, 1991).

Rank, Otto, *The Double: A Psychoanalytic Study*, ed. and trans. by Harry Tucker (London: Maresfield Library, 1989).

Read, Jacinda, *The New Avengers: Feminism, Femininity and the Rape Revenge Cycle* (Manchester: Manchester University Press, 2000).

Rehak, Melanie, *Girl Sleuth: Nancy Drew and the Women Who Created Her* (London: Harvest Books, 2006).

Renov, Michael, *Hollywood's Wartime Woman: Representation and Ideology* (Ann Arbor/London: UMI Research Press, 1988).

Robinson, Florett, 'Hiss-s-s-s Through the Years: Styles in movie villains change, but whether Western desperadoes, city slickers or Japs, they're all bad men', *New York Times*, 15 August 1943, p. 16.

Rosen, Marjorie, *Popcorn Venus: Women, Movies and the American Dream* (New York: Avon Books, 1973).

Schatz, Thomas, *The Genius of the System: Hollywood Film-making in the Studio Era* (London: Faber and Faber, 1988).

Schatz, Thomas, 'The New Hollywood', in Jim Collins, Hilary Radner and Ava Preacher Collins (eds) *Film Theory Goes to the Movies* (New York and London: Routledge, 1993).

Schatz, Thomas, *Boom and Bust: American Cinema During the 1940s* (Berkeley: University of California Press, 1999).

Schwitchenberg, Cathy (ed) *The Madonna Connection* (Boulder: Westview Press, 1993).

Sconce, Jeffrey, 'Narrative Authority and Social Narrativity: The Cinematic Reconstitution of Brontë's *Jane Eyre*', in Janet Staiger (ed) *The Studio System* (New York: Rutgers University Press, 1995).

Siegel, Deborah L, 'Reading Between the Waves: Feminist Historiography in a "Postfeminist" Moment', in Leslie Heywood and Jennifer Drake (eds) *Third Wave Agenda: Being Feminist, Doing Feminism* (Minneapolis: University of Minnesota Press, 1997).

Siegel, Deborah L, 'Nancy Drew as New Girl Wonder: Solving It All for the 1930s', in Sherrie Inness (ed) *Nancy Drew and Company: Culture, Gender and the Girls' Series* (Bowling Green State University Press, 1997).

Silverman, Kaja, *Male Subjectivity at the Margins* (New York and London: Routledge, 1992).

Smith, Murray, '*Film Noir*: The Female Gothic and *Deception*', *Wide Angle* 10 (1) (1988), pp. 62–75.

Stables, Kate, 'The Postmodern Always Rings Twice: Constructing the *Femme Fatale* in 90s Cinema', in E Ann Kaplan (ed) *Women in Film Noir: New Edition* (London: BFI, 1998).

Stacey, Jackie, *Star Gazing: Hollywood Cinema and Female Spectatorship* (London: Routledge, 1994).

Stanfield, Peter, '"Film Noir Like You've Never Seen": Jim Thompson Adaptations and Cycles of Neo-Noir', in Steve Neale (ed) *Genre and Contemporary Hollywood* (London: BFI, 2002).

Stanley, Fred, 'Hollywood Shivers', *New York Times*, 28 May 1944, p. 3.

Stanley, Fred, 'Hollywood Bows to the Ladies', *New York Times*, 7 January 1945, p. 1 and p. 3.

Stoneman, Patsy, *Brontë Transformations: The Cultural Dissemination of Jane Eyre and Wuthering Heights* (London: Prentice Hall/Harvester Wheatsheaf, 1996).

Tasker, Yvonne, *Spectacular Bodies: Gender, Genre and the Action Cinema* (New York and London: Routledge, 1993).

Tasker, Yvonne, *Working Girls: Gender and Sexuality in Popular Cinema* (London and New York: Routledge, 1998).

Tasker, Yvonne (ed) *The Action and Adventure Cinema* (Oxon: Routledge, 2004).

Tasker, Yvonne and Negra, Diane (eds) 'In Focus: Postfeminism and Media Studies', *Cinema Journal* 44 (2) (2005), pp. 107–133.

Taylor, Helen, 'Romantic Readers', in Helen Carr (ed) *From My Guy to Sci Fi: Genre and Women's Writing in the Postmodern World* (London: Pandora Press, 1989).

Truffaut, Francois, *Hitchcock* (New York: Simon and Schuster, 1967).

Ursini, James, 'Angst at Sixty Fields Per Second', in Alain Silver and James Ursini (eds) *Film Noir Reader* (New York: Limelight Editions, 1996).

Vernet, Marc, '*Film Noir* on the Edge of Doom', in Joan Copjec (ed) *Shades of Noir* (London: Verso, 1993).

Walby, Sylvia, 'Post-Post Modernism? Theorizing Social Complexity', in Michèle Barratt and Anne Phillips (eds) *Destabilizing Theory: Contemporary Feminist Debates* (London: Polity Press, 1992).

Waldman, Diane, '"At last I can tell it to someone!": Feminine Point of View and Subjectivity in the Gothic Romance Film of the 1940s', *Cinema Journal* 23 (2) (1983), pp. 29–40.

Walker, Michael, '*Secret Beyond the Door*', *Movie* 34/35 (1990), pp. 16–30.

Walsh, Andrea, *Women's Film and Female Experience 1940–1950* (New York: Praeger, 1984).

Walters, Suzanna Danuta, *Material Girls: Making Sense of Feminist Cultural Theory* (Berkeley and London: University of California Press, 1995).

Walton, Priscilla L, and Jones, Manina, *Detective Agency: Women Rewriting the Hard-Boiled Tradition* (Berkeley and London: University of California Press, 1999).

Ward, Elizabeth, 'The Unintended *Femme Fatale: The File on Thelma Jordan* and *Pushover*', in Alain Silver and James Ursini (eds) *Film Noir Reader 2* (New York: Limelight Editions, 1999).

243

Warner, Marina, 'The Uses of Enchantment', in *Cinema and the Realms of Enchantment: Lectures, Seminars and Essays by Marina Warner and Others, BFI Working Papers*, ed. by Duncan Petrie (London: BFI, 1993).

Wheatley, Helen, *Gothic Television* (Manchester: Manchester University Press, 2006).

Whelehan, Imelda, *Modern Feminist Thought: From Second Wave to 'Post-feminism'* (Edinburgh: Edinburgh University Press, 1995).

Wicke, Jennifer, 'Celebrity material: materialist feminism and the culture of celebrity', *The South Atlantic Quarterly*, 93 (4) (1995), pp. 751–778.

Williams, Linda, 'Feminist Film Theory: *Mildred Pierce* and the Second World War', in E Deirdre Pribram (ed) *Female Spectators: Looking at Film and Television* (London: Verso, 1988).

Williams, Linda Ruth, *The Erotic Thriller in Contemporary Cinema* (Edinburgh: Edinburgh University Press, 2005).

Williams, Linda Ruth, and Hammond, Michael (eds) *Contemporary American Cinema* (New York: Open University Press/McGraw Hill, 2006).

Wise, Naomi, 'The Hawksian Woman', *Take One* 3 (3) (Jan–Feb 1971), reprinted in Jim Hillier and Peter Wollen (eds) *Howard Hawks: American Artist* (London: BFI, 1996).

Wisker, Gina, 'Dangerous Borders: Daphne du Maurier's *Rebecca*: shaking the foundations of the romance of privilege, partying and place', *Journal of Gender Studies* 12 (2), 2003, pp. 83–97.

Wood, Robert E, 'Somebody Has To Die: *Basic Instinct* as White *Noir*', *Post Script* 12 (3) (1993), pp. 44–51.

Woodall, Joanna (ed) *Portraiture: Facing the Subject* (Manchester: Manchester University Press, 1997).

Wright Wexman, Virginia, *Creating the Couple: Love, Marriage and Hollywood Performance* (Princeton, Princeton University Press, 1993).

Wyatt, Justin, *High Concept: Movies and Marketing in Hollywood* (Austin: University of Texas Press, 1994).

Index